The Cost of Compassion

FIVE WOMEN WHO PAID THE ULTIMATE PRICE

Barbara Pawlikowski
Foreword by Joyce Rupp

Barbara Ann Muttra   Shirley Kolmer   Agnes Mueller

Kathleen McGuire   Mary Joél Kolmer

THE COST OF COMPASSION
Five Women Who Paid the Ultimate Price
by Barbara Pawlikowski

Edited by Gregory F. Augustine Pierce
Drawing on cover and previous page created by Pinaki15
Cover design & typesetting by Harvest Graphics

Published by ACTA Publications, 4848 N. Clark St., Chicago, IL
60640, (800) 397-2282, www.actapublications.com

Library of Congress Number: 2017962391
ISBN: 978-0-87946-657-2
Printed in the United States of America by Total Printing Systems
Year: 30 29 28 27 26 25 24 23 22 21 20 19 18
Printing: 15 14 13 12 11 10 9 8 7 6 5 4 3 2 First

♻ Printed on paper with 30% post-consumer waste.

CONTENTS

Foreword by Joyce Rupp.. i

Introduction.. xi

Four Minutes More... 1

Beginnings 23

Happier Times 31

The Call.. 33

Sister Barbara Ann Muttra 45

Sister Shirley Kolmer 113

Sister Mary Joél Kolmer 153

Sister Agnes Mueller... 177

Civil War, Return to Ruma, and Back to Liberia.............. 201

Sister Kathleen McGuire 241

Final Days 265

Final Hours... 297

Post Scripts... 319

Acknowledgments... 343

Appendices.. 345

DEDICATION

For All Those Who Serve Others
…and particularly for Bob

FOREWORD
BY JOYCE RUPP

To offer the heart is not like offering a fingernail
or a lock of hair we were ready to discard anyway;
it is to offer the core, most essential part of our being.

SHARON SALZBERG

In January of 1990 I flew to Monrovia, Liberia, to give a week-long retreat to missionaries of various communities serving in that country. When I accepted the invitation I had no idea what a profound experience this would be. Nor did I realize the impoverishment of the country, or that the women religious I stayed with would be my teachers of generous-hearted compassion.

I had never been in a developing country until I went to Liberia. My three week stay opened my mind and heart to a world vastly different than the privileged one from which

I came. So naïve was I about going there that I joked with friends about having to receive the required inoculations for yellow fever, typhoid, malaria, and hepatitis. My first evening sitting at table with the five sisters from Ruma, Illinois, quickly changed my mind. I listened to them comment casually about each one having had at least one episode of malaria and hepatitis, along with a worm fungus on a sister's arm, plus other illnesses that invaded their lives.

My appreciation of their acceptance of a totally different lifestyle came when I got into bed under netting that kept out mosquitoes from a nearby swamp, but not the finger-length cockroaches that managed to slip beneath the netting. Further confirmation of what the sisters experienced came with the next-door garbage dump's pungent odor wafting through my bedroom window. As I tried to go to sleep that odor, and the incessant noise of the congested marketplace, with its loud disco music playing on the other side of the sisters' residence, I was led to wonder: "How do they live with this?"

In the space of less than twenty-four hours I quickly recognized what these sisters were willing to endure in order to give so fully of themselves in service. The next morning I headed to the bathroom, anticipating a welcoming warm shower after the long trip overseas. Instead, Sister Joél met me with a bucket of water, explaining, "The water is often shut off here. We never know if we will have access to it or not." I understood, then, why tall barrels full of rainwater sat at the end of the hallway. Later, I noticed lunch being prepared with charcoals on the porch because electricity, like water, was shut off that day. When they did have access to running water, it was cold. Sundays were reserved for warm water because "It costs too much to keep the hot current on." While water and electricity were limited, insects were excessive. I watched one of the sisters spray a can of bug spray into a hole above the kitchen sink where the pipe fits in. A zillion bugs came swarming out.

But it was the gracious, dedicated, and difficult work of the sisters that most impressed me. They went about their ministries of education, health services, and pastoral care with amazing peacefulness, unrelenting joy, and an immense love of the Liberian people. Their ability to consistently be available to the people's needs touched me deeply.

In the coming weeks I would also learn of the hidden sacrifices they made to be so far from loved ones. At that time, no Internet existed. If mail arrived at all, it would be months, sometimes years, before it reached them. They had no phone, and transportation left much to be desired. Sister Shirley's old, beat-up Renault shimmied and shook like a tin can rolling down the street. The sisters often took taxis crammed with six or seven other passengers climbing in beside them.

Staying in the Bush

Because I wanted to know about the life of these missionaries before I led their retreat, I asked to spend a week in the bush with two of their members: Sister Toni, who did pastoral ministry, and Sister Barbara Ann, a nurse who worked in the clinic she had built with funds from a European agency. As in the city, I observed how fully these sisters gave themselves in service.

We always ate our evening meals late because Sister Barbara Ann worked long hours at the clinic with just herself and two local women she trained. She never left the clinic until seeing to everyone's medical concerns. I learned from her that one day 107 people arrived at the clinic and she stayed until all of them had been tended. One evening in the middle of our meal a man came to the door and begged her, "Please come, my daughter, she is very sick." Sister Barbara Ann immediately left with him and went to see what she could do. She told me later about when she worked in a clinic south of Monrovia. She would have to walk down a side aisle in church on Sundays because if the children saw her they'd start to scream—she had vaccinated many of them!

Sister Toni told harrowing stories of getting stuck in the bush when she visited people, almost getting washed away in her old Bronco truck by the flooding. She expressed sorrow for what was happening to the land. Because the rainforests nearby were being depleted of their gigantic trees, the heavy rains washed off the soil quickly, causing constant flooding. (The sisters cared not only for the Liberian people but for their land, as well.)

The Developing Danger

On the trip from the airport after I arrived in Liberia the sisters spoke of the country's "unrest" and that "things are not well here." The bloody coup was only in the north of the country at that time, but armed soldiers were on the streets in Monrovia. Curfews and check points had already been set up. Sister Shirley mentioned that the soldiers there were often drunk, so it was best to get to their place before dark. At the same time, she assured me that their community members were safe, that the American sisters were respected and appreciated for their service to the people.

Even with this insistence of their not being afraid I noticed how careful the sisters were regarding house burglary by having bars on the windows. As we left the house one day Sister Joél reminded me, "Close the wooden door. It's easy for someone to cut the screen." Whenever all of them were away, they left a radio on, and when coming home they pretended to say "hello" to someone inside as they entered.

An incident late one evening told me of the sisters' vulnerability regarding violence. I was awakened by a loud banging on the front door. It continued with increasing volume until I heard Sister Shirley say, "Just a moment. We can't find the key." About five minutes later she opened the door and found several intoxicated men there, without army uniforms, claiming they were soldiers and demanding money. The sisters explained that they were American nuns and gave them twenty dollars and a Bible, which seemed to satisfy them.

Eventually, the men left. (I learned later that Sister Shirley's slow response to answer the door was to give the sisters time to hide some Liberian women who lived with them and were at risk of being raped.)

After three weeks, when this dedicated group of sisters took me to the airport, they were even more concerned about getting back home before dark. Even so, when I bid them farewell I could not fathom any of them being harmed. They were such stalwart, loving women, willing to let go of their white-privilege status and the easy lifestyle of the U.S.A., giving of themselves fully in friendship and service to the Liberian people. The loving presence of these generous-hearted women rooted strong seeds of compassion in my soul. They taught me that compassion can demand a steep price, a cost that neither they nor I fully understood at that time. Two years later we would all know.

Joyce Rupp is well known for her work as a writer, "spiritual midwife," international retreat leader, and conference speaker. She is a member of the Servants of Mary community, author of numerous best-selling books, and the co-director of The Institute of Compassionate Presence. Joyce Rupp resides in West Des Moines, Iowa, and can be visited online at www.joycerupp.com.

*We pray the Lord that we might always try to be
women of the Lord;
women who laugh and dance and sing;
women who are not so conscious of what we have given,
but of what we have been given;
women who are struggling for justice;
…women who are warmhearted;
with a great capacity to accept and forgive all.*

SISTER SHIRLEY KOLMER, ASC
EXCERPTED FROM INSTALLATION SPEECH
AUGUST 15, 1978

INTRODUCTION

This is the story of five Catholic American missionary sisters who were killed during the early years of one of the most brutal conflicts in modern history. It is also the story of the 250,000 Liberians who died during nearly 14 years of civil war. The sisters, Barbara Ann Muttra, Shirley Kolmer, Mary Joél Kolmer, Agnes Mueller, and Kathleen McGuire were members of the Adorers of the Blood of Christ, a community of Catholic religious women. They would have been the first to admit that they were just a small part of a much larger tragedy playing itself out on the West African continent during the last decade of the twentieth century and the first few years of the twenty-first.

I first heard about the murdered nuns in July of 2010 while on a trip to Liberia to visit a friend who wanted my help with a writing project. He and his wife were administering a Catholic mission located in the town of Careysburg in Montserrado County, about an hour's drive outside of Monrovia.

While the civil war had officially ended seven years earlier, the scars of that confrontation were still highly visible; manifest in the ruined buildings that dotted the streets of the capital. Such effective destruction could not be contained in Monrovia alone. Like a broken dam, devastation had spilled forth destroying all in its wake. Burned-out buildings were just one legacy of the war; the more serious wounds went much deeper and were more personal. Everyone, it seemed, had lost someone—often in a most inhumane manner.

One evening, as my friend and I sat outside on the mission grounds, he recounted that he had learned of five American sisters who had been murdered during the civil war. He told me that the women were members of the religious order Adorers of the Blood of Christ and had been killed a mere 10 miles away from where we sat that very evening, by rebel forces loyal to warlord Charles Taylor as they advanced on Monrovia in October of 1992.

The story of these sisters was completely unfamiliar to me, and I wondered why I had not heard of them before. I determined to learn more, though it would be two more years before I was able to begin the project in earnest.

In the summer of 2012, I got in touch with Sister Raphael Ann Drone, ASC. Sister Raphael Ann was intimately connected with the murdered nuns as a friend, family member, and fellow Liberian missionary. I was invited to Ruma, Illinois—the very place where the five sisters had studied as young women and professed their religious vows—to explain my idea for a book to several members of their community.

Over the course of my research, I would be welcomed many times to interview members of the order who had been friends with the martyrs, as the five are known in their community. Two of the nuns I spoke with were blood sisters of two of the women who had died. In Ruma I would also be allowed to study in the archives and read original correspondence and journal entries kept by the Liberian missionaries. My original research would expand to encompass interviews with family, friends, and colleagues across the U.S. and ultimately in Liberia.

In Context

If you are familiar with the history of Liberia, or just anxious to jump to the meat of the story, you might be tempted to skip this section and go straight to Chapter One. My advice, however, is to take a couple of minutes to read these few introductory pages. It will help you understand this story much better from the start.

Even today it is difficult for the western world to comprehend the kind of violence that stalked the people of Liberia for more than half a generation. Simple, ordinary people were not only confronted with but sometimes forced to participate in acts of violence so depraved that my words cannot truly convey. Families were intentionally sundered by warring government and guerilla factions fighting for control of local populations. In some cases, the methods were heinous. Fathers were forced to rape their own daughters in front of their wives and other children. Children were forced to kill their parents or be killed themselves. Witchcraft, voodoo, and child sacrifice became associated with some of the uncontrolled and uncontrollable armies that ransacked village after village. Though their country is now at peace, Liberians will continue to pay the price for these actions as long as collective memory of these atrocities remains.

What follows here is a much-abbreviated outline that may help you understand some of the circumstances surrounding the civil war.

In 1822, almost forty years before the American Civil War, a plot of land on the West Coast of Africa was colonized by freed American slaves under the auspices of the American Colonization Society. These colonists expanded their holdings and eventually fashioned a government modeled on that of the United States of America. They named their new country Liberia and their capital Monrovia (after U.S. President James Monroe). The descendants of these settlers were called Americo-Liberians and became the ruling elite of the country. The members of the 16 tribes indigenous to the area remained largely uneducated. Consigned to lower class status, they were denied a voice in the national government. The lion's share of Liberia's wealth from natural resources was controlled by the Americo-Liberian class, though they made up only about 2.5% of the population. The injustices endured by the indigenous inhabitants continued to fester until 1980, when a lowly master-sergeant in the Liberian army brought a quick and brutal end to Americo-Liberian rule. Samuel K. Doe, an ethnic Krahn, led a military coup that overthrew and murdered sitting President William Tolbert, Jr. For the next decade, Doe ran Liberia with a ruthless energy. Under his rule, power was increasingly vested in supporters from his own Krahn tribe, and once again most of the other indigenous people were still left out in the cold. As this government became increasingly repressive of opposition, the dissatisfaction of ordinary citizens grew. In an effort to forestall any potential coup against his regime, Doe began to move against a number of ethnic groups—even those that had once backed him.

In December of 1989, Charles Taylor, a former Doe supporter, led a group of rebels dubbed the National Patriotic Front of Liberia (NPFL) against the government. Shortly thereafter the NPFL itself splintered and a new faction calling itself the Independent National Patriotic Front of Liberia (INPFL) under the leadership of Prince Johnson began vying for power against both Doe and Taylor. In 1990 the Economic Community of West African States sent a peacekeeping force to Liberia to stem the violence. Later that year, Doe was captured by Johnson's rebels and executed. After Doe's death, many of his former soldiers continued fighting, forming a group called the United Liberation Movement of Liberia for Democracy (ULIMO). Later still, even more insurgent groups arose among the ever-fracturing rebellion.

In 1991 rebel factions agreed to a ceasefire that allowed an Interim Government of National Unity (IGNU) to be established, with Amos Sawyer as president. Though Sawyer would keep the job for nearly four years, the peace he helped broker was short-lived. In October of 1992 Charles Taylor's rebels undertook a massive, multi-pronged assault on Monrovia in what would be called Operation Octopus. It was during this assault that Sisters Barbara Ann Muttra, 69, Mary Joél Kolmer, 58, Kathleen McGuire, 54, Agnes Mueller, 62, and Shirley Kolmer, 61, were savagely murdered by Taylor's forces in two separate attacks, the first on October 20 and the second on October 23.

Taylor would go on to defeat the government and was elected president in 1997. Peace during this time was uneven, with Taylor eventually facing a rebellion of his own. In 2003 he was forced to step down as president and left Liberia. This paved the way for new elections in 2005 that culminated in the selection of the African continent's first woman president, Ellen Johnson-Sirleaf.

But between 1989 and 2003 Liberia had suffered a total breakdown of civil society. One million people, almost a third of the population, were made homeless by the continued fighting, and a quarter million lost their lives.

In 2012 Charles Taylor was convicted by the United Nation's -backed Special Court for Sierra Leone of crimes against humanity for the atrocities he had helped perpetuate during the bloody civil war in that country. He was sentenced to 50 years in prison and is serving his sentence in Britain. Taylor has not been tried for any crimes committed in Liberia.

Why Nuns and Sisters Still Matter

In a me-centric, celebrity-crazed world prone to value flash over substance it is easy to overlook the people who do not crave attention for themselves but rather shy away from it. The five women religious who are the subject of this book were among them. It would be a tragedy to ignore what they have to teach us about how to live our own lives.

There are hundreds of different orders of women religious in the Roman Catholic Church. Typically, women entering religious life take life-long vows of poverty, chastity, and obedience. Some orders focus on active involvement in society (they are usually called "sisters"), while others choose a cloistered life of prayer set apart from the rest of the world (they are usually called "nuns"). The sisters in this book are subscribers to the first group, but I will use the two words interchangeably in this book, following popular practice.

The Adorers of the Blood of Christ, sometimes referred to as Adorers, ASCs, or Precious Blood sisters, can be found serving in communities throughout the world. Their stated mission is to "collaborate with Christ in his work of redemption," which is achieved "by witnessing to God's love and ministering that love to others, especially the poor, the oppressed, and the deprived."

The sisters featured on these pages took this message quite literally, choosing to be of service in one of the neediest areas on the planet: Liberia, West Africa.

For most people, Roman Catholic nuns belong to a little understood segment of society that chooses to live their lives on a spiritual plane we don't really comprehend. They are different from the rest of us. And that is a good thing, because for centuries women who wore the habit were trailblazers in areas normally prohibited to females. They founded and ran schools, orphanages, and hospitals during times when most women did not even have an education or opportunities outside of the home and marriage. They have left us a legacy that continues to this day. In perhaps one of the most paternalistic of organizations, the Roman Catholic Church, women religious have carved their own paths, choosing not to be limited in their service to others by their gender. Some, like the sisters in this book, recognized that "no" is just a word, not a permanent condition under which to live. It is unfortunate that so many people—including many Catholics—seldom recognize or acknowledge the extraordinary debt we owe these women.

The Five

If we look for real heroes in this world, we will discover a bold few who possess a certain restlessness of spirit and an expansive world view. They are drawn by their faith to follow one of Jesus of Nazareth's central teachings: to minister to the least among us. These kind of people follow Jesus' directive literally, traveling to far-flung parts of our country and the rest of the world, where decades—sometimes centuries —of poverty, war, and disease are entrenched. Missionaries are among these people, although they occur in all walks of life. They are people burning with zeal to serve, to spread the "good news" that God cares, as proven by the fact that they themselves have been sent to serve the poorest of the poor. No matter the cost of their compassion, these "saints," if you will, actively live out their faith. This is so hard for many of us to understand, especially those of us who wear our faith like a baggy old sweater, never quite satisfied with the fit. The five sisters in this book wore their dedication to God and others like a second skin. For them, faith was love and love is an active verb. For them, love without action was just a hollow husk demanding to be filled.

For 21 years, members of the Ruma, Illinois, Province of the Adorers of the Blood of Christ were a presence in Liberia, having first set foot on the African continent in early 1971. In that time, 17 women religious offered themselves as nurses, teachers, religious guides, and friends to the people of that country. As civil war began to rage in the1990s throughout Liberia, five of these women bravely chose to stand with their Liberian friends rather than abandon them. And though they would become known in Catholic circles as Martyrs of Charity, this was not the fate they would have chosen for themselves. They would have found that pious appellation off-putting. In truth they were five wonderfully dedicated, spiritual, funny, occasionally stubborn, sometimes exasperating, but above all human women with distinctive strengths and failings. They loved and were loved. They were, in many respects, just like you and me. This is their story, as best as I can tell it.

What sets Shirley Kolmer, Mary Joél Kolmer, Agnes Mueller, Barbara Ann Muttra, and Kathleen McGuire apart from the rest of us is not the way they died but how they chose to live in our bruised world. Though they were women of faith bound by certain conventions and traditions, within these conventions they found an incredible freedom and support that enabled them to venture forth to the remote parts of the world and do the things most of us only dream of doing. Each in her own way was a fiercely independent person who chose vowed religious life as her vehicle for expressing this independence. Each was a deeply religious woman who did not subscribe to the notion that spiritualty and autonomous thought are mutually exclusive attributes.

In a world that produces very few people so filled with near infinite goodness, the loss of these five, all virtually at the same time, was an egregious blow. Though their absence leaves a hole, they are still spectacularly alive in the many young Liberians, particularly women, they influenced, and in the many nuns (especially the ASCs), who continue ministering through their own lives of service and prayer.

FOUR MINUTES MORE

Thursday, October 22, 1992,
Just Outside Gardnersville, Liberia

Sister Barbara Brillant, FMM, sat at the back of an army convoy in a borrowed ambulance, willing it forward. That she was in a war zone in Africa with active fighting going on might seem an unlikely state of affairs for a Roman Catholic nun to find herself in, but it was precisely where she was determined to be. In fact, she was impatient to dive even deeper into the fray: The louder the guns, the closer she was to Gardnersville and the convent of the Precious Blood sisters she believed were trapped between two opposing armies.

Sister Barbara had not envisioned making the six-mile trip from Monrovia to Gardnersville stuck at the back of a military convoy. But it was the only way the ECOMOG soldiers, comprised of West African peacekeepers from Liberia's neighbors, would allow her to continue her journey into the outlying area around Monrovia. For the last seven days, the capital had come under siege by National Patriotic Front of

Liberia (NPFL) rebels loyal to warlord Charles Taylor. Under the brutal direction of NPFL General Christopher Vambo, aka "Mosquito," the area around suburban Gardnersville was being particularly hard hit by mortars and rocket launchers. West African peacekeeping soldiers had been deployed around Monrovia months earlier to forestall just such an attack by the NPFL, which was seeking to unseat the internationally recognized interim government of Liberia. The rebel assault was to be multi-pronged, thereby engendering the rather grandiose battle name: Operation Octopus. Monrovia and its environs would endure a 120-day battering at the hands of Taylor's forces, marking the dramatic end to a fragile year-and-a-half cease fire. The rebel offensive would help plunge the country into a devastating five-year death spiral.

As she inched her way towards Gardnersville, Sister Barbara had no way of predicting the scope of the devastation to come. All she knew for sure was that the thread-bare peace had been broken. And that her colleagues, Sisters Shirley Kolmer, Agnes Mueller, Kathleen McGuire, Barbara Ann Muttra, and Mary Joél Kolmer, all members of the Adorers of the Blood of Christ (ASC from its Italian name), were sitting right in the path of the rebel assault.

"We've got to move faster," she said to the man driving the ambulance. "The gunfire is getting louder. I don't know how much time we have to reach Gardnersville before it all goes to pieces." Exasperated, Barbara sat in the cab of the ambulance, praying that the line of vehicles in front of her would move faster, though she had about as much chance of setting the pace as a tail has of wagging the dog. She would have to accept that things were in God's hands and she was merely God's instrument.

Earlier that morning, prior to setting out on her fateful rescue mission, Sister Barbara, a Franciscan Missionary of Mary, had paid a visit to the United States Embassy in Monrovia to alert them to the fact that it was likely that five U.S. citizens were caught up in the renewed fighting between rebels and African peacekeeping troops. Reports from missionaries stationed in other parts of Liberia left little doubt in her mind that Taylor's rebels were cutting a cruel and bloody swath through the countryside towards Monrovia. Gardnersville, where the ASC sisters lived, sat right on the paved road that led directly into the capital. But the embassy was already aware that the sisters were unaccounted for. After the start of the October 15 attack, the embassy put its travel warning program into effect. By radio, the embassy staff began contacting pre-determined individuals about the growing danger of Taylor's new offensive on Monrovia. This group would in turn contact another group of individuals who would pass on the warning to others in ever widening circles, until all U.S. citizens had been contacted about the risk. By the next day, evacuations of Americans would be under way, with people being sent to Ivory Coast or Freetown in Sierra Leone. From there they would catch commercial flights to the United States. By October 20, hundreds of U.S. ex-patriots had been evacuated from Liberia, but the ASC sisters were not among them.

The fact that five nuns from the American ASC community in Ruma, Illinois, were in Liberia at all was more by happenstance than design. Prior to 1971 their community had no more than a tangential involvement with overseas missions. (Though there had been a few sisters to serve in China for a short period.) In the main, the order, popularly known as the Precious Blood sisters, had focused their energies in the heartland of the U.S. But a plea from an international order of missionary priests had brought a contingent of them to Africa.

The community's formal name—Adorers of the Blood of Christ—is rich and evokes an archaic mystical connection to the God-Son who chose to spill out his life force for the suffering souls among us. True to this calling, the sister Adorers were in Liberia in 1992 to help bind the wounds of people who had been traumatized by an especially bloody 14-month civil war begun on Christmas Eve 1989, when Charles Taylor and a few hundred supporters invaded his home country of Liberia by way of Sierra Leone. This would set in motion a years-long chain of events that would bloody and almost break the spirit of the people of Liberia. The ASCs, like scores of other foreign missionaries and nongovernmental organization workers, had found it necessary to flee the country in 1990, but the nuns returned in 1991 when a cease-fire was brokered among the warring factions. For Catholic missionaries, a call for their return was made

4

by the Archbishop of Monrovia, Michael Kpakala Francis, the highest ranking Catholic prelate in Liberia. The Adorers of the Blood of Christ answered this call by allowing four seasoned missionaries and one neophyte to return to Liberia in the summer of 1991.

Though there had been a tenuous cease-fire for over a year, it was by no means a comfortable peace. Taylor's NPFL controlled 90 percent of the countryside and other rebel factions held small strongholds, while an interim government controlled the capital. Operation Octopus was a ferocious rebel push to capture the seat of government. When it began on October 15 it seemed to catch most Liberians off guard. They were ill prepared for the mayhem that followed.

Operation Octopus lasted 120 days, cost 3,000 lives—including the five sisters—and made refugees of over 200,000 civilians. It was described in a 2013 article by the Coalition for Justice in Liberia:

> *Operation Octopus was conceived with the purpose of implementing a pogrom to ensure that the NPFL exerted full and total control over the City of Monrovia and its environs. This would become the NPFL's scorched-earth policy and template for prosecuting its senseless war throughout the '90s, making the city unsafe and unlivable for its inhabitants and meeting out unspeakable crimes to instill fear and submission in the populace.*

Prior to Operation Octopus most missionaries, including the ASC sisters, may have felt some danger in their situations, but they had not seen themselves as specific targets of the rebel armies. And while many could testify to having some close calls with the various armed groups roaming the country, the prevailing sentiment at the time was that the Liberian people welcomed the missionaries' help and would never harm them. But as the war ground on, the fracturing ill-trained armies became more and more lethal and the rebels, once celebrated as Freedom Fighters, became less about freedom, instead indulging in drug-fueled voodoo and cannibalistic practices. Looting, raping, and murdering became the new pastimes for thousands of rag-tag bands of child soldiers armed and then set loose upon their own people by various armies.

At the same time, paranoia was growing within the rebel ranks that all white people were either CIA spies or working for the interim government. In the face of these new realities, the belief that missionaries' respected status with the people they served would protect them from harm proved to be little more than a thinly-plated wish. Everyone was at the mercy of hop-headed, machete-wielding, gun-toting youngsters, and it turned out that the average Liberian people had no protection to offer the missionaries at all.

For days Sister Barbara Brillant had sensed the changing milieu in the country, and she didn't like it one bit. It was starting to feel more and more like 1990, a year marked by the downfall of one tyrant leader, Samuel K. Doe, and the rise of the nascent warlord Charles Taylor. Though initially declaring themselves to be "Freedom Fighters" standing up for the rights of oppressed ethnic groups, Taylor's NPFL proved themselves no better than the brutal regime they opposed. Within weeks of their 1989 Christmas Eve invasion, wholesale slaughter and mass murder of innocent civilians by both sides in the conflict became the norm. Now, almost three years later, the NPFL rebels were once more pushing towards Monrovia, and Sister Barbara feared a return to the earlier atrocities.

In 1990, in an effort to keep tabs on one another during this first stage of the civil war, members of the various Catholic missionary communities in Liberia had set-up twice-daily radio check-ins. With very few telephones in-country, the shortwave radio was their most reliable means of communication. These check-ins continued through the months of relative calm in 1991 and 1992. As the war drums began to beat once again in mid-October of 1992, the daily check-ins took on increased significance. The ASC missionaries were on the short-wave list, but for almost two weeks they hadn't been heard from. Most likely they had a bum radio, and it hadn't been much of a worry to the others. With reports of renewed fighting beginning to circulate, however, it became critically important for them not to be cut off in case of trouble. On the Sunday, October 18 check-in, Sister Barbara voiced her unease to some of her compatriots on the radio.

"Has anyone heard from the Precious Blood sisters?

They haven't checked in for days."

"No."

"Not me either."

"Haven't seen them."

The disembodied voices of missionaries stationed throughout Liberia responded.

"It's been almost two weeks," Sister Barbara told the others, and I'm getting concerned about them."

"Haven't heard of anything happening in Gardnersville," was one reply.

"Thank goodness. Still can someone go out there and tell the sisters their radio isn't working?"

"Will do."

Monday, October 19, 1992

The Gardnersville convent got the message and on Monday, October 19, Precious Blood Sisters Mary Joél Kolmer and Shirley Kolmer made the short drive from Gardnersville to Saint Teresa's convent in Monrovia where Sister Barbara Brillant lived near the campus of the University of Liberia. It was a place Sister Shirley knew well, having taught mathematics there on a Fulbright Fellowship years earlier during the 1977-1978 school year.

Sister Shirley and Sister Joél, double first cousins because their mothers had married brothers, were in good spirits when they arrived at Saint Teresa's. Sister Barbara did not detect any particular anxiety on the part of the women. The roads into the city were open. Though shelling of the capital had begun several days earlier, it was coming from a distance, and rebel armies had yet to reach the nearby environs. The scope of Operation Octopus, however, would be more fully comprehended the next day when refugees pushing in from the countryside ahead of the advancing armies brought news of the on-the-ground offensive with them.

When the women arrived at Saint Teresa's that Monday morning, Sister Barbara ushered them into the kitchen, where they shared cups of coffee and small talk. Finally, they handed their radio over for Barbara to inspect.

"It just stopped working," said Shirley.

"We don't know what's wrong with the darn thing," said Joél.

"Well I've got an extra radio," said Barbara as she went to find the spare.

But that was of no use either. "Darn thing doesn't work," she said. "Tell you what. You need professional help. Take these radios down the block to Electro Shack and see if they can get one of them working again."

Joél and Shirley stood and headed for the door. A short while later the cousins stopped at Saint Teresa's once again. "They couldn't fix it today," said Shirley.

"Well when will you have it? You don't want to be without a radio too long."

"They said to come back on Wednesday and it should be ready. We'll see you then. And thanks for the concern. Cheers,

Barbara." It was a signature Sister Shirley sendoff, complete with her gap-tooth smile.

But when neither Joël nor Shirley returned for their radio on Wednesday as prearranged, Barbara grew very worried indeed. Something was wrong, she knew, because her friends would have come back for their radio. She was sure of that. Especially since word was now reaching her that Taylor's men were moving closer to Gardnersville. The Precious Blood sisters, Barbara feared, were right in the line of fire.

And Barbara knew from personal experience just how dangerous their predicament was. Taylor's men were not model soldiers by a long shot. Army discipline was lacking. And the soldiers were in thrall to drugs and superstition. They were also ruthless. In 1991 Barbara had been captured for a time and held at gunpoint by an NPFL soldier who accused her of being an American spy. The situation was doubly dangerous because the man was high on drugs at the time. By the grace of God, she says, she had been spared, but it had been a near escape. She knew things could have gone either way, which heightened her concern now for the five sisters she assumed to be hiding in their convent in Gardnersville trying to stay safe.

What Sister Barbara and every missionary still in Liberia knew was that the potential for harm to any and all of them was real. They knew this empirically, yet most of them consciously set this knowledge aside so that they could continue functioning in a society that desperately needed what they had to offer. Even in the face of growing evidence to the contrary, these missionaries held on to the thin belief that the Liberian people—their people—would never intentionally harm them. Yes, harm might come to them but not at the hands of the people they served. That is what Barbara clung to as she prepared to retrieve the five Precious Blood sisters on Thursday, October 22.

Because she knew these five women, albeit some better than others, Barbara assumed that they had not fled the area ahead of the fighting but were trapped in their home. More than likely, she thought, they also had locals taking shelter with them. If she moved swiftly, Barbara thought, she might just get to them in time and pull them back to Monrovia where it was safer.

After first informing the U.S. Embassy about the sisters' situation, Barbara put her rescue plan into operation. She went for help to her colleagues at Médecins Sans Frontières (MSF), Doctors Without Borders in English. "I need an ambulance," she insisted. "I've got people in Gardnersville and it's about to be overrun by rebels. I want to evacuate them."

Her MSF colleagues knew Sister Barbara well enough to realize that trying to talk her out of the effort would be a fruitless exercise, so they lent her an ambulance and found a driver willing to accompany her into the center of the storm. A short time later, nun and driver were headed east out of Monrovia hoping to cover the short distance to Gardnersville before things deteriorated too badly.

Ensconced in the front passenger seat, Barbara prayed

as the ambulance headed for the sole paved road that would lead them to Gardnersville. But they were stopped outside of Monrovia, just beyond one of the many bridges that span the swamps surrounding the capital. There stood a newly erected barrier where armed Nigerian soldiers—part of the ECOMOG (West African peace keeping) contingent—were turning back traffic.

"We have to stop, Sister," said the driver. "They might not let us through."

"Oh, they'll let us through *all right*," said Barbara defiantly. She had already stood up to men pointing guns at her during this war, so she wasn't about to let a road block stymie her now.

"This is no time to back down," she said. And if it took a little finesse, or even an outright lie to get them through, she was up for it. She could always go to confession later!

"Jesus, we need you now more than ever," she prayed. "Help us through the guards up ahead, and please watch over the good sisters."

"You must turn back," insisted the soldier when they reached the barricade. "No one is allowed. There is fighting up ahead."

"I know that," said Barbara employing her *I'm in-charge voice*. "We've been called. You can see we are an ambulance and someone is hurt."

Her bluster was just good enough to get the barrier lifted. The ambulance continued on, with the sounds of gunfire growing louder.

But it wasn't long before they encountered another military road block. This one was more sizeable than the last. Probably a command center, Barbara reasoned as numerous trucks and soldiers idled in unison waiting for a directive.

Barbara thought it best to go with the truth this time, as she appealed to the guard who she took to be Senegalese. "There are five American missionary sisters trapped in Gardnersville. I've come to get them out."

"No, Sista. You cannot go. The fighting is too heavy," came the reply from the young soldier guarding the barricade. But Barbara would not be put off so easily and continued to argue her case. Soon another soldier, this time a commander, came to see about the commotion. He approached the ambulance. This is the man who could let them pass, thought Barbara, so she re-told her story with even more passion the second time. Perhaps it was the urgency in her voice or her determination not to be thwarted that finally convinced the commander. Or perhaps he thought she was more trouble than he had time for. Whatever the reason, he finally relented. As most sensible African men know, when a stubborn "Old Ma" will not be moved, it is usually best just to get out of her way.

"Alright," he said. "You can join our convoy. We are going in that direction anyway, but stay at the back!"

Which is how Sister Barbara and her driver found themselves bringing up the rear of a slow-moving military procession snaking its way towards the suburb of Gardnersville in the face of increasingly intense mortar fire. When she finally saw the cross atop Saint Anthony's Catholic Church in the distance, Barbara thought her prayers had been answered. She knew from experience that it was just a mile further to the sisters' convent. She estimated that at the rate they were going they should be there in another few minutes, four at the most.

It was then that the sluggish convoy ground to a complete halt as people who moments earlier had been sheltering in their homes were driven out into the open. Shells launched by rebels from the backs of rickety trucks proved to be equal opportunity assassins, maiming civilians and soldiers alike. ECOMOG soldiers charged with holding back the advancing rebel army returned fire. People now caught in the bombardment began to run helter-skelter for their lives, clogging the only road leading out of town, effectively blocking any further progress for Sister Barbara and her ambulance. Forced to pull off the road and into a gas station, she and her driver watched helplessly as a human sea of chaos rolled towards them.

Then a boy fell just in front of their vehicle. He had been shot. The driver helped Sister Barbara pick up the child and put him into the ambulance. With heavy hearts, they turned around and slowly made their way back to Monrovia. It was no use anyway. "We're not going to get any further today in all this fighting," Barbara told her driver.

All she could do was pray that her fellow missionaries were safe and try again the next day. What she could not know at the time was that two of the nuns, Sister Mary Joél

Kolmer and Sister Barbara Ann Muttra, were already dead. Killed in an ambush two days earlier on Tuesday, October 20.

Friday, October 23, 1992

Sister Barbara Brillant and her driver would make two more failed attempts to reach the Gardnersville convent. On Friday, October 23, they could not get even as close as they had the day before. Once again rocket fire forced them to the side of the road where they sat for hours into the night, waiting to see if the sisters might miraculously walk by. As they sat in the cab, they watched streams of people heading their way. Everyone, it seemed, carried whatever they could salvage of their belongings. Balancing their things on their heads, with their free hands holding on to youngsters, the crowds undertook the long walk to Monrovia. Anxiously perched in the front seat of the ambulance, Barbara eagerly looked for any sign that the Precious Blood sisters had joined the exodus.

But their wait proved fruitless. Around 5 p.m. that afternoon, rebels had attacked the convent of the ASC sisters, killing Kathleen McGuire, Agnes Mueller, Shirley Kolmer, and Abraham Nasser, a Lebanese shopkeeper and neighbor who was taking refuge on the convent grounds. Spared were the man's wife, another Lebanese family, and four young Liberian girls, aspirants to the religious life who had been living and studying under the sisters' guidance.

Saturday, October 24, 1993

Still believing, or at least hoping, that the sisters were alive, but more deeply concerned than ever for their fate, Sister Barbara made one final attempt to reach them on Saturday, October 24. That final day the wait was worse than ever. With hope waning and Taylor's forces flexing their muscles and advancing towards Monrovia, Sister Barbara and her driver had to stop even further away from Gardnersville than the two previous days. Again they waited by the side of the road as people passed them by, hoping against hope that they would catch sight of the sisters, thinking that perhaps they had merely missed them or that the sisters had escaped towards Kakata instead of Monrovia, trying to deny the sense of dread that was building in their hearts.

Barbara noticed that some of the people walking by were wearing rosary beads around their necks. They must have taken refuge at Saint Anthony's Catholic Church in Gardnersville, she reasoned, and that was near the convent. Surely someone would have seen the sisters. Excited she scrambled down from the vehicle and began to stop people. "Have you seen the sisters? Have you seen the sisters?" she asked over and over. But the answer was always the same: a shake of the head and then, "No, Sista."

No one had seen them because they were already dead.

In recent years, Sister Barbara Brillant would recall the events of those days with sadness, trying to make sense of why so many people had been able to escape from Gardnersville but the sisters had not. Why hadn't they joined the exodus on that first day, when they could have escaped? Why did they wait until it was just too late and the fighting too heavy to try and leave their convent? Why didn't the ECOMOG troops make them leave when they still could? And, when they finally did make an attempt, why did ECOMOG tell them to stay put? All these things Barbara learned much later.

But of course, Sister Barbara's missionary heart knew right away why the three remaining sisters: Agnes, Shirley, and Kathleen, did not just walk out. They were waiting for Barbara Ann and Joél to come back home. The two had gone out in their car on Tuesday afternoon and never returned. The remaining sisters feared the worst, but they continued to hope for the best. They prayed that the two were held up somewhere safe; even as each passing hour made that outcome less likely.

And finally, as each of the nuns in her own mind came to accept that the worst had most likely happened to Sister Barbara Ann and Sister Joél, they made the decision to pack their car and leave. Yet they still told themselves and one another that they might all meet up in Monrovia safe and sound. As people of faith they must have prayed long and hard over their actions. But they were caught up with no good choices before them: Leave too soon and risk abandoning Joél and Barbara

Ann; stay put and hope that their status in the town would protect them and the families sheltering with them.

"I know they made the best decision they could at the time, but still it must have been terrible, terrible," said Sister Barbara, even as she conceded that it could just as well have been her who was murdered that sunny October afternoon. "It could have been any one of us in their place," she said

After the sisters' murders, the atmosphere in Liberia grew even more threatening for Americans. Charles Taylor was convinced that Americans, including religious missionaries, were spies for the interim Liberian government or, just as treasonous, the CIA. Ironically, it is believed by some that since the early 1980s Taylor himself had been an informant for the U.S. Central Intelligence Agency. It has even been reported that the CIA went so far as to engineer Taylor's escape from a Massachusetts prison in 1985—where he had been awaiting extradition to Liberia on charges of embezzling from his home country—in order to facilitate his return to Liberia and promote another regime change.

But by 1992 the warlord viewed Americans as his enemies. And he passed these suspicions on to his supporters. However, it was not always clear in the fevered-minds of these fighters who were Americans and who were not. Often any person with white skin was treated as a spy. Many missionaries of all nationalities were threatened, held hostage, beaten, and robbed. For women, there was the added threat of rape.

Sister Barbara tells of another close call she had later in the war, hiding out on the Stella Maris campus in Monrovia with several female students, who were in the nursing program. Several soldiers climbed over the school's walls with the intention, she believes, of raping the women. By this point in the war, rape had become a commonplace and particularly brutal tool for terrorizing the population. Unknown to the soldiers, however, SMA priest Father Garry Jenkins had recently brought the residents of a leper colony from besieged Bomi County to shelter on the campus. As the soldiers advanced demanding the women, Barbara and the students hid. Remaining as quiet as possible they prayed for salvation. Meanwhile Garry and the lepers went out to the courtyard and blocked the soldiers' advance, insisting that there were no women on campus. In a display of great courage, the unarmed lepers marched towards the soldiers yelling, "Look at us! Look at us!" Terrified, the soldiers broke ranks and scrambled back over the wall.

The longer the war went on the more atrocities Barbara witnessed. "I saw people decapitated. I saw people with their skin peeled from head to toe. I saw mothers with the babies cut from their wombs. I came across evil, evil, evil in the war. Even though many of these acts were done by child soldiers, and even though they were high on drugs at the time, the fact is there were other people who knew what was going on and allowed it to happen. And that is the true face of evil."

With good and evil knotted up in the same people it sometimes became difficult to distinguish friend from foe. "Looking back I suppose we should have known that people are capable of these terrible acts, but at the same time I can tell you of half-a-dozen times when I was saved by people because they knew I was just trying to do good."

Safe and sound in the United States, a reasonable person may wonder why Sister Barbara Brillant continued to stay in Liberia, especially in time of war. The same question has been asked about the five slain ASC sisters. While the answer may be self-evident to a devoted missionary, it is anything but clear to an outsider.

For this, Sister Barbara ventures a simple explanation, "If you are a missionary and a healer, then that is your life. Put that together with the fact that you fall in love with the people and the place, and that is a good recipe for happiness. When you are away from your mission you cannot wait to get back to it because these are your people. What I know about myself is that I work well in a crisis. I think it was the same for the Precious Blood sisters. I'm sure that, like me, they saw that when people are down and out is when they need you the most. I would never think of staying away. They were the same."

Sister Barbara recounted these memories for me in a Skype interview in August of 2013. She was sitting in her office in Mon-

rovia, half a world away, on the Stella Maris Polytechnic campus where she ran Mother Patern College of Health Sciences. When she spoke it was with a Maine coast accent: "Wha da ya wan a know?" When she laughed, it was of the hearty "Haw, haw, haw" variety.

When Sister Barbara talks of the murdered Adorers of the Blood of Christ sisters, she is speaking about women she knew personally. Sister Barbara Ann Muttra, ASC, was a nurse like Barbara, and they shared a love of healing. The two women's paths had often crossed in a professional way. Barbara also knew Sister Shirley Kolmer because they both had been instrumental in the planning of Stella Maris, a Catholic university in Monrovia. The other three sisters were known to Barbara through gatherings that the five ASC sisters would host at their house in Gardnersville, Liberia.

When we neared the end of our interview, I wondered to myself how Sister Barbara can stand remembering all of the terrible things she has seen. As if reading my mind she told me in a ruminating voice, "Maybe that is why I'm still here at my age, to help restore the lovely values that were destroyed during the war." She saw these values in Liberia before the war, she said. She saw beauty and the ability of the Liberian people to work together for a common purpose. I silently wished her well in her current endeavors as we disconnected.

CODA

When the Ebola epidemic of 2014 was laying waste to the limited Liberian healthcare system, I would occasionally see Sister Barbara Brillant's name in on-line news stories. Still on the frontlines, I thought, still fighting the bad things that keep coming her way. And I realized once again how blessed we all are to have people like her in the world.

BEGINNINGS

The story of the five sisters began long before any one of them ever set foot on the African continent. It began decades earlier in small towns and rural communities scattered throughout the southern third of Illinois. Some of the communities, like Waterloo, rate a dot on the Illinois road map, but others, like tiny Pond Settlement, are unmarked, invisible to all but those who know where to look.

On display in most of these communities is at least one church steeple sprouting from the center of town; witness to faith as lush as the wild columbine and larkspur that cover the ground in spring. Hugged on three sides by two mighty rivers, the Mississippi on the west and the Ohio on the south and east, southern Illinois is a place apart from the north of the state where Chicago dominates. Chicago is liberal, rowdy, and cosmopolitan. It is big-city with skyscrapers and vibrant night life and scores of suburbs radiating out in three directions from the city's hub along Lake Michigan on the east. Beyond its radius of influence, in the smaller more conservative communities of Illinois, Chicago is often seen as a troubled and often troublesome co-tenant of the land named after the Native American tribe that originally inhabited it. Like unreconciled siblings, the global city and the provincial towns of Illinois have grown up and grown apart over the 200 years of Illinois' statehood. In some respects, this makes the idea of the tiny town of Ruma being a seat of international attention even more intriguing and compelling.

The course of events that would eventually thrust a small group of nuns from Ruma onto the world stage had been set in motion by hard working, faith-filled parents who taught their daughters two very simple rules—follow God and care for others. This dual mandate would be tested and further refined as these daughters committed themselves to the sisterhood as young girls. The commitments, or "vows" as they are called in religious life, would be sorely tested during the mid-twentieth-century post-Vatican II era of the Roman Catholic Church: a time when both men and women religious seriously reexamined their vocations. Though many chose to forsake their vows and re-enter secular life, the five Precious Blood sisters featured here recommitted themselves to lives of service in Jesus' name. It was a renewal that would lead a total of 17 of them to Liberia, Africa; five of whom, like the Savior they followed, would make the supreme sacrifice.

The women at the center of this story have been called many things over the years: brave, loving, self-sacrificing, foolhardy. To be sure, they were all of these, but what else were they?

Sister Barbara Ann Muttra, the oldest of the group at 69, was the longest serving member of the ASC community in Liberia, having come to Africa in late 1971. Barbara was a nurse who put caring for other people, especially children, way above concerns for her personal comforts or safety. She was a 5-foot-2-inch firecracker who could go toe-to-toe with anyone who stood in the way of good healthcare practices. A priest acquaintance called her a "soldier always pushing forward." Sister Barbara had a temper but would only show it in the defense of others. She was tough and not afraid to call things as she saw them, but she was also compassionate and full of love for those in her care. Though Barbara was a deeply spiritual person, she was not as intensely contemplative as Sister Agnes Mueller or Sister Kathleen McGuire. Full of kinetic energy, action was Barbara's go-to mode. If God needed a pair of hands to help heal this broken world, then she would willingly give hers to the cause.

When Barbara was diagnosed with ovarian cancer in 1990, it was but a pause in her ministry, not an end to it. She was operated on but because of health complications was not able to receive chemotherapy. Yet she pronounced herself "cured" and returned to Liberia in 1991. There was absolutely no quit in her.

Sister Shirley Kolmer, 61, complemented Barbara nicely; though physically they could not be less alike, both women had the kind of persona that made others sit up and take notice when they spoke. Like Barbara, when Sister Shirley decided on a course of action, she was rock solid in her conviction and pushed hard to get her way. She was a big woman; her 5-foot-10-inch frame and size 13 feet contained an even larger personality. Often generous, occasionally sharp, Shirley radiated an inner strength that made it easy for others to follow. She owned a gap-tooth grin that she flashed widely and regularly. As a child, she possessed a lively nature that sat just at the edge of impishness; it was a characteristic that Shirley never quite outgrew. Her mind was alert and logical as befitted the owner of a doctorate in mathematics.

Shirley was in all respects a formidable woman; eulogized as "large in body, heart, and spirit." She had served as provincial (a.k.a. mother superior) to her community in Ruma, Illinois, and was the leader of the small ASC community in Liberia. She has been called a visionary who was not content to settle for the status quo.

Sister Mary Joël Kolmer was 58 and a tall woman herself, though an inch or so shorter than her cousin Shirley. Thinly built, Sister Joël was a delicate reed next to Shirley's sturdy branch. Musical, artistic, funny, and with a trace of capriciousness, Joël possessed neither guile nor cunning. Often unconcerned with the practical aspects of the way the world worked, people considered her a bit naïve. Though she herself occasionally struggled with academics in school, Joël admired Shirley's prodigious intellect. Anyone who knew Joël respected the genuine goodness she radiated wherever she went. It was hard not to smile when one was in her company. For Joël, life was a beautiful adventure full of God's glory. She saw wonders everywhere, often stopping to sketch something that caught her attention. If she had no pen or paper, then she would sketch with her mind—a habit that got her into trouble on more than one occasion when it caused her to lose focus on the task at hand. She was sweet and tender, with a heart that generally overrode any inclination to judge others.

At age 62, Sister Agnes Muller felt that she had finally found the place she was meant to be in Liberia. Her early years as a religious nun had been marked by a sort of restlessness, as if she could not quite find what she was looking for. Trained as a nurse, she eschewed medicine after 14 years for a career as an academic.

A life-long learner with a prodigious intellect, Sister Agnes eventually earned two master's degrees in theology and entered parish life. She never stayed more than a couple of years in one place, however, seeming to relish the challenges of new people and places. Described variously by friends as "bookish," "intelligent," "curious," and "compassionate," Agnes was also a feminist who felt women should have a larger role in the Church. She insisted that women were not as respected as their male counterparts by Church leaders. Perhaps her most striking physical characteristic was an intense pair of eyes that one friend described as "alive."

Agnes had wanted to be a missionary since she was a child. Before she finally achieved that goal, she was well into her fifties and had lived her whole life in the United States. Though her own life was one of moderation, Agnes saw excesses of abundance in American culture that bothered her greatly. She found a completely different lifestyle in Liberia: one marked not by abundance, but by want; a life that was hard and devoid of most modern conveniences.

Yet Agnes found she was happy to be living in Africa, a place void of most consumerism. For her, life on the mission helped focus her ministry and allowed her to pursue what interested her most, which was creating a community-centered church and helping empower women as leaders. This was a passion her colleague Kathleen McGuire joined her in most eagerly.

Sister Kathleen McGuire, 54, had a shock of white hair that contrasted sharply with a set of deeply dark eyebrows perched over beautiful green eyes. Sister Kathleen was an avid camper and skilled in outdoor survival practices. She also held a doctorate in education. At the time of her death she had been a missionary all of 14 months.

Kathleen had come to Liberia to be with her four friends, all seasoned Liberian missionaries, and to help support their efforts in any way she could. If that meant directly ministering to the Liberian people, or cooking and cleaning in the convent, or doing any task that was asked of her, Kathleen was a willing helper living out the Gospel directive to serve others. She saw the importance of even the smallest gestures if done for the right reasons; no job, even ironing for the sisters when no one expected it, was beneath her. For Kathleen, all service had intrinsic dignity.

Those who knew her best called Kathleen "reserved." Though she was very friendly, she was not really a big fan of hugs. When introduced to someone new, she could take their measure in minutes then graciously put them at ease by flashing a wide grin that "spread from ear to ear." She was a "deep thinker" who would not be moved until she was sure of her course of action. But once convinced, "she moved and would not be swayed," according to one of her younger brothers.

Kathleen's assignment to Liberia was meant to be a short-term commitment, two years at most. Her real goal was to serve in Latin America, where the bishop and martyr Oscar Romero and other personal heroes of hers had made their mark fighting for the rights of indigenous people. An ardent crusader for social justice, Kathleen was possessed of a persuasive personality that she used to her advantage on many occasions. She brought a hesitant ASC community around to her point of view in the 1980s when she helped convince them to offer shelter to families fleeing conflict in Central America as part of a controversial sanctuary movement of the time.

Though we know the story of these five very able, very likable women will end tragically—at least by the world's standards—to look away from it would be an injustice to their memory. In some respects, their deaths might even have been predicted as the price of doing God's business. Father Pat Kelly, a retired missionary priest who knew Sister Barbara put the risk this way: "The Lord I believe in," he said, "promised us many blessings if you follow him. But he also promised we would be persecuted." Just as Jesus was persecuted and executed unjustly, those who follow him face the possibility of the same fate. Though most of us don't think about paying this price very often, if ever, and definitely don't seek out martyrdom of any kind, it is always there, lurking in the background "part of the life" of a missionary. Consciously or not, these five women freely accepted that risk.

HAPPIER TIMES

It is difficult to find a picture of the five missionaries all together. One gets the sense that they were too busy to be pos-
ing for group pictures. Most of the photos from that time are
little better than snapshots—blurry, off center. But one that
comes to mind was taken in December of 1991 at a Christmas party given at the U.S. Embassy in Monrovia, Liberia,
just ten months before their deaths. The sisters are joined in
the photo by a man identified as Michael Yunkis, from the
Catholic Relief Service. Everyone is smiling broadly, though
Sister Barbara looks pained, as if she is still feeling the effects
of the cancer surgery she had endured the previous year. Yunkis towers over Sister Shirley whose shoulder he comfortably
wraps his right hand around. Shirley's famous toothy grin is
on prominent display. She and her cousin Joél wear matching
round glasses that reflect the light from the camera's flash. As
usual, Sister Joél's thin face sports an infectious grin as she casually rests a hand on Sister Agnes, whose face is crinkled as if
she is laughing so that you can't even see her famous piercing

eyes. Sister Kathleen, who is wearing an African print blouse, stares dark-eyed into the camera, an unsure smile parting her lips. At this point Kathleen had only been a missionary for four and a half months.

Kathleen recorded this party in the Gardnersville annals with good humor: "Dec. 21: We attend a Christmas party at the USA embassy. Luckily we left before the drinks released inhibitions and some folks were thrown into the swimming pool."

During this party, however, outside the U.S. embassy compound, a precarious peace held on by a thread. The civil war that engulfed Liberia in 1990 and early 1991 had cooled down, though there were frequent ceasefire violations. Thousands of displaced civilians were trying to rebuild war-shattered lives on shifting sands. Everyone feared that fighting could begin in earnest once again. But inside the embassy these thoughts had been put aside for a few hours as a disparate group of citizens of the U.S. gathered to celebrate the birth of Christ with their friends and colleagues.

The joy of that celebration, forever frozen in the photo of these five women who look to all the world like a collection of everyone's favorite aunties on a group outing, is most likely the last picture ever taken of the five soon-to-be martyrs. But this was realized only years later. (The snapshot is reproduced as best as possible on the inside back cover of this book.)

THE CALL

When the first Precious Blood sister set her very sensible crepe-soled shoe down on the red earth of Liberia in January of 1971, her first thoughts were most likely that she had just stepped into a very crowded sauna full of people hustling a curious variety of wares to all new arrivals, including her. At that point in time, the country was enjoying relative calm, with civil war almost two decades off. Widespread unrest would not begin to crescendo for many years, although anyone with eyes could see restiveness beginning to simmer among some of the ethnic groups relegated to second class citizenship by those then in power.

The seat of government for Liberia rests in Monrovia, and in 1971 the country presented a formidable face to the world. It was a land rich in natural resources like rubber and iron and had a strong central democratically elected government modeled after that of the United States. Liberia was often referred to as the "pearl" of Western Africa in those days. It had an economy that rivaled any in Africa. But outside of the capital it was a different story, with abject poverty and illiteracy the general rule. It was these people that the Adorers of the Blood of Christ had come to serve, although in truth this had not been an idea of their own making.

Father Philip Bagnasco drove south on Illinois Highway 3 speeding by fields that mere weeks earlier had showcased mile upon mile of ripe corn. Stalks crowned with wind-whipped tassels had waved silky hellos to passing cars then. Now, with winter of 1969 in the offing, the fields were empty except for the occasional hay bales strewn like giant severed camel humps on bare ground.

Gray and rainy as the day was, Father Phillip was not about to let the gloominess affect his mood, not when he was busy about the Lord's work. The priest, who belonged to a community of religious men known as the Society of African Missions (SMA after its Latin name), was on a quest. He had long been a missionary serving the Liberian people in West Africa, and he knew first hand of the desperate plight of these all-but-forgotten children of God. Now he was going to do something really important about it.

The Society of African Missions was founded in France in 1856 with the express purpose of evangelizing the most abandoned people in Africa. The aim of those early missionaries was to establish an indigenous Catholic clergy who would in turn continue to spread the Word of God. The first SMA priests and brothers to journey to Africa had settled in Sierra Leone in 1858. They lasted just 13 months. Within the space of 26 days the fledgling community lost five of their group to yellow fever. The lone surviving brother was sent back to France, and for a time the spirit of the order was devastated. But it was not defeated. Within two years the SMAs were back in Africa, this time in Benin. Over the next 45 years, they established mission outposts in seven more countries, including Liberia in 1906.

For over six decades the SMAs ministered to the people of Grand Cess, Liberia, pretty much singlehandedly, but now they needed an infusion of new volunteers to address the growing educational and health needs of the local Kru population. Finding these volunteers would become a personal quest for the leader of the American Province of SMAs, Father Philip Bagnasco.

Armed with a list of several hundred religious communities of women spread across the U. S., Father Philip embarked on a long and grueling campaign to find missionary sisters who might answer the call. The story goes that the priest would sally forth for several weeks a year, visiting various Mothers General (the heads of orders of women religious) unannounced. This went on for over a decade according to an account the priest wrote in 1967.

"I visited seventy Mothers General. Some of them gave me donations for the Mission. Some of them gave me prayers. They ALL gave me a cup of tea. (And I hate tea.) But none of them could give us Sisters." As prospects faded, the priest good-naturedly joked that at least he hoped to "develop a taste for tea."

With this recent history in mind, it's easy to imagine that Philip might have been less than buoyant as he ventured into the rural countryside of southern Illinois to a place heretofore unknown to him called Ruma. But it is equally easy to imagine that his determination, inspired by the example of those first unwavering SMA pioneers, strengthened his resolve. They didn't give up and neither would he. And so it was that his journey brought the plucky priest to Randolph County, a 583-square mile region in Southwestern Illinois, population 34,000, with a rich Native American, French, and British history; though that probably never entered his calculations. Randolph County is a place of small towns and fertile farming communities, many bordering the venerable Mississippi River, but that probably wasn't important to him either. More significant to Philip's quest was the fact that this was a cradle of conservative Midwestern values, where hardworking people of the land and, most importantly people of faith, lived. Nestled in a tiny (less than half a square mile) of Randolph County was a town so seemingly insignificant that it would never make a vacation guidebook. The town was called Ruma, and in that little fraction of the Earth was Phillip's destination: the Illinois home of the Adorers of the Blood of Christ. Perhaps his prayers would finally be answered there.

As Philip drove the flat, empty highway it would have been easy for him to miss the turn-off that would take him to the convent of the Adorers. In truth, he would barely have had time to register the fact that he actually was in a town at all save for the abrupt end to the corn fields. Ruma, home to just a few hundred people, is featureless with only a few low-slung brick buildings hugging the empty highway in the heart of the tiny village. The priest's turn for route 155 would have come up quickly, just past the solitary restaurant. Then he would have made an easy turn west onto the small rural road. Within three-quarters of a mile he would have had to be sharp-eyed in the fading light to find what he was looking for: a sign on the left of the road bearing a white heart that marked the entrance to a narrow lane. That lane wound gently through open acres, eventually ending next to a burial ground where rows of regimentally aligned simple wooden crosses rose from a field of grass already being claimed by winter. The modest crosses, which would be replaced by modest stone markers in 1974, designated the final resting places of the Adorers of the Blood of Christ who had completed their earthly mission. The earliest dating of a grave at the time of Father Philip's visit would have been 1883.

Who would have imagined when the first ten Adorers of the Precious Blood sisters (as they were called at the time) emigrated from Germany to the heart of Illinois back in 1870 that they would eventually number a multitude? A deteriorating relationship between the Catholic Church and the German Empire may have further added to the sisters' number in 1873 when 49 more Precious Blood sisters settled in the United States. The exodus from their home country occurred at a time of state-sponsored religious oppression, with Chancellor Otto von Bismarck pursuing a policy of imprisonment, exile, and persecution of Catholics. The culture clash, little remembered today, was a 19-year struggle to reduce the power of the popular Roman Catholic pontiff, Pope Pius IX, within the German Empire. Many of those oppressed, like the Precious Blood sisters, chose to pick up and strike out for America, unaware of what lay ahead but willing to risk all on the hope of freedom.

It was not, however, a completely smooth transition for the early ASC pioneers. They had originally intended to make their home in Piopolis, Illinois, among German immigrant families. But it was reported that there was unease with the local bishop, and within three years the nuns had relocated to Ruma, 100 miles further west. There they eventually purchased a former school building and land from the local bishop. Finally, they had their foothold in the Midwest. From little Ruma, the sisters would continue to expand, adding sites in Missouri, Pennsylvania, and Kansas. With a missionary zeal that would have made their foundress, Saint Maria de Matias, proud, the sisters established and staffed schools, a university, a home for disadvantaged children, and hospitals. In later years their mission field expanded beyond their traditions of education and healthcare to encompass a number of social justice causes and—most important to our story—service in overseas missions.

As those first German Adorers died off, their numbers

were replenished by eager young women from small American towns and farming communities who burned with a desire to witness God's love to others "especially the poor, the oppressed, and the deprived" as the nuns described their particular charism as an order. The pioneers, many now lying beneath the soil of Ruma, had done their work well. They had established a community that continues to honor their foundress; a preacher and mystic, who in early nineteenth-century Italy resisted local custom by educating girls and women. In her own gentle way, Saint Maria dared to speak truth to power. It is a tradition her followers have continued to this day.

When Father Philip passed the graves, did he give thought to the nuns' rich history? Or to the fact that Mother Clementine Zerr, the first mother superior of the American group, was buried just yards away? Perhaps not. But he would surely have honored the collective resting place of the now silent sisters keeping watch over their successors. As a person experienced in the hardships of missionary life, Philip would have respected their sacrifices, especially as he came to ask even more of their heirs.

Immediately beyond the cemetery an impressive four-story, red brick building rose above its surroundings. At last the priest had reached his destination, the headquarters of the Ruma Province of the Adorers of the Blood of Christ.

Sister Marie Clare Boehmer, ASC, set the scene of what came next in her book *Echoes in Our Hearts*. It was already late in the day when Father Bagnasco arrived. He wasn't expected, so no one could blame him if he was a bit apprehensive of a welcome. He approached the imposing main building and climbed its 24 steps to the front door. Though he was probably weary, he was not yet ready to call it quits. He rang the bell. Sister Mary Ellen Brundza opened the door.

"Excuse me. My name is Father Philip Bagnasco and I am an SMA. I wonder if I might have a word with your Mother Superior."

"Do you have an appointment, Father?"

"I'm sorry, but I don't."

"Well then you will have to make one and come back another time."

"Please, I have been driving for so long."

Sister Mary Ellen took pity on the priest and went to find Sister Angelita Myerscough, head of the Ruma province. She returned shortly. "I'm sorry. But Mother's policy is that you need an appointment."

But Father Philip was not easy to deter. He had learned over these many years how to be a salesman, and now that he had the proverbial foot in the door he was not about to remove it so easily. He started talking, explaining the great needs of the people in Liberia to Mary Ellen, who possessed a missionary heart herself, and she began to soften. She thought to try her superior one more time, and leaving the visitor in the downstairs parlor ascended the stairs to Sister Angelita's office.

"Mother, couldn't you just come down and talk with

him? Just a little bit?"

"He's still here? Alright, tell him I'll be down in a minute."
As it turned out Angelita had a soft spot for the missions, too,
having once hoped to serve in China or Puerto Rico. Even so, as
she descended the stairs she was thinking it was best to let the
priest know where he stood right away. "Hello Father. I'm afraid
you are wasting your time here," she said by way of greeting.

Philip would not be so easily put off. He began explaining the great need that the people of Liberia had for the word
of God and for education and for healthcare.

The Mother General was just as adamant, "You don't
understand, Father. Our numbers are falling and many of our
sisters are in school themselves completing degrees. We've
even had to pull back sisters from the missions we serve here
in the United States."

The priest knew he could come across as a bit of a bother
at times (had someone even gone so far as to refer to him as
a pest?), but he considered being a bother in God's service to
be a noble calling. His speech grew more impassioned as he
spoke about the good people of Grand Cess, who had been
praying for sisters for years. People were dying there, even as
the two of them spoke, because they had no access to health
care.

What could Angelita say in the face of such a plea? When
the priest asked if he could leave behind some information
sheets and a film about the mission she acquiesced, although
not without misgivings.

Sister Clare attributes this quote to Sister Angelita: "It's ridiculous for me to let you leave anything here, Father. It's ridiculous because my head says the answer has to be no. But my heart somehow won't let me say a complete no."

If Angelita thought the matter finished, months later she was proved wrong. She bustled in on an assembly leadership meeting saying, "This priest keeps following me around. He won't go away! I told him we were not a missionary community but he showed up here anyway."

Indeed, the plucky priest had not been invited to attend the assembly, but he took it upon himself to drive the 330 miles from Chicago that morning to plead his case in person.

Sister Raphael Ann Drone recalls being at the assembly meeting when Sister Angelita hastened in and asked a question: "Is there anybody here who would be interested in going to Africa?"

It took only a moment for Sister Raphael and Sister Joél Kolmer to raise their hands.

"I wasn't particularly interested in going myself," said Raphael. "But I raised my hand because I thought somebody else would want to go." As it turned out, the mother superior took her up on the offer: Raphael would be one of the four original Liberian volunteers in 1971. Though Joél had been one of the first to raise her hand, it would take more than a decade before she, too, found her way to Africa.

The first two volunteers chosen were two women with their Master's degrees in education, Sister Bonita Wittenbrink and Sister Alvina Schott; picked to administer the SMA-run Saint Patrick's School in Grand Cess, a small, hard-to-reach community on Liberia's southern coast. It would be ten more months before Raphael, also a skilled educator, and Sister Barbara Ann Muttra, an experienced nurse, would join the tiny ASC missionary contingent. When they did, in November 1971, the contract that Sister Angelita had signed with Father Philip two years earlier (for four missionary sisters) would be fulfilled. Over the next 21 years, 13 additional ASCs would freely choose to go to Liberia to serve God's people. The deaths of the five ASC sisters in 1992 during the Liberian Civil War, however, put an end to the community's official participation in the mission, though Raphael would return two decades later to do pastoral work with the SMA fathers at their missions in Bomi and Tubmanburg. Most of the other ASCs who served in Liberia are now too old to return to the demanding lifestyle of the missions, but the imprint and love for the far away country of Liberia and its people have marked all the women religious of Ruma as surely as their baptism originally marked them for God.

In the odd way that fate works, when Sister Raphael Ann Drone was chosen for Liberia not everyone in her family was happy about it. Her aunt and godmother Pauline McGuire in particular often expressed concern for her goddaughter's safety. But it was not the welfare of her niece that Pauline need have worried about but that of her own daughter, Sister Kathleen McGuire, who would be one of the five ASC sisters to die in Liberia in 1992.

SISTER BARBARA ANN MUTTRA

It was a bright Midwestern June morning. I was headed down
to southern Illinois, which is what we native Chicagoans call the
vague open spaces south of Interstate 80. In truth, the road actually cuts across the northern fifth of the state. I was due in the
capital, Springfield, around eleven to meet with Joe Mudra and
his older brother Jim, nephews of Sister Barbara Ann Muttra,
one of the five Adorers of the Blood of Christ sisters murdered in
Liberia in 1992.

The trip should have taken about three-and-a-half hours,
give or take. I was preoccupied with thoughts of my upcoming
interviews (I had a full three days set up, starting in Springfield
then on to St. Louis, before winding up in Ruma). On the way to
the car, I rashly stepped on one of the dozens of deadly pinecones
that were littering the pavement. The resulting injury to my left
ankle was fast and furious.

The 215-mile drive to Springfield only aggravated my already
bloated ankle which looked like an over-stuffed sausage by the time
I arrived at Joe Mudra's neat ranch-style home on Bellerive Road.

*As I limped up the driveway, I noticed a motorcycle parked there
and had to smile. Sister Barbara Ann, the woman who could drive
anything, and did, would definitely have admired the machinery.*

*Inside I was greeted not only by Joe and his brother Jim but
by their cousin George Sabo (owner of the motorcycle) and Joe's
daughter, Theresa Maggiore, and her teenage son Porter. The
kitchen table held a delightful luncheon spread provided by Joe's
wife, Donna. It was a very gracious welcome. Teresa noticed my
discomfort went to the freezer and brought out a bag of corn she
claimed was already suffering from freezer burn and I gratefully
strapped it to my ankle before beginning our interview.*

*The memories they generously shared about their aunt,
whom Jim remembers fondly as Aunt Josie, helped put some meat
on the bones of Sister Barbara Ann's early days growing up in
Springfield as well as corroborated much of what I had already
learned from other sources about this remarkable woman.*

READY AND WILLING

The story of the Adorers of the Blood of Christ (ASCs) in
Liberia is, in many respects, the story of Sister Barbara Ann
Muttra. Though not the first ASC sister to step onto Liberian
soil, she was the longest-tenured, serving in all three mission
sites there beginning in late 1971 and ending with her death
on the Barnersville Road in 1992. The final third of Sister

Barbara's life, from 1968 on, was spent overseas; first as a nurse in Vietnam at the height of that war, then as a missionary in Liberia. Once she began working overseas, Barbara would be little more than an occasional visitor in her home country. Her longest consecutive stop in the U.S. would be a 15-month medical stay in 1990-91.

Barbara was born Josephine Mudra on May 11, 1923 in Springfield, Illinois, home of the sixteenth U.S. President, Abraham Lincoln. Illinois is proud of its connection to the Great Emancipator, going so far as to label itself "the land of Lincoln" on its vehicle license plates. Springfield is also the state capital and home to a bicameral legislature, the state Supreme Court, and the governor's mansion; not to mention numerous historical sites attached to Lincoln either by name or status (e.g., Lincoln's home and his tomb and his law office are all there).

Springfield was not always the capital though, usurping the honor from a smaller community to the south called Vandalia in 1839 (which had usurped it from tiny Kaskaskia in 1820) with the full support of a gangly young member of the state legislature at the time named Abe Lincoln, which goes a long way in helping to understand the city's filial affection for the man.

Growing up steeped in this culture it is hard to imagine any Illinois child, especially a bright one like the young Josephine Mudra, not absorbing at least some of her city's understanding of its place in American history and the social

justice implications of such a heavy legacy. As a first generation American, she would also have one foot firmly planted in
another culture, namely that of Austria/Germany, the home
of her parents. The time of their emigration to the U.S. in the
late nineteenth century had been marked by a period of intol-
erance and persecution of Catholics throughout the German
Empire. The quest for social justice and religious freedom
that affected the history of the Mudra family as it sought to
establish itself in a faraway country was one repeated over and
over by tens of thousands of immigrants who began flooding
into the United States around that time.

Whatever the final import of these twin legacies on little
"Jo," as she was called by her family, the woman she was to
become would be one marked with the indelible lessons of
acceptance, openness, and love of others.

Having emigrated as young adults from Austria in the
late 1800s, Alois Mudra and his bride Barbara spoke heavily
accented English throughout their lives. Mrs. Mudra would
pronounce the letter "d" as a "t", which led to some family
members, including the future Sister Barbara Ann, to accommodate this pronunciation by changing the spelling of the
family's last name to "Muttra" from "Mudra."

In 1923 baby Josephine joined an already well-estab-
lished family of five boys and a girl. Two of the boys were
teenagers; the two oldest, Tony 18 and John 16, were already
working in a local shoe factory. The fact that they were already
employed turned out to be a godsend when their father died

unexpectedly from heatstroke six months after baby Jo's birth. Alois, always a hardworking man, had been repairing the roof on his home when he died. He was just 45.

A skilled tool and die maker in his native Austria, Alois was not able to find work in this field in his new country and earned his living by the sweat of his brow as a miner for the Sangamon Coal Company. At the time, coal was a big industry in Springfield and the largest employer in the area, with 26 mines in operation. Old maps of the mines show that much of Springfield, except for the downtown area, was built over abandoned mines dating from as early as the 1880s. It was a dirty, dark, and dangerous way to make a living and, in this pre-mechanized era, backbreaking as well since a miner's main tools of the trade were the lowly pick and shovel. Mining was also sporadic—from September through April—and plagued with frequent strikes. It was a difficult career path but one followed by thousands of men with no better options. The family was lucky that all of Alois' sons would find other forms of employment; none had to follow their father into the mines.

In his free time, the industrious Alois built the family's large two-story, white-frame home on a triple lot at the corner of Wheeler and Moffat Avenues. He also dug his own well so the family could have water. The oversized lot afforded plenty of room beside the house, where the children played and where "Mother" (as she was called) kept a cow and an occasional pig. A summer kitchen "out back" was where meals were prepared over a coal stove in the warmer weather. In winter, meals were cooked over a combination coal-gas stove in the house kitchen. Jim Mudra, second oldest of Barbara and Alois' grandchildren, recalls that every time the gas was lit "it was like a bomb going off."

Across the street from the house was a railroad yard for the old Peoria and Northern line, and just east of that was the yard for the Illinois Central Railroad. Freight cars would come in and out day and night, steam engines hissing. The mighty engines were powered by the abundant Springfield coal. Growing up, Jim remembers that the train yard had what he termed a "zinc pit" where the coal for the engines was stored in water because wet coal made steam more easily.

In 1926 when Jo was just three years old, Springfield was at the nexus of the very first federal road project—construction of historic Route 66. In an age of multi-lane interstate highways, it is hard to imagine just how ambitious the venture was. Route 66 eventually crossed two-thirds of the United Sates, linking Chicago to Los Angeles. And Springfield went along for the ride, enjoying decades of tourists who would pass through and stop at its motels, restaurants, and shops. Even today, Springfield continues to celebrate the old "Mother Road" with a three-day festival every September.

The place and time that little Jo was born into was one of brawny industry flexing its muscles. Immigrant families from Italy, Lithuania, and Germany provided much of the brute force necessary to power the coal and transportation industries that flourished in Springfield. Their first-generation children straddled cultures and often struggled to assimilate. Yet there was one place where there was no struggle, where acceptance was unconditional—the local Catholic Church. For the faithful, like the Mudras, the local church was often a very close reflection of the one in the country they had left behind.

Every Sunday the clan would walk 15 blocks from their home to Saints Peter and Paul Catholic Church on Sixth and Mason. Established in 1849, Peter and Paul was the first German Catholic congregation in Springfield. It was also a place where German-speaking immigrants like Alois and Barbara Mudra could feel at home among their peers; though the church was a bit of a challenge to reach. The family had no personal car, not even a cart, and public transportation did not extend to their neighborhood, so the family had little choice but to walk the 15 long blocks to church, regardless of the weather. It was an experience that left its mark on young Adolph Mudra. "Dad said you changed your clothes three times on Sunday," recalled his son Jim.

After Alosis' untimely death, Josephine and her sister, Mary, three years older, grew up under the filial guidance of their big brothers. Yet the heart of the family was always their mother, Barbara. Difficult though it was, Mother somehow managed to stretch the income her two oldest boys brought home from the shoe factory where they worked. Even twelve-year-old Adolph pitched in at home by looking after his younger siblings, Carl, Joe, Mary, and Josephine, and by helping with household chores. Later he would also take up a paper route to add a few more pennies to the family coffers.

The family matriarch, Barbara Mudra, was a strong, big-boned woman, and a hard worker—she had to be. She kept a kitchen garden, so summer and fall saw staples like tomatoes and peppers aplenty. There was also a plum tree and a pear tree that had fruit as "big as your fist." But make no mistake, being a widow with little children was a real hardship, especially since there was no meaningful government aid at this time. Charity was considered to be the responsibility of the family, neighbors, or the local church. Food stamps did not debut until 1961 under the Kennedy administration. Little Jo was only six when the Great Depression hit in 1929, thereby assuring the lean years would continue. Soon economic woes began ensnaring even larger numbers of Americans, casting them into similar hardscrabble existences.

As the youngest child, Jo was most likely shielded from much of this reality by her cadre of big brothers, who would also ensure that she grew up a bit of a tomboy, often playing rough and tumble in the big side lot. She played softball but not basketball (her small stature was a disadvantage there). Later she would be a summer camp counsellor at Camp Star of the Sea. Here she would meet her first sister Adorers of the Most Precious Blood (a name change would eventually bring the community its current title, the Adorers of the Blood of Christ) and Jo's life would never be the same.

"I had planned to enter nurses' training at Saint John's in

Springfield," she later wrote as Sister Barbara Ann Muttra in a biographical sketch sometime in the mid-1980s, "but during that summer I volunteered to help the children at Camp Star of the Sea. There I met the Precious Blood Sisters and their work with children inspired me so much that I entered Ruma in August 1941."

A black and white photo taken of Jo and her brother Joe shows a smiling young woman dressed in a long, print dress with puffy sleeves. The dress looks to be homemade and is likely her high school graduation gown. Her brother, in a crisp white shirt that is rolled at the sleeves, scoots down in a rather awkward pose to accommodate the difference in their heights. Each has an arm draped casually around the other. They are friends—you can tell by the easy way they touch one another. Each is on the verge of adulthood. It is the summer of 1941. In less than six months the U.S. would be at war with Japan and Germany. Joe, fluent in German, joined the war effort as a translator for the Army. Josephine packed her bag and headed to Ruma, Illinois, to begin her novitiate.

Jo did not have to give up her dream of becoming a nurse. After her novitiate, the newly minted Sister Barbara spent three years, from 1943-1946, earning her nursing degree in Enid, Oklahoma. Her first assignment was a year at Saint Ann's home for the aged in Chester, Illinois.

Then in 1947, she was sent to Saint Clement Hospital in Red Bud, Illinois. There, as she put it, she "worked everywhere OR, OB, and general duty until 1950." The next year, she was assigned to the Children's Home in Alton, Illinois, caring for the under-five-year-old group. The young nun's training expanded further when she was sent by the ASCs to Chicago for a six-month operating-room training course. For the next decade, she worked as an operating room nurse and then as OR supervisor at Saint Vincent Memorial Hospital, which was established by the ASCs in Taylorville, Illinois in 1906. Barbara's time spent at Saint Vincent would play an important part in her professional development and provide her with the skills she would need later in Vietnam and Liberia. The year 1963 found her once again in the town of Red Bud; this time at Red Bud Hospital.

It was about this time that Barbara began to have questions about her religious calling, not unusual in the atmosphere of soul-searching ushered in by the Catholic Church's Second Vatican Council and an emergent feminist movement that influenced many women religious. According to a study published in 2000 by researchers at the University of Washington and Pennsylvania State University, there were over 181,421 American Catholic women religious in 1965, but by 1970, just five years later, that number had declined to 153,645, and by 1995 the number of nuns was 92,107. That downward trend continues to this day.

1964 would be a difficult year for the 41-year-old Sister Barbara. "I was going through a struggle, debating whether I could do better in the world than in religious life," she wrote. She ultimately recommitted herself to the sisterhood after attending a spiritual renewal program, or as she termed it "a spiritual summer," in 1965 at the Provincial House in Ruma. After that she returned to Saint Vincent's in Taylorville where she would continue her nursing career, paying special attention to sick children. Many people say it was always about "the little ones" with Barbara, and she had a reputation for high spiritedness that her young charges relished. It was said that she often showed up in the children's wards late at night, rousing the children from sleep just to play with them.

Then in December of 1967 a simple leaflet changed Barbara's life forever. The leaflet asked for nurses to volunteer in Vietnam under the auspices of Catholic Relief Services (CRS). Although there was a war raging in the Southeast Asian country, Barbara felt moved to volunteer. She knew she could be of great help there, especially to the thousands of children orphaned by the war.

INTO THE FRAY

"On March 17, 1968, I bid farewell to my sisters & friends and started my journey to Vietnam," Barbara wrote. The trip would be long and arduous, with the first leg from Springfield to Chicago and then on to Los Angeles, where she was joined by three additional CRS volunteers. The quartet would fly to Honolulu where they spent a whirlwind 12-hour lay-over "sight-seeing & enjoying the fresh pineapple & visit to Pearl Harbor." At 11 p.m. the quartet boarded a Pan Am flight to Guam and "in the interim had 3 breakfast(s)." After leaving Guam, the last U.S. outpost, they landed in Saigon at 10:30 the next morning, where they were met by the CRS Director Monsignor Robert Charlebois.

It was Monsignor Robert, distressed by the dire conditions in which the country's orphans were living, who had reached across the Pacific with the leaflet appealing for help from nursing sisters in the U.S. With a simple piece of paper, he had caught Barbara Ann's attention and touched her heart.

Now, with his new volunteers in country, the CRS Director could actually begin to do something for the children, though he readily admitted, "The recruits did not know what they were getting into. No one did."

Barbara's first view of Saigon was eye-opening. "We were taken through part of town where buildings & homes had been destroyed by bombs. On our way to our lodging people filled the sidewalks as this was their dwelling place of shelter because their homes were destroyed or invaded by the VC (Viet Cong)," she wrote.

Barbara's lodging in Saigon would be a simple affair located in a six-story hotel and consist of a cement-floored room furnished with a bed, a chair, and a desk. Though Spartan, it was lavish by local standards.

For the next six weeks, she and other volunteers received orientation and studied the Vietnamese language. At the same time, Barbara's emotions were being shredded by the constant stream of refugees she observed struggling to survive on the sidewalks of Saigon. Her compassion must have shown through, because she was often asked for help by the homeless. One particular incident stayed with her: "One day a lady came to me and asked me to take her baby as it was difficult to live on a sidewalk & shelter a baby." She does not record her response to the woman, but it is inconceivable that Barbara would not have given the woman some sort of aid.

A further testing of Barbara's compassion would come with her first assignment, the Go Vap Orphanage, which housed over 1,000 children. The orphanage was near Tan Son Nhut airbase, headquarters of the South Vietnamese air force. The U.S. military also used the base for operations from 1959-75. By the late 1960s, when Barbara was stationed at the orphanage, the airbase would be called the "busiest" airport in the world—and it was certainly among the most chaotic. Tan Son Nhut was a hub of activity, with commercial and military planes sharing the tarmac, often crisscrossing paths with military and civilian vehicles that moved in near constant streams across the airport's roads. As a military installation, Than Son Nhut was a ripe target for the massive Viet Cong-North Vietnamese Army campaign called the Tet Offensive that began on January 30, 1968, mere weeks before Barbara's arrival in country. Archival footage of the attacks show rockets being fired in a stream; schools of luminescent flying fish arcing across the darkened sky. Though the Tet

Offensive had been a surprise attack on 100 cities and towns throughout the south, it was eventually repelled by South Vietnamese forces and their allies, including the U.S.

To say that Sister Barbara Ann and the other CRS volunteers had walked into the thick of it would be an understatement. Within two months of their arrival "in country," a second attack on 119 South Vietnamese sites by Communist forces was launched. This would be referred to as the "May Offensive," or "Little Tet." Once again Than Son Nhut would be attacked, and for a time it was partially overrun by the Viet Cong.

In a brief account Barbara described the fighting: "In May of 1968 was the second Tet Offensive, so that brought on more problems and casualties and babies being found in rice paddies, churches, or left in a market—so we struggled again to restore some normalality (sic) for the children." It was a difficult task made more difficult in part because the volunteers' ability to move about the city was limited by nightly and occasional day-time curfews designed to keep people off the streets during the shelling around Saigon.

When Barbara and her comrades were introduced to the Go Vap Orphanage, what she saw incensed her. "We found 50 babies and children (2 yrs. under) lying in small cribs in one huge room, with rings of cries all over the room. Some were given bottles with diluted milk and huge holes cut in the nipples so that the milk streamed from the sides of their mouths." Instead of the milk nourishing them, the children's faces were raw from lying in the liquid that had pooled under their cheeks. The children had been all but abandoned for long periods because the regular staff were often not able to get to the orphanage due to the dangerous conditions. "Some were almost 2 yrs. old and could not even sit up." For Barbara, this was heartbreaking. It was also totally unacceptable, and so she did something about it.

Over the next three months, the CRS volunteer nurses and their Vietnamese counterparts worked to change things. They sectioned the big room off, ten babies to an area. They increased the children's diet, and "gradually got them up and walking." Though this might be considered a small victory, it was nonetheless an important moment. In the face of seemingly insurmountable odds Barbara and her counterparts had prevailed. She would act on the lesson that small gains can ultimately lead to big victories for the rest of her life.

A photo from that time shows Barbara smiling broadly —it is almost a laugh, really. She is trying to contain a fidgeting toddler in her arms while being surrounded by little children who are caught for eternity in untroubled poses as they aimlessly mill about her as if she is their center of gravity. Barbara is wearing a very simple blue frock and short blue veil set just far enough at the back of her head to reveal a glimpse of dark hair. Her eyesight is poor, a Mudra family trait, so she wears a pair of dark-framed glasses. Glasses as thick as "fruit jars" according to her nephew Jim. Soon after the photo was taken, Barbara replaced the glasses with contact lenses when she made a trip to Hong Kong to buy a pair for "practically nothing." The contacts revealed that her eyes were blue, like her father's.

By June of 1968, Barbara was on the move again. This time she and four others were sent to Cam Rahn Bay, about 180 miles northeast of Saigon. "We lived on a Special Forces compound in Ba Ngnoi (sic) a small village 10 miles from Cam Ram (sic) City.... Across the Bay were mountains which (we) were unsure of (held) friend or foe so (they) had to be guarded," Barbara wrote.

The bay emptied into the South China Sea where an island named Binh Ba "jutted out into the ocean. Around 4,000 refugees found quiet & peace here." The refugees built shelters of little more than cardboard boxes; some of the lucky ones added a bit of discarded tin or wood to their construction.

"It was a pathetic existence, but I spent much time on this island taking medicine & food to the people. I went by way of patrol boats," she wrote.

This was the first time that Barbara was called upon to ferry supplies to refugees of war, but it would not be the last. The dauntless campaigner that she would become in Liberia was being forged in Cam Rahn Bay, where she honed her medical skills and sharpened her powers of persuasion as well.

Barbara would become God's number one beggar if that is what it took to get the supplies, food, clothing, or money she needed for her patients. She did not mind at all humbling herself in this service. She had a knack for making friends and drawing others into her work. She already had a circle of supporters in the U.S., and now she began developing an even larger network that extended abroad. Her friends were many and would faithfully send her donations—some for decades—so that she could continue serving the poorest of God's children.

Barbara's family remembers her visits home to the United States over the years to gather medical supplies for her overseas ventures. She would go back to her old haunts, the hospitals where she had worked as well as area pharmacies, to collect medicines that were near to expiring. Even past-dated drugs can be useful when people have no medicine at all, she would tell people. Joe Mudra remembers his aunt telling him that one time she even went through the Vatican to help gather medicine for her Liberian patients. "She said she eventually got so much donated medicine that she could fill a 747. Maybe it was close to being out of date, but it would still be effective."

Barbara could be very convincing. "Persistent" was how her nephew George Sabo described her. He said she would get people to donate to her cause by consistently talking about the children overseas who needed their help. "She would just keep bringing it up until you decided to help," he said.

In Vietnam, members of the U.S. military also responded to Sister Barbara's calls for help. When she would run out of milk or rice at the orphanage, she would often approach a friend she had made in the U. S. Army, a man who just happened to be in charge of supplies. "He would send someone to the supply area to check if there were any 'damaged' goods or dented cans," recalled Sister Raphael Ann Drone. "Things that were not good enough for the military, he would give to Barbara." Sometimes, Raphael claimed, the soldiers even took their hammers along as insurance just in case there were not enough damaged cans.

It was this kind of generous behavior that endeared the soldiers to Barbara. She often held up their kindness to others, sometimes with mixed result. "In Liberia, she was always bringing this up," said Sister Raphael. The SMA fathers who ran the mission in Grand Cess had more meager resources than the U.S. military, and the comparison sometimes irked their pastor. "He finally yelled at Barbara that we were not the military and we did not have the money they did," Raphael remembers. The pastor's was an understandable reaction, but it never stopped Barbara from asking for what she needed to help the people.

When Barbara took a month's leave from Vietnam in March of 1969 to visit the U.S., she did not come home empty handed. "I brought 2 orphans to the States," she recorded. An 11-year-old went to a family in Madison, Wisconsin, and a one-and-a-half-year-old girl was adopted by a family in Medina, Ohio.

On her return to Vietnam, Barbara worked with older orphans in Saigon. Then in December of 1970, Catholic Relief Services discontinued their projects. Instead of heading back to the U.S., Barbara volunteered to stay and work with

Dr. Pat Smith, a well-respected American doctor working in Kontum in the central highlands. Dr. Smith was a favorite of U.S. service personnel and was described in a 1972 *Stars and Stripes* article as an "indomitable, blunt-talking woman the Montagnards call 'ya pogang tih'—'big grandmother of medicine.'" The article could just as well have been describing Dr. Smith's associate, Sister Barbara Ann Muttra, ACS.

When her hospital was destroyed during the 1968 Tet Offensive, Dr. Smith set up shop in a school house, turning it into an 87-bed hospital. This is where Barbara reported for duty in late 1970. The casualties from the war and disease were staggering. "I worked in the OR & spent hours sometimes picking shrapnel out of the bodies of women," Barbara wrote. She treated numerous cases of cholera and attended to fractures and lacerations. Their patients were almost exclusively Montagnard people—who had a deep-seated dislike for the Vietnamese, who viewed the Montagnards as savages. "The Montagnard people lived in this area," wrote Barbara, "and at night for fear of the bombs would come down from the mountain and fill the hospital floor and even surrounded the hospital in tents, as they felt secure here. I spent 3 months here and enjoyed caring for Dr. Pat's 3-yr.-old adopted son."

By the time Barbara left Vietnam in March of 1971, she had already committed to working in Liberia.

TOUCH DOWN LIBERIA

November 1971

Sister Barbara Ann Muttra stepped off the international flight directly on to the tarmac of Roberts Field outside of Monrovia. She surveyed the cacophonous crowd with a knowing look. She'd seen this kind of hustle and craziness before in Vietnam; but at least here no one was trying to drop a bomb on her.

"Sista, Sista," called a voice close by. "Carry your bag. Only one Liberian dollar," hands reached for Barbara's suitcase.

She preferred to keep her things close. "No. Thank you. I can manage," she said clasping tightly on to her bag. Following Barbara's lead, her companions, Sister Raphael Ann Drone and Sister Martha Goeckner, held firmly to their belongings too. The newcomers were swiftly plunged into a sensory stew of pungent odors and dissonance. Bodies pressed close as merchants hawked their wares. All the while, the thermometer pushed its mercury into the mid-90s, making it difficult for the three nuns to breathe in the heavy air. Liberia, their new home, had wrapped them in a muggy welcoming embrace.

"Whoa," said Raphael. She was used to the hot summers of St. Louis, but this was definitely more intense.

"Don't worry," said Barbara, "you'll get used to it."

The SMA fathers, the same order who had originally recruited the ASC sisters to Liberia in the first place, had sent Father Tom O'Donnell to the airport to gather them up.

Soon Raphael, Barbara, and Martha, who was on temporary Liberian assignment, were taken to the capital city, Monrovia, where they would spend their first few days acclimating to their new country. With no formal training program in place to introduce the newcomers to the various customs and languages of their new home, the sisters were more or less thrown into the deep end of the pool. Their training would be "on the job," provided by the SMA fathers, whose community had established the mission in Grand Cess 60 years earlier. Luckily for the trio, two members of their Ruma community, Sisters Alvina Schott and Bonita Wittenbrink, had preceded them to Liberia and were also eagerly awaiting their arrival. They would be a big help in acclimatizing their peers to mission life. Or that was the hope. Little did the new arrivals know that the two nuns were barely functioning. Both were suffering from the lingering effects of malaria, and shortly after the new missionaries arrived the two were sent to Rome for rest and recovery.

Liberia had not been an easy adjustment for Sisters Alvina and Bonita, the first ASCs to come to the country. In fact, within weeks of their landing in Grand Cess there had been a deadly outbreak of cholera, previously unknown in the region. So it was a harsh welcome for the newcomers and underscored the dire need for top notch medical care in their new home. Lucky for them all, help was on the way in the person of Sister Barbara Ann Muttra.

After spending a few days in Monrovia getting used to

their surroundings, Sisters Barbara, Raphael, and Martha boarded a red-and-white, five-passenger Cessna 195 for the flight down the coast to the Grand Cess mission. The little Cessna was a workhorse; capable of handling the numerous short-to-medium runs made necessary by Liberia's rugged geography. A journey by car from Monrovia to Grand Cess would have been virtually impossible at the time, since there were few paved roads and no direct routes to the more remote southern coastal areas. Located on the Kru Coast, Grand Cess is a village of 4,500 souls. It sits on the edge of the Atlantic in what can be described as tropical splendor. Its people are mainly ethnic Kru. They are hardy fishermen and self-sufficient subsistence farmers. Numerous small communities that lay further from the coast dot the dense forests that over-run the interior. The only way to access these interior areas is by foot or small boat.

The pilot for the sisters' journey down the coast was an SMA priest, Father Ed Galvin. In those days, bush pilots like Father Ed flew by sight, necessitating a low, coast-hugged journey. This proved a bonus for his passengers who were afforded a spectacular bird's-eye view of the land as the plane passed over. Sister Raphael remembers the hour and forty-five-minute flight as a visual feast. "We could see the villages and rivers below. We could even see rocks and palm trees and the waves on the ocean." And further off in the distance, "a tanker heading towards Monrovia."

Upon reaching their destination, Ed circled once around

the beach. The Cessna emitted a distinctive whistling noise that announced its arrival to anyone within earshot. The plane and its whistle were familiar to the townspeople, who were accustomed to its regular comings and goings between the mission and the capital. In what was a first look at their new neighbors, the sisters watched from their window seats as more than 200 gaily-dressed people stood along the beach and strained their eyes upward.

The people were rewarded as the little plane dipped towards the oceanfront strip. There was clapping and singing as the three ASC sisters deplaned to a truly joyous welcome. Everyone, regardless of religious affiliation, was more than pleased for the arrival of their very own nurse in Sister Barbara as well as a new teacher for the school, Sister Raphael. Though they had not anticipated a third sister, to everyone's delight the celebration quickly embraced Sister Martha as well.

The new sisters triumphant greeting mirrored the lavish welcome that had been afforded Sister Alvina and Sister Bonita 10 months earlier. A record of the arrival of the first ASC sisters in Grand Cess in January 1971 rests in the archives of Ruma. An account, though uncredited, is clearly written by one of the SMA priest present that day.

Shortly before ten o'clock all movement in Grand Cess

seemed to be in the direction of the airfield. School children in their uniforms, mothers with babies on their bellies and on their backs, old men, young fishermen and government officials, the choir of the Catholic and Methodist Churches in their church colors, and the ministers representing all the churches in Grand Cess made their way to the landing strip that is on the East end of town.

Local children were called upon to shoo the cows, which had free reign of the beach, away from the landing area. They were then ordered by their teachers to hustle back in line. A young boy in the brass band dropped his cymbals as the anticipation grew within the ever-increasing crowd. Then the plane circled the town and made a very graceful landing. According to the priest chronicler, Sisters Alvina and Bonita hopped out to a strangely hushed crowd. They were accompanied by the local bishop. But as the clergy and local government officials approached the plane "the sisters were swamped in a lively sea of vigorous handshakes, sparkling teeth, and cries of welcome!"

It was a slow, hour-long procession into town. The sisters reached the steps of Saint Patrick's School where, as custom dictated, they formally greeted the Paramount Chief, the high-priest, and other tribal officials. After the greeting, they were escorted to the stage in the school's auditorium.

"There were several speeches, songs, band selections, and finally the presentation of gifts." In what he called "the unique Grand Cess style," the priest goes on to enumerate the elaborate display that saw flowers, food stuffs, and other necessities given freely by the local people to their guests. A woman with a 50-pound bag of rice upon her head swayed rhythmically up the aisle to lay her offering at the sisters' feet. She was followed by 12 others "just as graceful and as rhythmic." They brought gifts of firewood, chickens, eggs, and even a bottle of scotch and one of gin.

Then, a moment of confusion ensued as running and shouting could be heard outside. "Finally there was a great roar as the source of the commotion was dragged in. This was the biggest gift of all—a bull, alive and kicking."

The priest continued his account: "A young teacher from Picinicess, an out-station of Grand Cess, presented some chickens on behalf of the Catholic Community of Picinicess. Many of them were present." He explained how the people of that village had left their homes at five o'clock that same morning so as to be sure of meeting the sisters at the airfield. "Picinicess is about a two hour walk from Grand Cess. The teacher introduced a man who walked with them. He is a leper. He has no feet."

The priest ends his report with a next-day meeting with "a feeble old man who had great difficulty speaking." Whispering in the priest's ear, the man said: "Now, Father, I am ready to die.... I have seen with my own eyes our own Grand Cess Sisters.... Tell the Bishop thank you."

Father Philip Bagnasco's assurances to Mother Angelita two years earlier that the people of Grand Cess had been praying for the arrival of Catholic sisters was no exaggeration. And so, when the final complement of "Grand Cess Sisters" arrived the following November, they, too, were greeted with much the same excitement.

"We landed to the singing of a choir made up of Catholics and Methodists and Pentecostals. The crowd escorted us to town singing the whole way," said Sister Raphael. The walk down the beach was about a mile, and as they entered the town one of the first things the sisters noticed was that the villagers had built an arch of palm leaves for them to pass under. After passing under the arch, the native "high priest" waited to greet them. Raphael recalls how the high priest, face painted white and wearing a feather in his hair, held out a cola nut to each of the newcomers in a traditional Liberian greeting. Unsure what to do, Raphael took only a small bite of the nut, which was just as well as it was "very bitter and full of caffeine."

Looking around them, the three sisters saw signs of a construction project underway. It was a new convent that was soon to be their home. It was supposed to have been completed before their arrival but wasn't. Still, the five bedrooms were already finished, albeit they lacked furnishings, and the chapel, too, was done. But since the kitchen was not, the chapel would pull early duty as the place where the sisters' meals were prepared and eaten.

Later still, Father Larry Haines, one of the SMAs in residence in Grand Cess, would plant two rows of flowering hibiscus along the front walk of the house. His efforts would be particularly appreciated years later by Sister Joél Kolmer. "He did a good thing!" she would write home in praise of the bountiful blossoms.

As the welcoming procession continued, the sisters saw an open area to the left of the convent that fronted the school and church, and behind, like a picture postcard, the Atlantic Ocean rose in swells as it cascaded onto the shore. The procession continued to the small cement block mission church, Saint Patrick's, which the SMA fathers had built around 1920. "All of us crowded in and there was a program to welcome us. Then each one of us was expected to make a comment," said Raphael. "I said I was very happy to be there and that they all had beautiful smiles. Barbara spoke about wanting to improve medical care."

All things considered, the seriousness of their commitment and the high expectations being placed on the new volunteers must have begun dawning on each of the nuns by this time as, most likely, was their lack of preparation for such an undertaking. Since they were not a traditional missionary religious order, the ACS sisters had not received formal training before leaving for Liberia. They would learn the customs of the Kru people and a bit of their language in the process of living with them. Though officially English is spoken in Liberia, it is a dialect and cadence that is difficult for the untrained ear to understand, and many people in remote areas only speak their tribal language. But the three sisters were eager. Before long, they would pick up enough to offer their new neighbors greetings and pleasantries in their own tongue. For all of the rest of their business, the sisters would employ a local person to act as translator. They would learn as they assimilated.

I called Father Brendan Darcy, who had been the pastor in Grand Cess at the time of the sisters' arrivals, to get his recollection of those 1971 events. Father Brendan, now retired from missionary work, left Liberia in 1983. He recalled how eagerly he had anticipated the sisters' arrival, especially that of Sister Barbara Ann, an experienced healthcare professional.

Brendan described the unhappy state of affairs before Barbara's arrival. "We had no doctor and no nurse, so we ran a little clinic ourselves on the porch early morning between Mass and school and again after school around 4 o'clock. None of us had medical training," he said referring to his fellow priests.

When a sick person came to the mission for help, one of the priests would consult a well-worn copy of *Merck Manual of Diagnosis and Therapy* to try and match the symptoms to a disease. It was admittedly a poor substitute for real healthcare, but it was the only thing available to them. The only medication at the do-it-yourself "clinic" was aspirin and some medicine for worms, something for malaria, and Imodium for diarrhea. If you got a cut, there were bandages (the Irish-born Darcy called them "plasters"), ointments, and salves. The more serious cases—the lucky ones—might be sent to a clinic 25 miles away in Pleebo for emergency care. But that was rare. The truly ill just died, said the priest sadly.

Infant mortality rates at the time were sky-high, with babies dying at an alarming rate. It seemed that the Grand Cess community was in a perpetual state of mourning, "but we couldn't do anything about it," another retired missionary priest, Father Joe Foley, told me. People were constantly bringing their sick children to the priests and it broke their hearts, especially when they were compelled to bury dead babies. It would be in this area that Sister Barbara would make her greatest impact, bringing down the death rate from 25 babies a year in the area to five.

The inadequacy of healthcare in Grand Cess had been demonstrated very clearly eight months prior to Barbara's arrival in Liberia. The sad tale is remembered by Jim McHale, a former SMA priest serving there at the time: "Fatha, I need help. My wife got running belly." It was early morning on March 3 and the man who had come to the mission seeking help was using a term that locals used to describe the effects of dysentery, which is spread through poor hygiene or contaminated food and water.

Jim described what happened next. "I consulted the *Merck Manual,*" he said. Since the symptoms the man described seemed to match those for dysentery, he was given medicine and sent home to his wife. "But that night," said Jim, "the man and his wife were both brought to the mission. They were dead. It was then we knew this was not dysentery."

As Jim and his fellow priests consulted the *Merck Manual* again, they found the man's symptoms matched another, much more serious disease—cholera. "But we had never seen any cases of this in West Africa before, so we were not quite sure. That's when we called upon Sister Sponsa for help." Sister Sponsa Beltran, OSF, was an American missionary sister who ran a hospital in Cape Palmas, 40 miles southeast of Grand Cess. She, along with Theresa Hicks, a volunteer nurse brought in from a clinic 25 miles distant, valiantly fought the outbreak in Grand Cess. In all, 65 people were sickened, and 15 of them would die. The only other person brave enough to treat the ill was a local man, called a "dresser," who knew how to administer the IVs necessary to keep the patients hydrated.

"The dresser, Sponsa, and Theresa were the only ones willing to put their lives on the line for these people." Jim explained to me. "Other nurses had come up from Cape Palmas, but they got out of there pretty quickly," as did a couple of doctors from Monrovia who confirmed the cholera but did not treat it, he said.

Because the two nurses had to be flown into Grand Cess by small plane from outlying areas, lives were lost. Cholera kills very quickly, and the delay cost 14 lives initially. But after proper medical treatments were undertaken, only one more person died.

The source of the cholera was eventually pinpointed to one of the mission's in-ground wells where water was drawn with a bucket and rope. People, who normally would drink the water from the well untreated, were now told to boil it before using. "The whole mission yard was turned into a mass of little fires where people could bring their water and boil it," said Father Brendan. Alternatively, bleach was added to water used for washing vegetables and for cleaning cooking and eating utensils.

Sister Barbara, already having experienced cholera outbreaks in Vietnam, would undoubtedly have recognized the risks of drinking from open wells had she been in Liberia at the time. As a skilled nurse with top-notch medical credentials, her arrival in Grand Cess was met with rejoicing from the villagers as well as from the much-relieved SMA fathers who would no longer have to run impromptu clinics or bear the weight of diagnosing ailments beyond their limited skills.

Barbara also brought with her an expertise both in the operating room and as an infant-care specialist. And thanks to the three years she had served in war-ravaged Vietnam, she was also a seasoned field medic. The experience of having treating the severest of wounds and ailments with limited resources in Vietnam would serve her well in Liberia. In addition, the people of the Grand Cess area and its surrounding villages got an advocate who would fight any and all impediments to achieve good healthcare practices. Anyone who got in the way of those efforts, as the town mayor was soon to learn, could be subject to a display of Barbara's righteous outrage.

A ROCKY START

Sister Martha Goeckner planned to stay in Liberia only six months, just long enough to help establish a small kitchen garden so her fellow sisters could grow their own vegetables. It would turn out to be an exercise in frustration.

The agricultural conditions in Grand Cess proved challenging to say the least. The unfamiliar climate, soil, and especially insect activity combined to upset Sister Martha's most sincere gardening efforts. Not willing to let the bugs get the upper hand, she devised a plan. Rather than plant directly into the ground where the bug activity was most intense, she put dirt into 55-gallon drums then poked holes in the bottoms. Next, she built fires underneath the drums in an effort to smoke out the bugs. It seemed an ingenious strategy. After that she and Sister Raphael planted their tomatoes and beans. When the tomatoes reached six inches, the sisters celebrated. It looked as if the plan had worked. Alas, the next morning all the plants were wilted—their roots eaten by avaricious insects.

All the time Raphael and Martha were battling the bugs,

Sister Barbara was focused on her clinic. The final weeks of 1971 and early 1972 were consumed with fashioning a clinic out of a 20 x 25 foot "broken down shed." The make-over would be nothing short of miraculous. Assisting Barbara in the transformation efforts was Father Dominic Donahue, a young SMA priest skilled in construction. Barbara would repay Father Dominic's kindness a few months later by saving his life. At least that's how Father Brendan Darcy remembers it: "Dominic kept snakes," he said. "He would defang the snakes he kept, but sometimes fangs could grow back and with a small snake you might not notice the new ones."

To the dismay of some, but no doubt delight of the local children, the young priest would frequently take his snakes for "walks" along the edge of the porch on the priests' house. One afternoon, while Dominic was holding a rather small green mamba of about 18 inches in his hand, a cat came around the corner of the porch and startled the snake. It bit Dominic on the hand, surprising the young priest. Before long he was feverish and, to Barbara's clinical eye, in real trouble. As he lay on his bed perspiring, Barbara administered all the anti-venom serum she had available, but it wasn't enough. The mission plane and its pilot, Father Ed Galvin, were in Monrovia at the time, so Barbara radioed, entreating him to hurry back to the coast with more anti-venom serum.

The drama continued to build with Sister Barbara fretting the serum and Father Ed fretting the setting sun. By now, it was getting dark and since small planes flew visually, that meant it could be a dicey couple of hours' ride. A friend of Ed's, who also had a small plane, volunteered to fly down the coast, buddying-up with the priest for safety. As they neared Grand Cess the two pilots strained to see where to land. Suddenly, out of the darkness a row of lights appeared directing them safely to the beach-front landing area. People from the town had come to the airstrip with hand-held lanterns to guide them in!

Now all that remained was to get the medicine to Dominic. Barbara wasted no time in administering the anti-venom serum. During the whole ordeal, though, Barbara dealt with an uncooperative patient as the young man indignantly protested that he was just having an allergic reaction to the bite and was not truly poisoned. According to an account in the book *Echoes in Our Hearts*, it was a rare occasion on which Barbara doubted herself. "Maybe I acted too soon. Maybe I shouldn't have called Monrovia," she is reported to have said.

Whatever the case, by the next morning the priest was well enough to be transferred to the hospital in Cape Palmas, where he recuperated fully. There were ramifications. Upon hearing of the incident, the local bishop ordered Dominic to get rid of his fanged pets.

Father Dominic died in a boating accident less than two years later at the age of 36. The priest drowned in the dangerous Grand Cess River when his boat capsized as he was on his way to say Mass for the residents of a small mission outpost. It would be four days before local fishermen recovered his body. This time there would be nothing Barbara could do to help.

At the priest's funeral Mass, his brother Father Brendan Donohue, also an SMA priest, would call Dominic's life a gift and a "sacrifice for us." If the ASC women missionaries had not fully realized before now just how precarious everyday life could be in the remote areas of Liberia, Dominic's tragic death surely drove that point home.

But that tragedy was in the future, unknowable to Dominic and Barbara in 1971 when their only concern was how they could turn a junk room into a first-class clinic— a task that was made all the more challenging due to a lack of electricity and running water at the site. When sunlight waned, they worked by kerosene lamp. When they needed water for scrubbing up, the mission boys would haul buckets from the nearest well. In spite of these challenges, the two missionaries persevered, and by December supplies and furniture that Barbara had ordered months earlier from the U.S. began to arrive.

According to her own notes, Barbara had stopped in Grand Cess in June of 1971 on her way back to the United States from Vietnam. Her plan was to assess what would be needed for her clinic as well as for the new convent then under construction. She discovered that they needed virtually everything. Believing she had been given carte blanche by the SMA fathers in charge of the mission to purchase whatever was necessary, Barbara went on a spending spree when she got back to New York City, buying beds, mattresses, sheets, pillow cases, and chairs for the convent, and stopping at an Army surplus store where she ordered cots, canteens, army blankets, and more for the clinic. She ran up quite a bill.

Years later, Sister Raphael chuckled at the memory: "We got everything we needed, and then Barbara sent the bill to the SMA fathers." When their American provincial superior received the bill, he was "furious," according to Raphael.

Apparently, says fellow ACS missionary Sister Rachel Lawler, Barbara had initially been told that the "sky was the limit, which was the wrong thing to say to Barbara Ann." Eventually the waters were calmed when the Adorers of the Blood of Christ in Ruma agreed to pay half of the expenses and the SMA fathers the other half.

When furniture and clinic supplies began arriving in Liberia by ship in December of 1971, it was quite a process. The furniture initially arrived from the U.S. by ship to the harbor in Monrovia, where it was transferred to a smaller boat that carried it down coast to Cape Palmas Harbor. There the goods were transferred a third time to wooden Fanta fishing boats for the final leg of the journey to Grand Cess.

Over 40 years later Raphael sat in the comfort of her apartment in Bellville, Illinois, recalling the rather incongruous vision of a huge fisherman walking down the beach "with a wet couch on top of his head." The cushions, she said, arrived later by plane.

When Sister Barbara's clinic was finally ready, Raphael was called upon to put on the finishing touch with a hand-painted sign designating it as the "Cabrini Clinic." And with that, a clean, well-run medical facility opened its door for the first time in Grand Cess. Word of the new clinic spread quickly and soon people were traveling great distances, sometimes as long as seven hours on foot, to get treatment for themselves and their children.

Barbara wrote of the opening: "63 patients welcomed me. Jeannie Weah and Mrs. E. Minikon were the ladies to assist me. Soon after I hired 3 girls—one to register patients—2 to interpret and assist with medicines and dressings."

The clinic was open six days a week from morning until just before supper. When Barbara was out making calls in other villages, local women she trained handled patients. Sunday was reserved for worship and rest. Even so, people still knocked on the convent door on Sundays, and though she was loath to do it Barbara would tell them to come back the next day. Unless there was a sick child involved. The sound of a baby's cry was like a clarion call to her, Sabbath or no Sabbath.

"She would always help if she heard a baby crying," said Raphael. "And if she helped the baby then she would help the parent, too. I think sometimes people would pinch their babies to make them cry just so Barbara would open the clinic."

With Barbara, the children always came first. It was on their behalf that she became enmeshed in a running argument with the town mayor over sanitation and the penning of cattle. Many townspeople kept cows that would roam about the streets. So ubiquitous and free were the bovines that they often climbed right onto a person's front porch leaving the kind of presents cows usually leave behind.

Excrement was everywhere. Even the walls and dirt floors of homes used cow dung to patch holes. When children played outside or sat on the ground polluted with cow droppings, they often contracted worms. "That made Barbara mad," said Jim McHale.

To keep the children from being infected, Barbara wanted the mayor to require all cows be penned on the outskirts of town. Though Barbara was "hard-nosed" about trying to clear up the omnipresent waste, this was a fight that flew in the face of accepted local practice. People's wealth was tied up in their cows, and they were unwilling to enclose the animals on the outskirts of the village and out of sight. Theft was a real concern, as the ASC sisters learned firsthand when the bull they had been gifted by the people of Grand Cess on their January arrival was stolen and eaten by neighboring villagers.

Jim counseled Barbara to be more patient: "In Liberia there is a saying. 'Softly, softly catches the monkey,' meaning change takes time."

Eventually, Barbara's appeals were at least partially successful when some villagers did put up fences to restrain their cows. But there were even bigger battles ahead.

There were two particularly abhorrent practices Barbara fought against. The first, termed "peppering" a newborn, consisted of rubbing a mashed pepper concoction on the roof of the baby's mouth. The pepper was of a small African variety and very hot. "Parents thought they were giving the child some kind of immunity," ventured Father Brendan Darcy by way of explanation. But in reality, their actions burned the child's mouth and made it difficult for the baby to nurse. In the second case, a newborn's umbilical cord would be rubbed with mud before it was cut. It was a practice that perplexed the western missionaries. "Perhaps this was meant to be a sign of solidarity with the earth or a kind of baptism," hazarded Jim McHale. Such action often resulted in the newborn contracting tetanus.

While these observances were abjured by westerners, they were long-standing traditions in the Kru community. The practices were enforced by local shamans who held sway in their villages, where animism and belief in spirits and magic often marry with more traditional religious beliefs. If a mother chose not to follow these traditions and her child were to become ill and die, she could be accused of killing it. The irony of course is that a mother who followed these habits actually increased the likelihood that her baby would become sick. The battle against these harmful, yet fully enculturated practices, was one that Barbara embraced. Using every weapon at her disposal, she would devise a multi-pronged effort to save the babies from harm.

To do this, she oversaw the training of a cadre of local women who were then dispatched to act as midwives to their own villages. Classes were held for mothers-to-be to educate them in proper pre- and post-natal care. Mothers were bribed with powdered milk for their babies and awarded with a new infant blanket if they followed Barbara's instructions. They were cajoled. They were admonished.

Even so, Barbara was also a realist, so any baby she suspected of having its umbilical cord rubbed with mud would get a tetanus shot within its first week of life, thereby cutting the risk of infection. Eventually when mothers began to follow the healthy child-care practices they were being taught, the rate of newborn deaths would decline an astonishing 80 percent.

AT HOME IN GRAND CESS

When Sister Barbara Ann Muttra and the other Adorers of the Blood of Christ began their ministry to the people of Grand Cess, Liberia, and its surrounding communities, the population was around 4,500 and widely dispersed. The mission itself was comprised of Saint Patrick's Church and School, a priests' house, a sisters' convent, and the new Cabrini clinic, and it was ringed by thatch-covered huts. The Atlantic Ocean was their front yard. In a 1982 letter, Sister

Joél Kolmer described the setting: "We are about a quarter of a mile from the ocean…and so at night we hear the roar of the ocean waves. We can even hear them throughout the day if it's not too noisy, but at night, it is wonderfully peaceful and quiet and so the sound of the waves is very soothing."

A visitor might look around and upon seeing the sandy beach and waving palms call Grand Cess, Liberia, a tropical paradise. But anyone who made more than a cursory stopover knew that if this was a paradise it was one of the hardscrabble variety. Every soul in this idyllic setting worked hard to survive.

At first light, the fishermen of Grand Cess would begin loading their dugout canoes with nets and lines in preparation for seizing the early offshore winds that would carry them out to the best fishing areas. Since many of the men who took to the sea did not know how to swim, they were careful to stay within sight of land. Their sturdy canoes, each hand carved from a single log, were rigged with sails made from flour sacks. Many were big enough to accommodate two or three men, yet often held just one as the Kru preferred to fish alone. After a day on the water, when the breeze turned to shore, the fishermen would head home. There, on the beach, the day's catch of herring, sardines, or carangids would be displayed for sale. At twilight, the fishermen would head home to their families, where they would smoke some of the fish they had saved for their evening meal over an open fire. The next morning, they would begin it all again. It was hard and often dangerous work, not glamorous or idyllic.

By far the largest occupation in Liberia is farming. It is estimated that 70% of the population grow their own crops, most often for their own consumption, especially in rural areas. In fact, the southern coast was once termed the "Pepper Coast" in honor of the melegueta pepper, which was highly valued by European traders of the fifteenth century. Early on, the region was prosperous, but inter-tribal rivalries brought on by an active slave trade (in which some native peoples participated) and the raiding of natural resources by foreigners led the coastal area into decline. It has never recovered its previous status.

Today, farming in Liberia is mainly done to sustain the family. In the Grand Cess region, the farms are clustered together some distance from the town. Women, in particular, provide the sweat and toil necessary to raise food crops of cassava, rice, and vegetables. The work is backbreaking and done with rudimentary hand tools. On this score, not much has changed since the Precious Blood sisters called Grand Cess their home. Sister Shirley Kolmer gave a vivid account of a 1985 trip she and another sister made in the company of a young man they knew as he went to visit his family's farm:

> We walked to the farm all the way.... The man could not get a canoe so we walked all the way. It must have been three hours of walking one way.... At one point we crossed a river. They did not expect much water since

*it is dry season, but we had rain for two nights straight
and it was quite swollen. They cross on a tree that fell
into the river some time ago. This lies about 6 to 8 feet
above the bottom of the river. Well, now the water was
about 4 feet above that tree.... We had met up with
some others who joined us. This one fellow helped me.
He had a bag with my shoes and Zita's and his things
in it. This in one hand and me holding his other hand
and sometimes holding him by the shoulder too. It was
something. And of course a tree is not that smooth. Only
after we had come across and were on our way did I
realize what we had really done and what danger we
were in. The river was deep and fast. But we made it
and walked home another way.*

When at last the small group arrived at the farms, the
people were surprised and happy to see them. Shirley called
it "an experience to see the farms," which in no way compared
to the wide expanses of farmland she had grown accustomed
to in Illinois:

*They cut the bush and then burn it. Then clear it of the
tree logs and then plant between all the tree stumps. The
place looks more like a refuse pile than a farm. I could
not believe the scene. The men do the cutting and burning and sometimes the clearing, but I think sometimes
the women have to do the clearing and the planting.*

Shirley went on to relate that the farmers they visited had young children with them and resided in small shelters that she described as "really quite fancy." The people, she said "are rather artistic in their craft." When she asked some of the women if she could take their picture they agreed and proudly beamed for the photo while holding up the primitive tools they had just been using to till the soil. The hoes, Shirley said, "have about 14-to-18-inch handles and a little piece of metal for a hoe end."

It was here, among these hard-working people—people a callous world had all but disregarded—that the Precious Blood Sisters found their truest home in Africa.

ROUTINE

At 5:30 every morning the sisters would awaken, perform their morning ablutions, then make their way to the convent's chapel to pray the psalms and the traditional readings assigned for each day—the same ones their ASC counterparts back in the U.S. were also praying. Just after 6:00 a.m., the sisters would head to Saint Patrick's Church for Mass and by a quarter past six they could be found seated in their pew, each deep in personal prayer. By 6:30 one of the SMA priests would be at the small wooden altar ready to offer the daily Mass in English.

Afterwards the women would head home for breakfast, exchanging pleasantries with any and all along the way, perhaps attempting a few words in the local dialect. They would nod and smile. In return, their neighbors would greet them warmly, proud that these women had chosen to live and minister among them. Though English is the official language in Liberia, it is less commonly spoken in the rural areas, where a variety of local dialects dominate. In such an atmosphere nods, smiles, and gestures step in to help bridge the language gap.

Breakfast was a hearty meal consisting of homemade bread baked by local women. The sisters would toast the bread on a skillet. Local papaya and fresh eggs laid by their own chickens would round out the meal. The chickens, like most of the domestic animals in Grand Cess, were free-range, which sometimes provided for an amusing state of affairs since the birds would lay their eggs wherever they chose. As a result, it was not always a sure bet as to whose eggs were whose. Some of the more enterprising children would gather up all the eggs they could find and then sell them back to the sisters for a small fee. Even if they suspected they were buying back their own eggs, it was a deception the women pretended not to notice.

After breakfast, Sisters Alvina Schott and Bonita Wittenbrink would walk the 50 steps over to Saint Patrick's mission school where they were joint principals; accompanying them was Sister Raphael Ann Drone, who was teaching there. The school ran from kindergarten through ninth grade and had 600 students. Many of the indigenous teachers had no formal education degree, and books were a rarity at the school. They tended to be prized possessions and as such were guarded against overuse. Raphael recalled that when she first got to Grand Cess and inspected the school library she discovered that most of the books had pages with holes in them where they had been eaten through by insects. A lack of printed materials was not just limited to Saint Patrick's or even to the bush communities. Throughout Liberia, as well as large chunks of Africa, books were, and remain, scarce commodities.

Even so, the students at Saint Patrick's were being given a "great education" according to Pastor Brendan Darcy who credits the ASC sisters with having a "big impact" on improving the school. While Alvina, Bonita, and Raphael tended to the education, academic as well as spiritual, of the local children, Sister Barbara tended to their health needs.

If she wasn't expected to call at another village, Barbara would spend her day in Grand Cess treating patients at the Cabrini Clinic, opportunely situated next to the church and the boys' residence.

On her Grand Cess mornings, Barbara's diminutive figure could be seen hurrying across the village center, where sultry ocean breezes might play across the open space; a sudden gust could send her veil billowing across her face—a teasing invitation to dawdle. But Barbara would be all business on clinic days, because she knew a line of people had already formed to await her arrival. Some would have walked great distances to see "Sista." Those who could not walk for themselves might be carried to the clinic over rough footpaths by anxious family members on a homemade stretcher or a chair. So dawdling for Barbara was out of the question.

Besides the short veil that signified her as a religious sister, Barbara's customary ensemble was a knee-length blue shift with oversized pockets. Capacious pockets were a requirement in her line of work. It was where she kept bandages, aspirin, and tissues readily to hand. And if in her estimation a garment did not have adequate space for her necessities, then she would sew on more pockets. The feature was so integrally a part of Barbara's makeup that she was reportedly dubbed "Pockets" by some of her associates. Now in her adopted country she would earn another honorific when some of the local people began to call her "Old Ma," a term usually reserved for well-regarded native matriarchal figures.

Barbara ran the clinic with characteristic efficiency. Three local women were employed as her helpers. She trained these women well enough so they could see patients even in her absence. Indeed, her efforts as a teacher would bear much fruit, as one of her early trainees would eventually go on to excel in the healthcare field and assume the running of a government clinic.

In addition to clinic duty, there were several days each month when Sister Barbara would head into the bush to see patients, as she wrote:

The mission plane came every Saturday to take me to Barclayville for the weekend to see patients. Then once a month Father Yates took me in a boat up the river 1½ hr. to a small town called Filoken where I often treated over 100 patients—one time 186 patients. Then once a week I would walk to Picinicess with the three girls who worked with me in the clinic.

Eventually, through the generosity of friends back in Percy, Illinois, Barbara got a red Honda motorbike. With her medical bag securely strapped to the back, she would head out to the far-flung villages. To get to communities located on the other side of the wide Grand Cess River, she rode across on a rudimentary ferry. It was not until 1976 that a road was finally built connecting Monrovia to the further reaches of the coast. But the road terminated on the western bank of the Grand Cess River. To reach the town of Grand Cess, vehicles had to be loaded on to a chain ferry and hauled across the wide expanse of water. The ferry was made up of a dozen 65-gallon drums lashed together. Planks were then secured over the drums to provide a large flat surface where people, vehicles, and cargo could stand as the ferrymen pulled hand-over-hand on a wire strung across to the other bank. It was an arduous task.

The ferrymen were pressed into even harder service when the Liberian government made an ill-conceived effort to construct a local hospital in Grand Cess. With much hoopla, President William Tolbert visited the area and, using some government money as well as $26,000 collected locally, he pledged to build the hospital for the local people.

The project required cement to be transported from Monrovia to Grand Cess on the newly constructed road. At the western bank of the Grand Cess River, the bags of cement were offloaded and put on the ferry to be taken across. Then the ferry would transport the truck; once across, the vehicle had to be reloaded with the bags of cement for the two-mile drive to the hospital site. It was a grueling affair, and during the rainy season, when the river was running especially high, no vehicles at all could cross the river.

When a 50-bed hospital at last opened two years later, it appeared to have been a worthwhile effort. But it was short-lived. Sister Barbara initially called the hospital "a great asset for the area." That is until the hospital's "medicines were depleted and patients all drifted back to the mission clinic." Unlike the government clinic, Barbara had personal resources and was able to call upon her many friends in the world-wide Catholic community as well as friends in the United States to help replenish her medical supplies.

Barbara continued her excursions into the interior and, though she was an excellent driver, her trips were not without risk, especially when riding her motorbike on the rutted footpaths she regularly traveled. There were times, especially during the rainy season, when even her best efforts could not overcome an impassable road. The story is told of one trip when Barbara's bike skidded out from under her. She fell and cut a deep gash in her leg. Methodically and calmly, the nun reached for the medical bag that was secured to the back of the bike and sat in the middle of the dirt track and sewed her own wound. Then she remounted the motorbike and continued on her way to tend to the people awaiting her. Though this is just one small vignette, it demonstrates the unyielding stuff at Barbara's core. Some called it grit, some courage, but whatever the name it allowed her to push forward in the face of adversity again and again. And when civil war loomed and challenges grew bigger and more personally dangerous, Barbara would draw on this reserve, somehow finding the nerve and strength of character to stand up to armed soldiers—and eventually, to her own cancer. It was her defining characteristic—one that, for better or worse, would have a hand in determining her fate as well as that of four of her fellow sisters.

STEADY HANDS

Sister Barbara would spend a decade in Grand Cess. She trained local women as healthcare workers. She educated the indigenous residents, as well as members of the mission community, in proper health practices. Some of the things she taught were simple—like proper sanitation practices such as boiling drinking water and regular hand washing that could prevent illness and save lives. Some were larger efforts—like convincing a local chieftain to chlorinate the well water in his village. And then there were truly heroic efforts.

Because Barbara was basically the best-qualified medical expert for miles around, she was pushed to tackle complex medical problems she would never have been expected to handle back in the States, where doctors are plentiful. But in Liberia, where the full complement of doctors in the country of almost three million could be numbered at little more than a few dozen, her expertise in the operating room and in the nursery would prove life-saving time after time. She did anything and everything—including pulling teeth when need be—loving each new test even when the odds were not in her or her patient's favor. Clear-headed and competent, Barbara would make decisions solely on the basis of her judgment of the benefit to her patient. Compassion, not government regulation, was her watchword.

In one particularly remarkable instance Sister Barbara Ann was called upon to perform emergency surgery on a young man who had partially severed his nose in an accident. Doug Gilbert was an SMA seminarian. Sister Marie Clare Boehmer, ASC, in her book *Echoes in Our Hearts*, described the accident. Gilbert was standing on the zinc roof of Saint Patrick's School checking it for problems when a section of the roof gave way under him. As he fell, a piece of zinc sliced through his nose and nearly severed it. Jim McHale, pastor at the time, and Philip Wymola, another seminarian, hurried Gilbert over to Barbara's clinic in the waning light.

In a phone interview, Jim McHale recounted the story with gusto. "He smashed his nose like a tomato! It was an awful mess." Barbara, he said, was anxious when she saw the extent of the injury. Her little clinic was not equipped to handle this kind of an emergency. Still, she had no choice but to try her best for the young man. She gave her patient local anesthetic then chose a very fine thread and meticulously began sewing the nose back together. The job was made more difficult because it was getting dark and there was no electricity in the clinic so Jim and Philip held kerosene lamps aloft. Insufficient as the light was, it would get even worse as the two lantern bearers began to feel queasy watching the surgery. The light wavered; then failed as the young seminarian fell to the ground. "I almost fainted, too," said Jim. Barbara revived the young man and then, unfazed, continued working on the nose of Doug Gilbert.

Barbara's surgery was so expert that when a doctor in Monrovia finally examined Doug's nose days later, he pronounced it a "job well done." Over the next several months, Barbara was dutiful in applying Vitamin E ointment to the wound every day so as to lessen any scarring. It was, according to Jim "a magnificent job."

Jim McHale, clearly a fan of Sister Barbara's grace under pressure, recounted another emergency where the nun's professionalism was put to the test. This time it was a middle-of-the-night birth, outside in tall wet grass. Jim recalls being awakened about two in the morning and called to the side of a woman in distress. When he got to the scene he discovered that the woman was lying outside her home in the grass and "had already given birth." The baby was still attached to its umbilical cord, and the mother was having trouble delivering the placenta.

"We called for Barbara, who came over quickly," Jim said. "She tended to the baby first. She got it wrapped up and brought inside, then she took care of the mother." Later the mother would tell the priest that this was the eighth baby she bore but only the second one to survive.

A PAT HAND

One particular story about Sister Barbara bears repeating—not merely for its entertaining aspect but for what it says about her in those unguarded moments with friends. These were the times Barbara felt free to display her playful side. She was, as this encounter shows, not beyond making a bit of mischief. The tale was related to me by her friend, Sister Raphael Ann Drone.

According to Sister Raphael, if you were just observing the event you would have seen Barbara fly down the dirt path in hot pursuit of a receding male figure. As she ran, the pitcher she was clutching splashed its contents onto the surrounding scrub grass.

The figure, Father Laurier (Larry) Haines, one of the SMA fathers, knew better than to slow down. If he dared to cast a look backward, he would have seen what looked like a mad woman chasing him towards the garden gate. Fearing his pursuer was gaining ground, he veered off the path. A moment later he crashed through the wooden fence that surrounded the convent yard and never looked back as he sprinted for the safety of his own home.

Incredulous at the destruction wrought by the priest, the nun stopped in her tracks and dumped the water she had been carrying onto the ground. Then she emitted a peal of hearty laughter. The guffaws grew even more robust when Sisters Raphael Ann and Mary Gaspar caught up with Barbara and joined in the chorus.

Moments earlier Father Larry had been calmly seated with the trio around their kitchen table. A sturdy oilcloth covering provided the canvas on which a newly dealt hand of cards sat ready in front of each player. The game that evening was International Rummy, a perennial favorite of the missionaries. Games, especially card games, filled a vital entertainment role at the little sea-side mission. The players gathered up their hands, and as the evening sky began to grow darker a kerosene lantern was lit. Its dim offering cast a yellow pall over the cards. A puff of cool air from the Atlantic rattled the screen door; a welcome reward after the day's punishing heat. (There were some perks to living on a beach in a sticky tropical climate, and an ocean breeze was definitely one of them.)

As Barbara considered the cards she had been dealt, Larry bent his head ever so slightly in her direction to get a quick glance at her hand. A few moments later, Barbara cast a surreptitious look in the priest's direction.

Sister Raphael Ann, who had been watching the cheaters' duet, shook her head. "You both know you are looking at each other's cards, don't you?" she deadpanned.

Larry feigned indignation, "What gives you the right to look at my cards, Barbara! You always have to win!"

But Barbara would have none of his holier-than-thou censure. Without warning, she picked up her water glass from the table and threw the contents in the priest's face, astounding him and the others.

Dumfounded, but quick to recover, Larry indulged in some tit-for-tat when he picked up his own water and threw it at Barbara. For Barbara, whose temperament generally bent towards winning, it would be impossible to let him get the upper hand, so in one swift movement she picked the water pitcher off of the table and emptied its contents onto his head. The escalation promised to continue when she ran to the sink and began to refill the container as the other two nuns present, Raphael Ann and Mary Evelyn, watched the action with astonishment.

Larry, now drenched, recognized that the evening had toppled into chaos and made one last plea. "No, Barbara. Don't." Then the priest, still a young man in his thirties, sprinted for the back door. In his haste, he pushed out the screen and ripped off the door lock before clearing the house and making a break for the garden gate with Sister Barbara Ann Muttra, ASC, hot on his heels.

GARDNERSVILLE

By the early 1970s, it was clear that the ASC community's foray into Liberia was a success. Health, education, and religious ministries were making positive impacts on the lives of local residents in Grand Cess. A decision was therefore made back in Ruma to support a second site in Liberia—this time in a suburb of Monrovia called Gardnersville. Preparations for the new site began in August, 1973 with Sister Alvina Schott taking the lead in preparing the convent. She would be temporarily assisted in the effort by her old friend Sister Bonita Wittenbrink. Besides Alvina, two newcomers to Liberia, Sisters Virginia Walsh and Mary Evelyn (Gaspar) Nagle, would join the Gardnersville mission by the end of September.

Gardnersville is located about six miles from Monrovia. It is one of a number of small towns that encircle the capital, just beyond a swampy region at the outskirts of the city. A paved road, known locally as the "hard road," connected the suburb with Monrovia. The road, a two-lane affair that never lived up to its original four-lane design, was known as the best road in the area. Once it reached Gardnersville, dirt paths split off from the hard road leading to various clusters of homes.

In the area around Gardnersville, gritty businesses that are the undercarriage of commercial life provide jobs for the local populace in places like the chicken-soup factory, the aluminum factory, and the battery factory. The people who live in the area make just enough money to get by. In the mid-1970s, when the ASCs first arrived in the area, there was a middle class of sorts living there, too. People had cars and sent their children to the Catholic school, Saint Michael's, in the nearby town of New Georgia. The parish in Gardnersville, Saint Anthony's, was run by the SMA priests, the same organization that had been working so successfully with the Adorers in Grand Cess. The expectation was for another fruitful pairing of the two religious groups.

The home where the sisters were to set up housekeeping was described as an "old house" owned by of one of the teachers in the parish. "It is interesting to note," said the convent's journal, "that this house served as this parish's first church and first school and now the first convent!"

The Gardnersville mission marked its official opening with the arrival of Sister Virginia and Sister Mary Gaspar on September 28, 1973. The next day, the Gardnersville ASCs made their first short-wave radio call to their fellow sisters in Grand Cess. The newcomers also received a hearty welcome from a decidedly less congenial following. "Ants!" wrote the chronicler on October 1. "Inside and outside! On the walls, floors, furniture, clothes, food! The Battle of Ants was on." Though the women tried every weapon at their disposal, they were unsuccessful as the ants "kept coming." To add insult to injury, the next day the women were beset by bats. The creatures had descended upon Mary Gaspar in the night through a hole in the ceiling. Ultimately the "ugly creatures were killed and the hole closed." Though one bat did escape and torment the sisters just when they thought they were in the clear. And by October 4 the Liberian Health Organization came to the rescue and exterminated the ants.

But there was another type of local parasite that no amount of pesticide could eradicate. These were known as rogues, or local thieves. So, on October 5 the sisters hired a night watchman. They knew three women living alone were vulnerable. "There are no houses around and the Sisters are at the mercy of anyone who might wish to harm them or steal from them," was written in the convent journal.

Finally, the women settled in. Sister Bonita Wittenbrink would put her educational expertise to work at Saint Michael's school, Sister Mary Gaspar Nagle would take care of the household, and Sister Virginia Walsh, a trained nurse, would work at the Catholic Hospital in order to "get acquainted with some of the African sicknesses."

Their proximity to Monrovia would prove providential as visitors traveling to and from the U.S. then had a place to stop before venturing further down the coast or inland. In addition, the ASCs in Grand Cess could avail themselves of the fellowship of their fellow community members and would make frequent visits. Plus, the Gardnersville group could more easily obtain supplies and foodstuffs and send them down the coast to the more remote Grand Cess. It would not take long for the new mission site to become a hub of activity, not only for the ASCs but also for other missionaries and ex-pats, who were always welcome to visit.

BOMI TERRITORY

Life in Gardnersville and Grand Cess was good, and that made Sister Barbara Ann Muttra restless. Barbara and her friend Sister Toni Cusimano had never ventured into the Bomi Territory before January 12, 1982. But at the invitation of missionary priest Father Gareth (Garry) Jenkins, SMA, they undertook the journey. The visit proved historic as it laid the groundwork for the founding of the first Catholic mission established by religious women in Liberia.

The two started out from Monrovia early that morning. The drive, 30 miles to the city of Bomi Hills, took about an hour due to the generally questionable condition of the roads outside of the capital; though according to Barbara's written account of the visit at least part of the way consisted of "good blacktop." The blacktop was probably a relic from the days when the Liberia Mining Company was active in the mineral rich hills of Bomi. The road would have been built over a generation earlier to enable Liberia Mining to transport the iron-ore it excavated in the hills to Monrovia's seaport on the Atlantic Ocean, where it was then shipped to the United States.

Away from the mining sites, however, blacktop turns to a network of frowzy laterite roads and footpaths that wind their way through an undulating landscape connecting small villages one to another. Here, roads bordered by a riot of dense green vegetation harbor hidden potholes that turn into swimming pools during the rainy season, catching any number of vehicles in wheel-deep mud holes. Though just over a score of miles from Monrovia, the Bomi Hills are unlike the city and its environs by almost every measure.

While Monrovia is the gateway to Liberia's global trade, Bomi is the gateway to the country's interior. The capital city's chaotic energy is epitomized by an international port of call and crowded dock-side markets where thousands of people joust daily in a battle for commercial dominance, leaving in their wake effluvia from discarded goods and foodstuff. The Bomi Territory, by comparison, presents a bucolic face with its rolling landscapes blanketed in shades of green and by rivers and streams, valleys, plateaus, and numerous small villages.

Monrovia, the low-lying giant, is festooned in watery garlands; on its west, the mighty Atlantic beats a ceaseless tattoo against a narrow sandy shoreline, while the city's remaining quadrants are ringed by mangrove swamps and lagoons. But just 20 miles to the northwest the landscape sheds its boggy skin like a snake as it begins its slow crawl over ground hardened by ancient sedimentary rock. Here the hills are bursting with natural resources: gold, diamonds, iron-ore, stone, timber. Natural resources buried for eons lure strangers into the hills to exploit their riches. Yet deals made between outside companies and the Liberian government to harvest these treasures have never benefitted the local populace.

The people who live in the Bomi Territory are mostly from four native populations: Gola, Vai, Kpelle, and Mandingo. In everyday affairs, not germane to the national government, the people rule themselves through a hierarchy of village chiefs, clan chiefs, and paramount chiefs. In this manner, the leaders wield authority over any interventions in their communities by outsiders.

Fortunately Father Garrye belonged to a religious group, the Society of African Missionaries (the SMAs) that already had a long history of working respectfully and successfully with local village leaders to establish churches and schools throughout Liberia. It was in 1977 that Garry was directed to establish a mission in Bomi Hills, the largest city in the Bomi Territory, with a population of 14,000. (Today, Bomi Hills has been renamed Tubmanburg in honor of the country's nineteenth president, William Tubman.)

Quite likely, Sisters Barbara and Toni looked on this trip into the roughhewn Bomi Territory as a bit of an adventure. After all, neither had ever been to this part of Liberia before. For Barbara, the last 11 years had been mainly spent along the coast of the Atlantic. And idyllic as that may seem, 11 years was the longest time in her professed life that she had spent in one place. It's a safe bet that with the Grand Cess clinic and its attendant healthcare programs running well Barbara felt the need for a new challenge.

From her own accounts, it is clear that Bomi's pull on Barbara was immediate; it would also be long lasting. What made the area, especially the little village of Klay where she would ultimately settle, so special to her is not entirely clear. But what is certain is that the attraction never faded, and on more than one occasion she would willingly risk her safety and even her life in service to the people of the Klay District in Bomi Territory.

Pre-civil war the people of Bomi Territory lived largely in self-sufficient communities. This would have appealed to the can-do spirit of Barbara and Toni. The people the sisters met on their 1982 trip raised their own crops, fished the local rivers, and constructed their own homes, much like the Kru natives of Grand Cess did.

But Barbara also noted another aspect of the Bomi natives. For all their independence, and the natural riches around them, they were a people in need. And that captured her heart.

While Garry's main mission campus was in Bomi Hills and consisted of a church and school, the flock of parishioners he attended to was much more wide-spread. Barbara described the vastness of the congregation: "Outside and surrounding the Bomi Hills is a network of dirt roads leading to numerous towns and villages which Father services. His mission extends to Robertsport, which is 55 miles from his residence."

The first stop Garry made with Barbara and Toni on the Bomi tour was a marred landscape riven with circular roads snaking their way up barren hills. A short five years earlier the area had been alight with frenetic activity; now it was a lunarscape. Lured by the promise of a mother-load of iron-ore buried within the stony hills, heavy machinery had systematically gouged and ripped the lucrative mineral from its sedimentary home. It took a mere 26 years, from 1951-1977, for the Liberia Mining Company, an American entity, to take what the hills had steeped for eons. When it had exhausted the majority of the iron-ore and sent it overseas along with the lion's share of the profits, the company departed, leaving in its wake a cratered land that locals nicknamed "Bomi Holes."

The barren landscape, startling as the sight must have been for a first-time visitor, was of apparently small interest to Barbara, who merely wrote, "...we were taken on a tour of the iron-ore mines which were operable until a few years ago." Clearly, she was no environmental activist. Her true interest and concern had always been centered on people, not places, as revealed in her very next passage she wrote to her sisters, which goes on at some length.

"Father toured us to five of the nine villages which he comes to weekly for Mass and instructions. When we reached

Melima, a Gola tribe people, Father pointed out a school of 2 classrooms and an unfinished clinic building." She goes on to describe the villagers and their desire for missionaries. They spoke to her heart almost immediately. She states that the villagers had been "begging the bishop to send them a nurse and some teachers." It was a plea that had gone unanswered. The chief of the village, wrote Barbara, went on to recount to his visitors how the first missionaries had come to the little village 60 years earlier. "There were 2 priests. The chief himself was their first mission boy. Unfortunately because of lack of medicine, the priests died within 3-6 months after their arrival. The chief said that they had been waiting all these years for missionaries to return.... The chief said the people built the clinic and school hoping some missionaries would come to help them."

When no Catholic missionaries returned, notes Barbara, the townspeople all became Muslims. Even so, promised the chief, if a Catholic mission were to be established they would be more than willing to have their children instructed in the Christian faith.

When Barbara wrote the next lines, it was as if the deal was being sealed: "Then the problem was presented about the lack of health facilities and medicine." Impressed by the people's sincerity, Barbara, apparently on the spot, informed Garry of her interest: "With this we partially committed ourselves...to come and help these people. Sister Antoinette was enthused about the pastoral ministry."

The very next day the two women ventured to Monrovia for a meeting with Catholic Archbishop Michael Francis, where it was agreed that the ASC sisters would start their own mission. The site eventually decided upon would be in a tiny village called Klay, which lie near the southern entry into the Bomi Territory and where a small government clinic already existed. The plan was to use Klay as their home base while extending their ministries to a number of local communities, much like Barbara and her fellow Precious Blood Sisters had been doing in Grand Cess since 1971. Their Klay mission would be about 15 miles south of Father Garry's church in the village of Bomi Hills.

Meanwhile, the Grand Cess mission, still staffed by Precious Bloods Sisters, was in capable hands. Barbara and her staff at the Cabrini Clinic had made great advances in the health and care of the people of Grand Cess, especially the babies. She was sure the women she had so carefully trained could carry on without her, especially if Sister Shirley Kolmer, her Provincial, sent another nursing sister to administer the clinic.

The remainder of 1982 would be a flurry of activity for Barbara and Toni. They asked for and received permission from Sister Shirley to establish the mission in Klay. Shirley, who had served in Liberia from mid-1977 to mid-1978 as a teacher at the University of Liberia, approved their request wholeheartedly. In fact, this was just the sort of expanded outreach that Shirley had envisioned for her community from the moment she became Provincial.

The Klay mission was significant in that it would not just be staffed by ASCs; it would be the first Catholic mission *founded by* women religious in Liberia. In the years to come, the mission and its people would claim a special part of Barbara Ann's heart.

October 1983 saw Sister Antoinette Cusimano living in Bomi Hills in a convent belonging to an order of Catholic Dominican sisters. The accommodations were temporary while she oversaw the renovation of a mud and brick residence in Klay that she and Barbara would be renting. The house, while not overly large, had three bedrooms, and a living room, dining room, kitchen, and bathroom. "Eventually," wrote Toni, "we'll get a little linoleum to put on the cement floors."

While their new home was under construction, Toni was busy establishing herself in the area. She traveled to outlying villages: "Father Garry and I and a couple of boys go to Mano. It's about a two hour drive on a dirt road." There she helped out with the liturgy and offered support to the people who had suffered a devastating mud slide a year earlier that had claimed 200 lives. In another village, Gbama, a young teacher "has been begging us to come," Toni wrote. The nun enthusiastically responded by regularly leading prayer services for children and adults in Gbama. To help communicate with the local people, Toni wrote that she was "trying to learn a bit of the Gola language."

Toni's job was to help the SMA priests evangelize the people of Klay and its remote villages, "taking the Good News to places where it is brand new." Barbara's job was once again ministering to the health needs of isolated populations. She would supervise the running of the clinic in Klay, where the nursing staff had been "improvising without adequate equipment and supplies." She would also spend two days a week traveling to outlying areas deep in the bush in her mobile clinic, a large blue Toyota Land Cruiser donated by a charitable organization in Germany. Once again, Barbara had demonstrated her remarkable ability to solicit funds and donations to further her work.

Ray Studer, a volunteer living in the Bomi Territory at the time, remembers that clinics were "pretty sparse" and the quality of the medical personnel were mostly of the "brown bag" variety. Barbara, he said, raised the bar, even though it was not very convenient for most people living in the outlying areas to get to her clinic. "People had to walk," Studer said. "We would see people walking miles and miles carrying someone on a stretcher," all to get to Barbara Ann Muttra's little 3-bed clinic.

CODA

Towards the end of her life, when she was barred from anything more than supply runs to Klay because of the civil war, Barbara ached for "her mission" as she still called it. In a May 1992 letter, a few months before her death, she wrote: "I have not been able to settle down as yet in my own mission, as Taylor keeps sending different rebels in our area." Though she would continue to serve Klay and the hundreds of refugees sheltering there as a volunteer of the Catholic Relief Services, Barbara would never again be allowed to live at the mission that she and Antoinette had founded in Klay with such faith, hope, and love.

SISTER SHIRLEY KOLMER

I was making one of my several trips from Chicago to Southern Illinois, or "downstate" as it is often called. I had just been in St. Louis where I interviewed Sister Elizabeth Kolmer, ASC, about the life of her sister Shirley and their early years growing up on a farm near Waterloo, Illinois. Now I was breezing further south towards Ruma where the ASCs have their archives. I was driving at a good clip, maybe even a bit over the limit, because, really, how long can a soybean field hold your attention? About 25 miles into my drive I was suddenly struck by what seemed to me a whole slew of features on the outskirts of Waterloo, a town of middling size. New construction was everywhere. It was as if the town had traded in its work boots for a new pair of high heels. And that got me thinking, would Sister Shirley Kolmer even recognize this as her childhood stomping grounds?

When the Arthur Kolmer family lived on Rural Route 3 about five miles north of Waterloo, there was a lot more corn and a lot less town. Since then, a line of franchise businesses has sprung up along the town's eastern border on Highway 3; nascent signs of prosperity courtesy of Walgreens, Applebee's, and Pizza Hut. Even the highway has gotten a makeover, widened to allow for quicker ingress and egress in and out of the city. A stoplight at Market Street, the town's southern terminus, marks the last vestige of urban activity before the highway once again resumes its country demeanor and cars and trucks pick up speed. The road plows steadily onward through miles of flat-featured farmland. That part of the scenery hasn't changed much over the decades.

About a dozen miles south of Waterloo another modest burg, Red Bud, blooms on the horizon. Low lying buildings poke their noses up and over a sea of golden tassels signifying the abrupt end of the cornfields. But here the results seem a bit tired; shiny new businesses have yet to make much of an appearance. It takes only a few minutes to work through Red Bud's diffident commercial district and continue on Route 3 for the last five miles of the journey to Route 155 in Ruma, an even more non-descript town which brings to mind the caustic Gertrude Stein appraisal about there being "no there there."

One could be nearly forgiven for this assessment but for the existence of the beautiful, sprawling, pastoral campus tucked down a private road belonging to the Adorers of the Blood of Christ (the ACS sisters). Over the years hundreds of dewy-eyed young girls were driven by anxious parents down that road to attend Precious Blood High School where they would be left to board and contemplate entering the religious life. Many would leave after high school, but the select would stay and ultimately enter lives of service as Catholic nuns. Some would come to lead lives of extraordinary diversity and unique attachments that they could have never envisioned for themselves when they first stepped on to the quiet campus as young teens. They would grow into women who would touch lives in areas of the world both near and remote, both ordinary and exotic. This was merely their first stop in their education and formation for their future work.

Two of those teens belonged to the Arthur and Carmelita Kolmer family. Once a month, on "visiting Sunday," the Kolmers would make the drive from their home near Waterloo to Ruma to visit their girls. The drive in the 1940s would have been leisurely, more of a picnic-pace than the race car velocity of today. Back then there was a war on, so road speeds nationally were capped at 35 mph as part of an effort to save on rubber and gas. Most likely Arthur would have been behind the wheel with Carmelita in the front seat and two or three children packed into the back for the 25-mile ride to the convent where Shirley and her younger sister, Elizabeth, eagerly awaited them.

JULY 1944

Mother was in the mood to bake a pie, so Shirley and her younger sister Elizabeth were sent to pick some cherries from a stand of trees that bordered the house. The trees were old but could still produce enough fruit for a pie or two.

When they reached the trees, the girls climbed up and

began to work in amiable silence, enjoying one another's company and the beautiful day. It was one of those lovely summer gifts when the temperature in Southern Illinois was just right and the humidity was manageable. One by one the girls twisted the ripe cherries from their stems and dropped them into a waiting bucket.

Shirley had to be careful as she balanced among the branches. At 13 she was just shy of her ultimate 5-foot-10-inch height. She had grown so rapidly that at times her arms and legs seemed to have minds of their own, moving in opposition to one another rather than in concert. Her clumsiness often exceeded that of her classmates at Saints Peter and Paul grade school, but then so did her sense of playfulness and academic prowess. As in most things, Shirley was outsized.

Soon a new chapter would begin for Shirley. In a few short weeks, she would start high school. It was assumed that she would attend school in Waterloo, just like her older siblings.

With their task done, the girls climbed down from the trees. Elizabeth had something on her mind and decided this was as good a time as any to break the news to Shirley. "I'm going to enter the convent next year," she said. She was only 12 years old and had another year of grammar school to go, but her plan was already firm.

Unfazed, Shirley leaned her long back against one of the branches, turned her famous gap-tooth grin on her sister and said coyly: "Oh, I'm going to do that this fall. I'm going to go to high school in Ruma." Shirley said it as if the idea had just occurred to her.

It took Elizabeth a moment to recover but when she did her first question was, "Well, have you told Mom and Dad yet?"

But, of course, Shirley hadn't since it wasn't in her nature to get too far ahead of herself with details.

"Have you even applied yet?" Elizabeth pressed.

"No" again.

"Well you better hurry up. School starts in just a few weeks!"

Whether or not Shirley took her sister's admonishments to heart, she did step up her preparations to secure a place at the ASC's Precious Blood High School. However, the first hurdle for her was to convince her reluctant mother, Carmelita, that she was not too young to go away to a convent boarding program.

The youngest Kolmer sibling, Joe, was 14 years Shirley's junior. He doesn't have a firsthand recollection of the summer of 1944, but he does remember the family conversations about it. In a phone interview, he explained it this way: "Mom did not want her girls to enter the convent, but before long she became proud of their decision." On the other hand, their father was the reflective sort and less likely to speak his mind. "Dad never said anything about the convent one way or the other," said Joe. Arthur Kolmer was "a man of few words."

Apparently, the two oldest Kolmer daughters, Mary Lou

and Dorothy never expressed an interest in going away to school, let alone a convent school. Shirley would be the first to break that ground. Fortunately for her, even at a young age she could display a determination as unstoppable as a runaway train. Joe summed up that feature of his sister's personality this way: "If Shirley wanted to do it, she would do it."

As a woman who knew her own mind, Carmelita must have recognized that same characteristic in her third daughter. Perhaps it even gave her comfort that Shirley was so sure of herself.

In August Shirley received her acceptance letter to Precious Blood High School.

Over time, the gangly young girl would evolve into a mature, thoughtful woman. The little-girl stubbornness would mellow into resolve and her childhood cleverness grow into wisdom. Shirley would become a teacher and mentor who inspired and challenged her students and colleagues to do great and important things. Hers would become the voice others listened for and followed.

As for Elizabeth, true to her word, she would enter Ruma the following year, thereby bonding the girls not just by birth but by a shared desire to lead lives devoted in service of Jesus Christ.

BEGINNINGS

There was just a whiff of obstinacy in the air when Shirley Ann was born on December 15, 1930, to Arthur Kolmer and Carmelita Vogt Kolmer. Born into two families with deep roots in the Waterloo, Illinois area, the girl would grow up surrounded by an abundance of aunts, uncles, and cousins spread like seed throughout the tight-knit German farm community.

The knot was drawn doubly tight between the Vogts and the Kolmers when two Kolmer boys, Arthur and Harry, married two Vogt girls, Carmelita and Alma.

Between 1926 and 1945, Carmelita would bear a total of eight children: Mary Lou, Lee Roy, Dorothy, Shirley, Elizabeth, John, Jim, and Joseph. John and Jim died in infancy.

When Carmelita's third daughter (and fourth child) was born, she was determined that the baby be named Shirley—a prospect that had been thwarted earlier for various reasons. Carmelita had wanted the name for her second daughter, but pressure from her parish priest to adhere to Catholic tradition dictated the child be named for a recognized saint. And there was no Saint Shirley. In the end, Carmelita acquiesced and named her second girl Dorothy after an early Christian martyr.

Carmelita had learned a thing or two about mothering by the time her fourth child was born. With experience comes confidence, so when it came time to christen this new baby she was ready to pick up an old argument. This time, when she said she wanted to name her baby Shirley, Carmelita was unwavering. Though she did make a small concession; the child's name would be Shirley Ann. Since Saint Ann was a bona fide saint of the church, it was a compromise both she and her pastor could abide.

The name dustup was a mild affair and did nothing to diminish the rock-solid devotion the Kolmer family had for their Catholic faith, which was manifest in Saints Peter and Paul Church and School. For decades, an assortment of Kolmer and Vogt cousins would grace the parish's four-classroom grammar school. Here, under the tutelage of sisters belonging to the Adorers of the Blood of Christ, Shirley would be introduced to women living in a religious community. It was a way of life she wanted to explore more fully.

Years later, Sister Elizabeth Kolmer related how her sister Shirley would laugh at the story of the skirmish over her name. "Oh, that's all right," she would say. "I'll be the first Saint Shirley." Elizabeth never forgot that jest. After her sister's death in 1992, a priest referred to the five sisters as saints. "I remember thinking when I heard him say Saint Shirley," said Elizabeth, "well, that's what she said she would do."

The years 1934 and 1935 would prove to be critical for the Kolmer family. In October of 1934 Harry Kolmer, just 26

years old, would die from an asthma attack, leaving behind his wife Alma and three little children, two boys and a girl, Orlou Rose, just seven months old. Baby Orlou would grow up to become Sister Joél Kolmer who, like her cousin Shirley, would be murdered in Liberia in 1992.

In January 1935, just over three months after Harry's untimely death, Catherine Kolmer, the family matriarch, died. Her last request to her surviving son Arthur was that he move in with his aging father to help with the farm. If Catherine feared that her husband would be lonely knocking about the big farm house by himself, she could not have been more off the mark.

Overnight Henry Kolmer would go from sole master of the large white house, seated like a statesman on a rise, to one of a dozen extended family members in residence. Touchy of nature in the best of times, the new living arrangement would prove a trial for Henry, who could become downright "crabby" according to family reports. This was an eminently understandable point of view, since eight members of the newly reconstituted household were under nine years of age. Beside Arthur and Carmelita and their five children, the newcomers also included departed son Harry's widow, Alma, and her three children—now part and parcel of Arthur's family. At least there was one consolation for Henry, tight quarters or not, he kept the master bedroom on the first floor that he had shared with Catherine all to himself. It was, after all, still his home—one he had built in 1894.

The wood-frame structure sat on the crest of a hill on property that had originally belonged to Henry's father. The land also accommodated other buildings, including a log cabin that had been home to the area's first settler—which faced the Kaskaskia trail, now Illinois Route 3—and a building originally intended as a permanent family home that had been abandoned and left unfinished. Portions of the uncompleted construction had been furnished in walnut, which Henry had later reclaimed and used in a hutch for his chickens. The sight of such high-end wood dressing up a chicken coop provided no end of amusement to his son Arthur, who teased his father: "Not too many people have a walnut chicken hutch!"

Besides the first-floor master bedroom, Henry's house had three additional bedrooms upstairs. Arthur and Carmelita's girls: Mary Lou, Dorothy, Shirley, and Elizabeth shared one of the rooms. Lee Roy, the only son at the time, had his own room, and Arthur and Carmelita had the third; Alma and her three children shared a large space at the end of the hall that they transformed into their living area. As far as modern conveniences, there were none. There was no indoor plumbing or running water (an outhouse and water pump were located outside) and there was no electricity (kerosene lamps and gas jets lit the house at night). For the time and place, though, this was all quite natural. It was not until 1937 that the national government, as part of Franklin Roosevelt's New Deal, would begin running electricity out to the rural areas of the country. It was a prospect that Henry Kolmer, a staunch Republican, wanted nothing to do with; though he did eventually relent and allow electric poles to be run across his land.

Supper was always a family affair. For the first couple of years, the expanded family circle would gather around a large table in the basement kitchen. Grandpa Henry would sit at the head, with his son and two daughters-in-law and their eight children rounding out the table. There the family would talk as they ate by the dusky yellow glow of kerosene lamps. After cleaning up the kitchen, the older children would huddle around the table to do their homework by lamplight. Upstairs in the sitting room and bedrooms, the house had a more welcoming attitude as gas jets supplied a brighter and whiter light. Then, in 1937, Alma remarried, and she and her children moved out of Henry's house. This allowed for a bit more elbow room around the dinner table. Later still, the kitchen was relocated upstairs when Henry finally permitted the home to be wired for electricity.

In the early years, Carmelita would pile her growing gang into the family's 1931 Chevy for the five-mile ride to Saints Peter and Paul grammar school. The car, basically a rectangular box, had horsehair bench seats that prickled, especially in summer. What's more, there was no heater, so the ride in the winter months could be bracing to say the least. The children did not really mind the old-fashioned vehicle too much. Perhaps that was due in part to the clever way Carmelita orchestrated their ride.

"We would sing songs," recalled Elizabeth. "Mom sang western cowboy songs. We would sing with her. Or we would recite poems—Longfellow or Oliver Goldsmith." The practice worked well for passing the time and keeping the children engaged. Carmelita would employ this same methodology when cleaning house with her girls, all of them singing along with their chores.

In 1940, the family upgraded to a "sleeker car." About a year after that, 15-year-old Lee Roy, now in high school, took over chauffeuring his siblings. While Lee Roy may have been a young driver, he was quite legal. The minimum age for driving in Illinois at the time was 15, as established in 1919, and it was not until 1939 that Illinois enacted its first law governing the licensing of drivers. In those days, cars were less plentiful, roads were far less crowded, and the process of accrediting a driver was fairly informal. A license could be purchased for about 50 cents at the local filling station.

Saints Peter and Paul School would be where Shirley would leave a youthful mark. Elizabeth recalls her sister as bright and rambunctious and a "real live wire" often at the center of one sort of commotion or another. Shirley's quickly growing frame made her rather clumsy, though that didn't stop her from seizing the spotlight whenever possible, dancing and clowning her way into her classmates' affections. She and her friends could be quite rowdy.

Sometimes after hearing reports of her daughter's exploits, an exasperated Carmelita would threaten to send her mischief-maker to boarding school if she didn't shape up. Although when presented with the reality a few years later, Carmelita would balk at the idea of allowing Shirley to go away to high school.

In the early years, Carmelita sometimes indulged her desire for a longed-for set of twins by dressing Shirley and her older sister Dorothy alike. She would pair up the girls for chores too. Dorothy and Shirley anchored one crew, while Elizabeth teamed with the oldest girl, Mary Lou.

The two teams alternated chores: cooking, cleaning house, and—as they got older—feeding the hogs and chickens and gathering the eggs while trying not to get pecked. Shirley especially disliked housework, which she found boring. Of course, this dislike counted for little; she was still obliged to do her share, though Elizabeth freely admitted that both she and Shirley would drag their feet on occasion, especially when it came to ironing. That chore was not only time-intensive but also inexact, since the iron had to be heated on a wood burning stove. During the steamy days of summer, ironing could be positively unbearable.

The girls' brother Lee Roy was spared the household chores. He mainly helped his father with the dairy herd and the crops. Farm life then, as now, was a physically strenuous business. But there was also balance in the Kolmer home between physical labor and education. The children were a bright lot, with each expected to keep up with his or her schoolwork. Most evenings found them studying together after dinner. Their father had a desk where each child would place his or her report card. Then, one by one they would meet with him to discuss their grades. Arthur commented on each one, though he was careful not to push too hard. It was a routine that paid dividends when several of the children went on to earn advanced degrees. Shirley would receive a Master's degree in mathematics from St. Louis University and a PhD in mathematics from Catholic University in Washington, DC, in 1964.

Besides providing a solid base in their Catholic faith and a love of learning, probably the most important legacy that Carmelita and Arthur bequeathed their children was strength of character, though their approaches were polar opposite. Arthur favored the strong and silent version of idealized masculinity and would bide his time before sharing his thoughts; Carmelita would let you know what was on her mind from the get-go, but she was never all talk. She led by action, helping anyone in need. Through the diocesan women's association and parish societies, she reached out to the less fortunate in the community by distributing used clothing. To the seasonal workers who lived in a trailer at the edge of town she would drop off eggs and other supplies. Her good works provided a powerful example to her children of how to live in a world that is less than fair.

Like her mother, Shirley was tall and big-boned. Their voices, too, were eerily similar; so much so as to be almost indistinguishable on the telephone. And if Carmelita truly wanted something, she would always figure out a way to get it. Shirley was much the same way.

When Shirley declared in the summer of 1944 that she wanted to go to Precious Blood High School and Carmelita said "no," the stage was set for a test of wills. Just exactly what Shirley's winning argument was that changed Carmelita's mind is no longer remembered by the family, though Elizabeth recalls that the next year, when it was her turn to face her mother and declare a reason for wanting to go to the convent, "I could never really explain it well." In all likelihood, Shirley may have found it equally hard to describe her reasons for wanting to enter the convent too.

A vocation or calling to religious life is a hard thing to pin down for most people, especially when they are young. Those who feel God wants them to be a priest or brother or nun generally believe it but can't necessarily provide empirical evidence for it. A religious sister once described it this way: It's like falling in love, you may try to deny it but you usually will get caught up in it eventually.

In truth, it was probably not the arguments she made to her mother at all but the determination Shirley showed in making them that caused Carmelita to relent and permit her daughter to enter the convent high school in Ruma. Even as a young teen, Shirley's dominant personality was becoming a force to be reckoned with.

In late August of 1944, when 13-year-old Shirley entered Precious Blood High School, she donned a modest knee-length jumper belted at the waist and a small black veil that she wore perched at the back of her head. The uniform was an outward manifestation of the choice she was making to pursue a life different from that of her friends back in Waterloo. Over the years, as she moved through the various stages of religious development, Shirley's uniform would change from school-girl attire to a more somber nun's habit; a reflection of her deepening commitment to religious life.

COMMITMENT

On July 1, 1946, Shirley Kolmer entered the novitiate of the Adorers of the Blood of Christ. The step was significant in that it indicated her acceptance into religious life. The black veil she had worn for two years as a postulant was replaced by a white one. In addition, along with her new status she would choose a new name. She would no longer be known as Shirley but as Sister Mary Kenneth—a name she would carry for three decades until the mid-1970s when, like many other sisters of that era, she reverted to her birth name. (*In an effort to reduce confusion, I will continue to refer to her as Sister Shirley rather than Sister Mary Kenneth throughout this book.*)

The next July, Shirley made her first profession of vows and received a red tasseled sash that she wore cinched across her waist. There would be five more years of study, prayer, and reflection before she made what are called her "perpetual" vows, in which she pledged her life irrevocably to God. A letter to the candidates of her class in February 1952 from their Provincial—recorded in *Echoes in Our Hearts*—reminds the young women of the seriousness of the commitment they are about to make:

> *Pray fervently to the Holy Spirit that he may give you the necessary strength to be faithful unto death.... Perpetual vows means a lifelong obligation, despite all the difficulties and hardships that may come into your religious career sooner or later.*

The 21-year-old Sister Shirley Kolmer would make that most sincere pledge "to be faithful unto death" on July 1, 1952.

Under the auspices of the ASC community, Shirley continued her education, and in the fall of 1953 she enrolled at St. Louis University to major in mathematics. Mathematics was a field that suited the young woman. She had a natural inquisitiveness and imaginativeness that the discipline satisfied because it allowed her to explore "how pieces fit together." It was reported that one of her favorite sayings was, "Mathematics is beautiful!" Though she loved pure theoretical mathematics, she was also very practical. Shirley would go on to teach mathematics first in high school and then college. She gained a reputation as a "hard but fair" teacher who could make a difficult subject accessible and even fun. Her naturally happy demeanor made her a student favorite. She was described by those who knew her well as "gregarious, open-minded, and liberal."

Shirley's first assignment after earning her undergraduate degree was to teach math at Saints Peter and Paul High School in Waterloo. The new job would place her in proximity to family once again. Even though it would bring her daughter close to home, however, Carmelita fretted. Their tight-knit German-speaking community was loaded with Kolmer and Vogt cousins, not to mention children of close friends who attended the high school where Shirley would teach. How would her daughter handle disciplinary problems so they wouldn't spill over into family conflicts? Carmelita need not have worried. The new educator had a way of combining fairness and discipline with an easy manner that won over the unruliest students. Even a family cousin, viewed by some as a "wild hare," fell into line when subjected to the young teacher's methods. Everyone, it seemed, loved Sister Shirley.

All the while she was teaching high school, Shirley was attending classes part time at St. Louis University in order to earn her master's degree in mathematics, which she did in 1960. Soon after that the Province sent her to Washington, D.C., where she earned her doctorate in mathematics from Catholic University of America four years later. The fall of

1964 would find the new PhD on the campus of St. Louis University once again; this time as an associate professor of mathematics. It was the start of a 13-year career at the university.

Living in a religious community also meant that its members had numerous obligations to their order that went beyond their everyday, secular jobs. So besides teaching at the university, Shirley was appointed to help guide several of the younger women among the ASCs preparing to take their final vows. An assessment of her qualifications for the job reads in part: "She seems to have common sense, good insight, a genuine supernatural love for others, and the capacity to inspire confidence and a sense of joy and optimism."

For the women who lived with Shirley and knew her best, she was a fun companion, a practical joker, and a true friend who helped out anyone who asked. Sister Marita Toenjes, a classmate of Shirley's, is quoted in *Echoes in Our Hearts*: "I never liked math. She explained it to me and helped me." With Shirley's guidance, Sister Marita went on to earn an A in her class.

Shirley's highly analytical mind would be a boon when she was appointed to lead the Ruma Province in 1978, enabling her to examine problems from all sides. She also had no need for a physical calendar because she could keep her busy schedule in her head. But perhaps the most impactful year in Shirley's life was 1973. This was when she accompanied her then Provincial Superior, Sister Irene McGrath, on a visit to the two missions in Liberia then staffed by her fellow ASC sisters. Not only would Shirley visit the Grand Cess and Gardnersville sites, she would also pay a visit to the University of Liberia in Monrovia. And with that, the seeds for her eventual return were planted.

LIBERIA CALLS

When she returned home, Shirley resumed teaching at St. Louis University, but it was becoming less satisfying for her. Her brother Joe recalls a kind of restlessness in his sister about this time. "I remember her saying that teaching college just wasn't enough for her. She wanted to make a difference, and it was not going to happen teaching college in the U.S."

The important work Shirley had seen her fellow community members doing in Liberia excited her, and she discovered it was something she wanted for herself. In 1976, she applied for a Fulbright Grant, and the following year got her wish when she was awarded a Fulbright Fellowship and secured a teaching position in mathematics at the University of Liberia. By the summer of 1977, she was ensconced in her own little apartment in Monrovia near the campus of the university. In a letter to her parents dated September 13, 1977, she talked about her busy schedule: "My big class of 97 just had a test and that was a chore to correct.... I am having a test tomorrow in another class but I only have 44 in that class." Then, as if that were not enough, she added, "I have also been teaching a small child to read."

The message is on thin blue airmail paper, the kind popular for overseas letters at the time. Her handwriting is slightly cramped, words jam-packed from edge to edge, threatening to cascade off the page. Shirley has a lot to tell her family about the people she is meeting and her new life. She is excited, not only by her experiences but by the prospect of sharing her new life with her parents in person. She exhorts them to visit her in Liberia: "When you come in December," she writes. Yet a letter dated February 16, 1978, makes it clear that Shirley, even now hopeful, is still awaiting their visit: "But do let me know about your coming, like dates and flights. I'll be preparing for you end of March." Her next letter dated March 15 no longer mentions the planned visit. Apparently, the trip has fallen through. If she was disappointed, she hid it well.

A line later in the same letter registers delight that Shirley had not been appointed to serve as Provincial Superior for her community. "Cheers for me, I can stay here. I am so relieved." Apparently, she had been in consideration as a candidate to run the Ruma Province. That honor went instead to Sister Anne Irose, who was named to succeed Sister Irene McGrath in the five-year term as Provincial of the Ruma ASCs.

Alas for her, Shirley's celebration was to prove premature when Sister Anne took ill. Shirley was informed in June of 1978 that she would be the next superior. She was directed to return to her community in Illinois and her life in Liberia was put on hold. The vow of obedience Shirley had taken so many years earlier superseded her personal desire.

Sister Shirley Kolmer's installation as the new Provincial in Ruma was marked by a speech that was short, barely a written page, but powerful. In it, Shirley laid down a gauntlet for her fellow sisters. She wanted them to throw open their windows and doors, as it were, by challenging the ASC community to follow her into an unknown future. She termed the stance she wished for them to be one of "readiness." Here is an excerpt of what she said: "Readiness creates a healthy tension between the present but an insecurity and, at the same time, confidence in the future. I say it is a healthy tension as it is sensitive, but not anxious; it is radical but not extreme."

And then in a beautifully poetic string of couplets, Shirley, who by now had been seasoned by a year of living in Liberia—and had felt the personal call to do more—exhorts her sisters:

*We pray the Lord that we might always try to be
women of the Lord;
women who laugh and dance and sing;
women who are not so conscious of what we have given
but rather of what we have been given;
women who are struggling for justice;
women who are faithful in prayer;
women the Spirit continues to disturb;
women who are warmhearted,
with a great capacity to accept and forgive all,
mindful that we all belong to the same human
but wonderful family.*

The five years Shirley would spend as Provincial Superior would be a time to exercise her leadership skills. It would
also be a time when she literally threw open the windows and
doors of Ruma. She would remake what she had always seen
as a dark and ponderous building where the sisters lived and
worshipped into a more welcoming and warm home for the
residents and their guests. Shirley wanted the Adorers' home
to reflect a more cheerful attitude; she thought her colleagues
deserved as much. To that end, she began a remodeling project that would take nearly a decade to complete. During her
tenure, Shirley rid the place of much of its heavy old furniture, had better lighting installed, and renovated most of the
first floor including the kitchen and dining areas. The result
was a cheerier living arrangement. One that reflected Shirley

Kolmer's own sunny disposition.

Many thought of their new provincial as pleasant, even happy-go-lucky, but she could also put the full force of her personality on display when need be. She had a vision in her head of where she wished the ASC community to go, but not everyone was in agreement. Sometimes change needed to be massaged for the more conservative members of the community. Shirley was quite capable of this, but she could also be sharp and impatient with those who did not share her ideas or were just too slow to keep up. There is evidence of this in a letter she wrote much later, after she had already given up leadership of the Ruma province.

It is early 1987, and Shirley is back in Liberia but still very much concerned with the running of the ASC community. It seems there had been talk among the sisters in Liberia about restructuring the American chapters of the ASC. Shirley reports in the letter, "We sent a proposal to the general chapter (in Rome) for restructuring/reorganizing of the provinces." (Shirley, deeply disappointed, had not been invited to serve as a delegate to the meeting in Rome.) "I think it says something about how closed the province is, or maybe afraid or shall we call it 'sheep.' Anyway I plan to be there." Apparently, Shirley did attend the meeting in Rome, and in a letter to Ruma a few months later she wrote that the proposal from Africa "seems to have sparked real interest." But she couldn't help a bit of a brag: "Of course it was my proposal which everyone here agreed to and I think were happy to send."

It is also clear that Shirley understood that she and her supporters were often viewed with ambivalence by some within the larger ASC community: "...they can't live with us and can't live without us. True enough."

As provincial, Shirley was ambitious. She wanted to expand the Adorer's scope beyond their comfort zones of Illinois and Missouri and pressed for more outreach in Liberia, approving the opening of a new mission in Klay, and two sites in New Mexico during her 5-year tenure. She saw answering the plight of the needy, regardless of geography, as a crucial responsibility for the ASCs and pushed her fellow sisters to go beyond their everyday ministries, to dig more deeply within themselves to address the cares of others on a wider, even international, scale.

By pushing her fellow sisters towards a state of "readiness," Shirley was in essence working the soil and encouraging her community to be open to even larger challenges to come. In 1985, Shirley's good friend Sister Kathleen McGuire proposed to the ASCs that they become part of the controversial Sanctuary Movement for refugees from Central America. Though it took a considerable effort, the majority of the Ruma sisters agreed to offer refuge to families fleeing violence there.

As head of the Ruma province, Shirley dedicated herself fully to her work. Yet Liberia was always in the back of her mind. During her tenure as Provincial she was able to make a stop in the country in mid-1979 on her way home from a leadership meeting in Rome. The visit was just a few months after the violent "rice riots" of April 14 in Monrovia. The riots were a response to Liberia's president at the time, William Tolbert, hiking the price of the country's main food staple. Protesters were shot and businesses were looted in what would mark the beginning of the end for President Tolbert's government. This time is significant as the seeding of tumult in Liberia. Old grievances against Americo-Liberian rule were now being stirred up in underrepresented communities. The upheaval to follow would last a generation. Of course, none of that would be evident to the ASCs then serving in the missions of Grand Cess and Gardnersville in 1979. Meanwhile, Shirley returned home to the U.S. after the visit and once again took up her duties as head of the Ruma province, secure in her belief that her fellow sisters were valued members of their adopted communities in Liberia and recognized for the good work they were doing.

Then on April 12, 1980, an army master sergeant named Samuel K. Doe and a handful of followers assassinated President Tolbert and his entire cabinet. And everything began to change. For the ASCs in Liberia, that April day dawned as one of joy and celebration. They were to mark the silver jubilee of one of their own, Sister Mary Evelyn Nagle. There was a Mass, with 22 concelebrating priests and 70 guests— fellow missionaries from other communities—gathered in

Gardnersville for what Sister Barbara Ann Muttra called a "wonderful evening." But around midnight, she wrote, "We heard guns being fired in the distance. Soon we heard big army trucks flying wildly down the road."

The next morning they learned of the coup. It would be five days more before Sister Barbara and the other Grand Cess missionaries would be allowed to make their way back down the coast. "We only went for Mass in early morning.... Soldiers were invading homes of the expatriates and forcing them to give money, their valuables.... It was quite a distressing time." It would be over a year before things settled enough for a 6 p.m. to 6 a.m. curfew over the entire country to be lifted.

Worrying as the new military rule was for Liberia, there was apparently no attempt on Shirley's part to curtail any of the order's missionary work in the country and no indication of fear for the personal safety of the ACS sisters. In fact, when her five-year term as head of the Ruma province was complete, Shirley was happy. She had already applied to renew her Fulbright Fellowship in order to return to teaching at the University of Liberia. There remained but one final item on her agenda: a party. Since each incoming administration was honored with an installation dinner and party, Shirley, always up for a good celebration, suggested that her outgoing team of councilors should be honored with an "outstallation" party. It was, of course, a great success.

LIBERIA AGAIN

By the end of January 1984, Shirley was back in Liberia. Math classes at the University of Liberia had been moved off the main campus in Monrovia and onto a new campus further outside the city. So instead of having an apartment in the capital as she had before, Shirley decided to live with the ASC community in the suburb of Gardnersville. There she joined Sisters Mary Evelyn Nagle, Martha Wachtel, and Raphael Ann Drone, as well as Josephine Wernah, a young Liberian studying for the sisterhood. The five other ASCs in Liberia at the time lived on the Grand Cess and Klay missions: Sisters Joél Kolmer, Rachel Lawler, Julia Lengermann, Barbara Ann Muttra, and Antoinette (Toni) Cusimano.

Though small in number, these nine women from a nondescript town in Illinois were beginning to make their presence very well known in Liberia. Two in particular, Shirley Kolmer and Barbara Ann Muttra, would garner special attention as leaders in the fields of education and health care respectively.

Shirley's return to Liberia, however, was proving to be challenging for her. Everything, it seemed, was in a state of flux. In a letter dated February 2, 1984, to her sister Elizabeth she writes: "I am in Gardnersville. I will probably stay here at least for a while, i.e. a year or 6 months. Maybe longer. It might be handy and it might not." She questions whether she will need a car, "I am not sure if I can manage without a car or not. We shall see." The phrase "we shall see" crops up often in Shirley's correspondence and is usually indicative of her anticipating a problem. By her next letter in March she has already decided on getting a car. "This is expensive but I believe worth it."

Shirley also remarks on the improvements she sees in the country and people since her initial stay in 1977. It is now almost four years since Samuel K. Doe wrested control of the national government from the Americo-Liberians. "I can't believe the improvements.... They have two buses really nice ones from Germany.... They have new bus signs too. The people here dress better and put their clothes on better. It is good to see."

Politically though, the atmosphere around President Doe was beginning to turn toxic. Doe distrusted progressives as well as most other people, including those from other indigenous tribes. Of the 16 ethnic groups in Liberia, Doe really only relied on two for support: the Krahn (his own tribe) and the Mandingo. Thomas Quiwonkpa, Prince Johnson, and Charles Taylor—all once aligned with Doe—now fled the country. Each would return and attempt to oust Doe. (Quiwonkpa would be killed for his effort.) All of this was bubbling in the background when Sister Shirley returned to her adopted country in 1984. Her letters, however, do not indicate that she understood these early markers of unrest or the hellish turmoil in which she would be caught. And to be honest, had she suspected the future, we might certainly question if she would have done anything differently anyway.

Shirley was back where she wanted to be, though she did admit that five years away from West Africa made for a bit of readjustment. The pace of life was quite different from that of the United States, and Shirley was finding it difficult to power down her lifestyle. She confided to Elizabeth in a May letter: "It gets a little boring sometimes. I am used to much more activity. It will take a little time."

The Gardnersville convent had an old black and white television for entertainment, though the viewing choice was decidedly limited, according to Shirley: "We have one channel here." Luckily, there was also a working VCR for videos. So after the evening news there might be a show of *"Dallas, Taxi, Sanford & Son, Dynasty....* It is amazing what one watches now and never did before." Shirley then described her evening activities: "...evening Mass at 7:00 PM then we eat & then news. I usually do not work after supper...short wave news at 9:00 PM. I lie in my bed and listen.... One thing I think I get enough rest. One can't do much else. The heat makes one tired and sleepy."

On weekends Shirley liked to travel. One of her early stops was a visit to the new ASC mission in Klay, which she had approved as Provincial. There she attended a house-warming party for Sisters Barbara Ann Muttra and Toni Cusimano, founders of the mission. The house, Shirley described as "country," meaning it was made of mud and sticks. "Lots of people came and brought lots of things.... We sat outside under the cover made for the cars—Barbara has a mobile clinic and Toni a car for pastoral work." Then Shirley added, "People really enjoyed being in the country."

By July, Shirley had once more adjusted to life in West Africa. "In fact," she writes, "it was too fast last week—the last week of school. This is exam week." Shirley was already hatching a new assignment for herself for the following school year. She wanted to address remedial learning. Her experience at the university had uncovered that many students had severe deficits. The best way to address this, she felt, would be to train high school teachers better. "Should be interesting as I will get around the country, I hope, visiting the hi (sic) schools," she wrote. As always when Shirley saw a problem, she also saw an opportunity to fix it.

LETTERS HOME

There is a treasure trove of written communication from Shirley to her sister Elizabeth and to others as well. Letters, lots of letters were exchanged, because this was before email, or texting, or social media. After her mother's death in the summer of 1985, Shirley made sure to write her father every week. Reading those letters, one can feel the care she took in writing to him. The tone is gentle, her sentences short and simple, and any concerns she expresses are minimized so as not to worry him. The letters to Elizabeth are meatier and occasionally a bit gossipy. In each case, the closing is the same: *Cheers! Kisses! Shirley.* Later she would amend the valediction just a bit, dropping the Kisses she would sign merely *Cheers! Shirley,* with an occasional *Cheerio! Shirley,* added to the mix. Even after war broke out and her letters took a much darker turn with reports of rebel activity and shootings, Shirley always managed the gay little good-bye. Perhaps it was her way of reassuring Elizabeth that she was coping, or maybe after so many years of this trademark closing she dared not change it lest she reveal too much.

Early on the letters are handwritten; later, more often than not they are typewritten. The typewritten ones, while more legible than the handwritten ones, prove to be an endless source of irritation for Shirley, mainly due to the obstinacy of a string of typewriters that show a distinct aversion to working in the Liberian heat and humidity. "You can see the problem with my typewriter," she complains. "Some of it of course is me." The short note is full of strikeovers, handwritten corrections, and juxtaposed letters. It is a pattern often repeated in other correspondence, so frequently as to become humorous. Clearly, typing was not a skill that Shirley ever truly mastered.

Occasionally politics creeps into her letters. In a May 11, 1986 missive, Shirley reflects on the October 1985 national election for president that Samuel K. Doe won. Prior to the election, Doe had been the de facto head of state for five years after the bloody 1980 coup. "There are more problems than I was aware of.... The political parties never did settle down after elections.... Everyone knows that Doe stole the election and they are still calling for a re-election." The letter continues to say that the Liberian people are upset with the human rights abuses being perpetrated by the Doe government and will not stand for it any longer. "It is good. It makes me happy to see it. Though it could get messy."

The following month Shirley relates the monetary troubles plaguing the country. Teachers are being especially hard hit since their salaries are paid by the government. "Many people here (University of Liberia) were not paid since December or January. Now they are promising that all will be paid up by the end of June." Liberian currency is losing value. "We have the American dollar for currency but they (the government) mint dollar and 5 dollar pieces. Now there are so many of them that we think we are on two different currency standards." Businesses that deal in imports are being pressed to pay for their goods in American dollars, which are often difficult to obtain. "It will be interesting to see what happens in several months as they cannot get more money made," she adds a bit cynically.

By August teachers in the government-run schools had still not been paid and threatened to walk out. Opposition to the national government continued to grow. "We hear rumors that dissident troops are being trained in Ivory Coast. It is hard to know what is true. But one always knows something is happening." Things were definitely happening, and not for the better. Because of the unrest, foreign investment in the country began to decline sharply and unemployment rose to over 50 percent—a previously unheard-of number.

Political commentary would assume more prominence in Shirley's correspondence as things continued to deteriorate in the country. Still, it was often the outreach of her fellow missionary sisters that held her attention. In a letter to her father she talked of visiting Klay and traveling around to several smaller villages with Sister Toni. "We went to one village which seemed at the end of the world. I asked Antoinette how she ever got to find the place. She said that someone told (her) that there was a man building a church in that village and (he) wanted someone to help him. So Antoinette went to talk to him. Most of the people in the area there are Muslims." Later she explained how her companion gave communion to a small group of Catholics in another village "to the few who can go to communion."

One particular outreach that would claim Shirley's attention was when her cousin, Sister Joél Kolmer, relocated from Grand Cess to the Gardnersville convent in July of 1985 to run the Aspirancy program for local girls wishing to become Precious Blood sisters. Shirley had encouraged Joél's transfer from the remote Grand Cess mission. She wanted her nearby. Joél's tenderness of spirit could lead her into sadness sometimes, and in those moments it was good for her to have Shirley around to talk to.

1986 was declared the International Year of Peace by the United Nations. It was marked by various observations throughout the world. In Liberia, however, there would be little peace and even less justice. Shirley recounted the trial of three men accused of sedition. They had dared to oppose the Doe regime. When it became obvious that the jury was about to find the men not guilty, the judge left the court declaring he was ill, without releasing the men. The jury protested. "Now they say they will have another trial," she wrote, adding that she only knew of these happenings through Voice of America or BBC broadcasts. "The local station carries very little."

The year wore on with teachers at the university still awaiting months-old back paychecks. Students rioted as the start of classes were delayed time and again. There was no direction. No planning. No one knew what to expect. For an ordered, goal-oriented person like Shirley, the chaos must surely have been mind boggling.

To add to her troubles, she was worried about the health of her father, Arthur, who had suffered a stroke earlier in the year. She had taken an extended leave to be with him back in the U.S. One can only imagine that upon returning to the disruption in Liberia Shirley must have felt that she was jumping into a blender running at high speed.

By the first of June, Shirley was still not back in class, but she kept busy with revising the remedial math program she had designed the year before for university students as well as monitoring teachers in three outlying cities: Robertsport, Buchannan, and Sinoe. "I can drive to the first two but have to fly to the last one," she wrote.

The traveling could wear her out. The roads were largely unpaved, sometimes harboring hidden potholes or other surprises like wandering wildlife. Driving them required an attentiveness that was draining. After several days on the move she wrote: "It is tiring to drive the roads here, so I had to take a good rest on Friday."

On June 3, she wrote: "We are hearing rumblings that the univ (sic) may start soon.... Before anything can happen the faculty must be paid for March. Can you imagine." This last sentence is not a question. Shirley's growing frustration is showing. She is talking to her sister Elizabeth, an academic herself and university professor in the U.S.

As she awaits the opening of the university, Shirley busies herself in writing a paper that she plans to present at a peace symposium marking the International Year of Peace. She sends a draft of the talk to Elizabeth for some editing help, which her sister sends back "in very good form." When at last school begins on June 23, Shirley is pleased. So are the students who she said are "eager to learn." There was just one snag. Of the thousand new students admitted to the university in 1986, most needed remedial math. "I am in charge of that program," she wrote laconically.

By October, Shirley seemed worn down. The strain was showing in her letters home. "We are finishing the semester and it is hard as my heart is not in it. I will be glad when it is over." It is becoming clear that she has had enough of the government run university. "Our 2nd semester should start mid-November. I hope it does or if not then not until after Christmas as by then my contract is finished."

But school did not start in November or even December. The school year was "messed up" according to Shirley: "We are supposed to start in January and have a whole semester. I can't believe it."

She had other worries, too. Her cousin, Sister Joél, was sick with anemia and needed to go home to the U.S. for treatment. Shirley fretted that Joél might need a hysterectomy. In her absence, Shirley promised to cover for her, no matter how long she was away. "I am staying with the aspirants in her absence," she told Elizabeth.

When it came time to deliver the speech she had painstakingly researched and prepared to mark the International Year of Peace, Shirley was too ill to deliver it herself. Instead, Sister Raphael Ann Drone read it for her. The speech, titled *Human Suffering and its Consequences for World Peace* is written from Shirley's heart. By now she has been back in Liberia for two years. She has seen firsthand the injustices that produce soul-crushing poverty. She talks of "our brothers and sisters who live a life of suffering, an existence that borders on the intolerable every day…. Their total energy is absorbed by the task of surviving every day." Yet Shirley is not just presenting a litany of indictments. She knows, and has known going as far back as those early days with her mother giving care to the poor in Waterloo, that the world is an unfair place. What Shirley, the problem solver, asks of her audience is to look through the eyes of those who suffer in the hope that it "will move us to do something about that vision." Peace, she contends, is "never done" and is "never a finished task." Nor is it "static;" it is, in her eyes, "a way in which women and men interact with each other to form a truly human community." But for a peaceful community to be successful "justice needs to be deeply imprinted on our hearts so that it is always there within to guide and uplift our spirits as we go about our peace-making." In other words, peace without justice is not possible.

She writes that those who suffer cannot just accept their state of affairs either but must struggle to realize that together they are not powerless. They must recognize their political, economic, social, and religious rights. She suggests that the way to do this is to follow the example being set in Latin America where "small Christian communities are led by one of their own members." In these communities, they share the scriptures and reflect on its meaning "for themselves here and now." This helps to form the basis for the group's direction and action. "This experience of the small Christian community brings about a change in the person's manner of relating to oneself, to others, to the surroundings, to the world."

These 1986 remarks would become a blueprint of sorts for a cooperative effort three years later between the ASC missionaries in Gardnersville and the new pastor of Saint Anthony's parish, Father Michael Moran, SMA.

According to Father Mike, the sisters wanted to help to create a "community-centered church," which he wholeheartedly supported. "They were really, really interested," he said. The principle was to break the parish into smaller groups of 15-20 people who would meet weekly. There were 15 basic Christian community groups. The groups would reflect on scripture and then decide how they were going to make that scripture reading come alive in their community. If the "scripture was on helping the sick, then they would visit the sick," he said. The people in each group "would have to come up with a concrete action" based on that week's reading.

Women emerged as leaders in these groups and were elected as chairpersons alongside the men. It was "about fifty-fifty" according to the priest. The people took their roles seriously and understood that each one of them had a responsibility to the group. Mike stated that developing women as leaders was not a primary goal of the groups but something that arose organically as members recognized the leaders among them. Liberian women were beginning to understand their power and nothing could please the ASC sisters more.

Later, as Sisters Agnes and Kathleen became active in this endeavor, the parish groups grew to about 30 members each. The small Christian community capable of bringing about change in people and how they relate to their world that Shirley had envisioned in 1986 was no longer a vision, but a reality.

When Shirley had talked so eloquently at her installation speech in 1978 of praying that members of her province have a stance of "readiness to follow the call of the Lord...so that much time is not needed to get ready when we are called," or when she envisioned her province "sitting in an easy chair, relaxed, carefree, and loving the comfort" but "ready to get up and go at a moment's notice," she was effectively speaking to herself. When she described her fellow community members as women "struggling for justice" and described them as "warmhearted, with a great capacity to accept and forgive all" or as "women who dream dreams and continue to promise," she was describing her best self.

It was this dreamer of big dreams who led the way for her fellow sisters in Liberia.

SISTER MARY JOÉL KOLMER

When the people I interviewed spoke about Sister Mary Joél Kolmer, it was as if I could hear a smile in their voices. To a person, I could feel a lift in their spirits when I mentioned her name. She was described as someone who saw wonders everywhere; someone who saw life as a beautiful adventure full of God's glory. And when something glorious caught her attention, she would often pause to sketch it or, lacking paper and pen, she would sketch with her mind; though that could lead to trouble when she got distracted from the task at hand.

Sister Joél, as she was always called and is referred to throughout this book, was sweet and tender, with an open heart that possessed no guile. Many said she was naive because for the majority of her life Joél could only see the good in people. At least, that is how it seemed. She shed some of that innocence as time wore on, but even when she saw the worst possible face of mankind in Liberia, she never gave up on its people.

When offered the opportunity to remain in the U.S. during Liberia's civil war, Joél balked. She chose to return to her adopted

153

homeland so she could minister to the suffering in their time of need. With that decision, she exposed a steel core that lay hidden beneath a soft surface.

EARLY YEARS

Sister Joél Kolmer was born on March 1, 1934 on a family farm just outside of Waterloo, Illinois. She was the third child—joining brothers Cyril and Kenneth—and first daughter of Alma Vogt and Harry Kolmer. She was christened Orlou Rose, a disharmonious legacy bestowed upon her by her father, who would die at 26, just seven months after his daughter's birth. She would shed the name, of which she was less than fond, for Mary Joél when she professed her vows as a Precious Blood sister. Displaying a fanciful flair for names herself, she added the French *accent aigu* over the 'e' and pronounced her name with an emphasis on the last syllable.

As a young widow with three children, Orlou's mother, Alma, needed help and was fortunate that there were lots of Vogt and Kolmer family members living in the area around Waterloo. Alma and her children were soon welcomed to live with her sister Carmelita's family on their farm just a few miles away. Carmelita's husband, Arthur, had been Harry's older brother, which made the personal bonds doubly strong. During the two and a half years the families lived together, the seeds of a close, life-long tie were sown among a younger generation of Kolmers: Shirley and Elizabeth, Arthur's girls, and their little cousin Orlou Rose, with all three eventually joining the ASC/Precious Blood community.

Shirley was nearly three years old and Elizabeth a year younger when their aunt and three young cousins moved into their small family farmhouse in October 1934. The following year, the expanded household moved as a group to live with their recently widowed paternal grandfather, Henry. That January, their grandmother Catherine Kolmer had died, and her last request of her son Arthur was that he move his family in with Henry—ostensibly to look after the homestead but perhaps to stave off any loneliness the new widower might be feeling, too.

In what would prove to be a rather extreme remedy for the blues, in the summer of 1935 a contingent of Kolmers consisting of three adults and eight children moved en masse into the large farmhouse that Grandpa Henry had built in 1894. The strain of incorporating so many young children (the oldest was just nine years old) into his home proved difficult for the old man. "Grandpa wasn't an easy person...even when he didn't have kids living with him," observed Sister Elizabeth later. "It was quite a challenge for my parents."

The arrangement would last about two years, until Alma remarried. Though there may have been difficulties for the adults in adjusting to clan life, Elizabeth remembers these early years as a time when close bonds were being forged among the cousins. Little Orlou, she said, was so sweet natured that everybody called her "Honey." This familial closeness would eventually extend itself to include the five children to be born to Alma and her new husband Herb Weltig over the next several years: Bill, Betty, Mary, Myrtle, and Vic. "They may have been half-siblings but were never considered as such," said Elizabeth. Indeed, all through her life, Joél referred to Herb simply as her father and, affectionately, as "Pop."

When Alma married Herb Weltig, the family moved out of grandpa's house and back down the road to Arthur's vacant farmhouse. After about a dozen years of struggling to make a go of farming, Herb decided it was too difficult to make ends meet, so the family moved to Waterloo and into a large house situated in the middle of a big piece of land owned by the city. The lot was open but overgrown, so the children played hide and seek and tag in the street that dead-ended near them. By that time the three oldest, Cyril, Kenneth, and Orlou, were in high school.

By the age of 13, Orlou Rose felt called to the life of a religious sister and entered the high school run by the Adorers of the Blood of Christ in Ruma. It was, she said, a desire she had first felt in the fourth grade when she sought to model herself after her teacher, who was an ASC sister. "She was young, vivacious, and so very personable," reflected the grown-up Joél. "I found that her character traits were what I myself wanted to possess."

But in her junior year of high school, Orlou Rose began

having severe sciatic pain; the effects were often debilitating. The pain would grow more severe and affect her ability to walk, causing a limp. To make matters worse, she was further plagued by severe weight loss and her studies began to suffer. By the middle of the school year, weekly appointments with a chiropractor in St. Louis took her away from class so often that the young woman was compelled to leave Ruma. Apparently, the sisters thought the problem too severe and likely to leave the girl crippled. Orlou was sent back home, where she finished high school at Saints Peter and Paul in Waterloo.

"I was about six when she came home," recalls youngest brother Vic. He said his sister's problem turned out to be a pinched sciatic nerve that caused so much pain that she could not concentrate on her studies. After Orlou left Ruma, the family believed this to be the end of her religious vocation; especially since their mother Alma did not want her daughter to return to the convent school.

"I remember my mother saying that she did not want to hear any more about Orlou returning to the convent until she turned 21," recalled Betty Cole. And for the next five years, that was the rule. Orlou never mentioned convent life, but she obviously kept the hope alive inside. "She never complained," said Vic, not even about her pain, which eventually improved with chiropractic treatments. It would take four years of weekly, and then monthly, doctor's appointments before the pain truly subsided. During that time, Orlou finished high school and got a job working as a secretary in Waterloo and then the next year in St. Louis as a file clerk. She also began dating, though apparently, there were no serious entanglements. When she turned 21, she announced her intention to resume her studies in Ruma.

"Everybody was shocked," says Vic. But Betty knew better. "I made a bet with my brother Kenneth that she would go back. He said she wouldn't. But deep down that was her calling."

Orlou's years at home were a gift to her younger siblings; a chance to reacquaint themselves with their big sister. It was an opportunity that would have been denied them had not illness intervened. Because of this stolen time, the Weltig siblings have vivid recollections of growing up with Orlou as an essential part of their lives. Betty remembers how her big sister would pitch in and help out at home after school by watching over the younger children and starting dinner. And then she would draw. Orlou began taking a series of mail order art classes and often would stay up late into the night sketching. "She drew all the time," said Betty. She drew anything that caught her fancy, including every cartoon character of the day represented in the funnies from Dotty to Brenda Starr. When Orlou drew, she was consumed. Nothing else seemed to matter, not even the dinner that she would so conscientiously begin and then summarily forget, burning more than her fair share of meals in the process.

Orlou's artistic side was not just consigned to the visual arts but included music as well. She became accomplished on

the guitar and as a singer. And she loved fashion. Suppos-
edly the style of the Precious Blood habit was one that had
appealed to the young girl the most, thereby cementing her
choice of religious community, though later in life fashion
became much less important to her. When she, like her fellow
sisters, finally gave up the habit, Joél dressed simply, caring
little about what she wore. Perhaps all the years of wearing
heavy religious garb had been fashion statement enough.

Her youngest sister, Myrtle Merriman, laughed when
she recalled the style depths to which her sister had sunk in
her middle years. She recounted how on one visit home, Joél's
bags were lost, leaving her without a change of clothes. But
Joél "scrounged around" and found some mismatched things
to wear. She looked like "a homeless person." Myrtle protested.
But Joél was unfazed. "As long as she had clothes to put on it
didn't bother her at all" what she wore, Myrtle insists.

When the teenaged Orlou was sent home from Ruma,
she was given a place on the second floor; not a room per se,
it was more of an open space with a stairway dividing her
area from that of her six-year-old brother, Vic, who slept on
a cot on the other side of the bannister. Orlou didn't seem
to mind sharing the space at all. In fact, it gave her a chance
to get to know her little half-brother better. "We would talk
sometimes before we went to sleep," said Vic. "She was very
encouraging to me. She was the one, even in my young age,
who would encourage me to be artistic or to study music. She
did this more than any of my other siblings."

As a child, Vic saw his oldest sister's spiritual side more than most of the family, because he would hear her praying at night. Then, as he lay in bed, Orlou would talk to him "about how to pray and how to act and how to be more concerned for others and more charitable and contemplative." Always, always "deeply thinking" herself about something, about everything, Vic remembers.

When Orlou finally returned to Ruma, it was as a postulant. She was already 21 and most of the other girls in her class were just seniors in high school, but that didn't bother her. "Everyone looked at Joël as the mother of the group. The oil that made the group run well," said Sister Terese Ann Kiefer, ASC. Everyone loved Joël's joyful nature. She never gossiped about anyone else. She never made snap judgements and always gave others the benefit of the doubt, and as Sister Terese puts it, "there was an innocence about her that people really respected."

Joël was also lots of fun; the "type who would try anything." She could often be found, in full habit, leading her little group in a game of softball, roller skating to waltz music in the auditorium, playing a game of volleyball, or even sledding down a snow hill with veil flying in the dead of winter, caring little that she had just torn her shawl on the way down. Wherever there was a bit of lightheartedness to be had, Joël would be there.

In one autobiographical sketch, Joél even tattled on herself: "As a Junior Sister I had the misfortune of breaking an auditorium window with the volley ball." She turned herself in to Sister M. Louise Utar, ASC, who seemed "very strict." Joél, "shaking in my shoes" recounts the "torture she went through just to tell the story" of the accident. And what was the penalty for her transgression? Forgotten. Apparently, anticipation was punishment enough.

But things were not just fun and games. Becoming a Precious Blood sister was serious business that required years of discernment and spiritual exploration. Joél dove into this exploration with abandon, calling God a "Pied Piper of human hearts" who "turns human lives inside out like a glove."

Preparation for the sisterhood also required that the young women get college educations so they could pursue careers, usually as teachers or nurses. Besides being worthy career-paths in themselves, it was a way for every able-bodied Precious Blood sister to earn a salary that would help support the community at large.

For Joél, the career route would be in education, although she found college studies difficult. While her dear cousins, Shirley and Elizabeth Kolmer, seemed to be breezing through master's degrees and doctorates, Joél often found herself scrambling to keep up in the classroom. Her cousins' seemingly effortless successes may have cast a shadow over her own accomplishments, though she was never heard to complain about this and was extremely proud of their achievements. Joél worried, however, that she would not measure up to what she wanted for herself. But she never said these things out loud. Only those who knew her best would surmise the personal doubts that occasionally plagued her. She was quite aware of her own shortcomings in the classroom and they upset her, but instead of giving up she pushed herself hard and then harder still. One of Joél's spiritual directors described her as a "person who has always overachieved her capabilities."

In 1969, Joél earned her bachelor's degree in Education from the University of Missouri. Her minor was in Art. And, though she did make an attempt at a master's degree in counseling at the University of Illinois, she did not finish the program. Her first experience as an educator was a year spent teaching 48 first graders in Cahokia, Illinois. In those days, young teachers, especially religious, were very often thrown in the deep end of the pool. Lucky for Joél there were those like Sister Rose Anthony, ASC, her fellow first grade teacher, who took Joél under her wing and helped her "get a good start in teaching. I am eternally indebted to Sister Rose Anthony," she said.

The next year found her in Columbia, Illinois, teaching second grade. There were four new sisters assigned to the parish at the same time and that made for a good deal of conviviality. "We had a good, full year of laughing," wrote Joél. "We laughed so much that we had a special laughing chair."

A year later, the young sister was reassigned to Holy Rosary Elementary in Fort Dodge, Iowa. This time the transition would be hard. Joél admitted that she had some serious "run-ins" with her superior whom she found "a little difficult." These were sufficiently problematic for Joél that she felt her "whole religious life was crumbling." But she was able to resolve these differences and bounce back "with much joy," saying she was "all the better for it!" It was a typical Joél response. When faced with adversity she somehow would find the wherewithal to turn it into a learning experience, benefitting in the process. She was a woman who counted her blessings while minimizing her problems. Which is not the same as saying she didn't recognize a problem when she had one.

Her tenure at the Catholic Children's Home in Alton, Illinois, as a child care worker would be perhaps one of Joél's biggest challenges. Here, she "agonized" over the best ways to help the children, all of whom had troubled backgrounds. The children's home had originally been founded by the Precious Blood Sisters in 1879 as an orphan asylum in Piopolis, Illinois. In 1884, the orphanage relocated to Alton, where services shifted over the years to focus more on residential programs for dependent and neglected children. The job would be a 24-hour-a-day commitment—emotionally draining and, in Joél's own words, "sometimes very depressing; yet vital to the lives of those we serve there."

Joél's good friend, Sister Mary Alan Wurth, ASC, said, "When she was at the children's home, big heart that she had, every one of those children's problems was her problem." Joél herself admitted as much: "I feel so helpless so often in the work that I am doing now." It was not just a struggle with outside forces but with interior ones that she was facing. "This type of work has made me realize, she said, "that, in all I do, it is Jesus doing in me what I do, and not me doing it." She talked about getting rid of her "old" self and not counting merely on herself but on Jesus, who "alone can make the difference." There were many dark days at the children's home —actually, "very dark days" is how Joél phrased it. "I've felt there was no hope in what I was doing as a child care worker," she said. But another ASC sister, Ruth Marie Boeckmann, "carried me through." Like before in Cahokia, when Joél needed help the most a friendly hand reached out to her and pulled her along. It would be a lesson she would take to heart and use time after time in the years ahead.

Vic Weltig recalled how his sister wanted to provide the troubled boys in her care with a little fun, so one day she decided to take them on an outing to their brother Bill's farm in Waterloo. One of the boys, who had a tendency to wander, was left behind. "He just walked off," said Vic. Sister Joél, knowing the boy well, also knew he would return in his own good time. Instead of getting the police involved, which could cause trouble for the youth, she gave him space, saying, "He will get home when he gets home." Which he did...two days later. With a naïveté both striking and precious, Joél chose to take the heat herself and spare the boy. Perhaps in defense of her actions one can only shrug and say that, after all, it was the 1970s!

Joél's experience at the Children's Home convinced her that institutional life was detrimental for a child. She even expressed a wish to one day work in foster care where children might experience living with a family and see "what true family life should be." It was a subject Joél knew very well, having maintained strong ties with her many brothers and sisters.

Joél's occasional visits with family members over the years are remembered as a treat by all. Her visits home from Liberia would be preceded by a conscious effort on her part to gain a bit of weight. She didn't want her thinness to alarm her family. Slender by nature at 5-feet 8-inches and 120 pounds Joél always had a hard time keeping the weight on in Liberia. To be truthful, she was also self-coconscious of her wispy brown hair—that, like her figure, tended towards the thin side, so she often concealed it beneath a baseball-style cap.

When she was with her brothers and sisters, though, she was still as charming and entertaining to them as ever. Watching television with Joél "was a trip," they say. Her viewing habits were boisterous, especially when she kept up a running commentary about the action on screen, often questioning the characters and telling them off when she thought they were being dumb. And when something tickled her fancy, she would let loose with her trademark "wahoo." Instead of being annoyed by this, Joél's family found her "more fun to watch than the television!"

DRIVING LESSONS

For Sister Joél Kolmer, teaching seventh grade at Holy Rosary Elementary in Fort Dodge, Iowa, was almost idyllic. In all, the young Joél would spend seven years teaching in that junior high, and she would number that time among her happiest. Many years later, when she looked back on this experience, she could find no particular explanation for this feeling except to say the kids in the school were not "so terribly bad" and the "ladies" she lived and worked with were "level-headed" and she respected and loved them dearly. Yet, while Joél could prize level-headedness in others, it was not a characteristic she always displayed herself, as evidenced by the following story.

It was 1966 and full-on summer in Fort Dodge. One fine day, Joél along with ACS Sisters Alvina Schott, Antionette Cusimano, and Flora Santel, decided to head out into the countryside for a picnic. Transportation was their only issue, but the sisters managed to convince their pastor to make them a loan of his automobile. Joél, the only one of the four to possess a driver's license, got behind the wheel. But there was one problem. She hadn't counted on the priest's car being a stick shift. The three pedals on the floor brought back memories of her step-father, Herb Weltig, trying to teach her to drive. They weren't particularly pleasant thoughts, since she was a less than stellar pupil. The best that can be said for Joél's driving is that her mastery of the motor skills was wanting.

If anyone had asked Joél's youngest sister, Myrtle, about

the wisdom of putting Joél in the driver's seat that day, she would surely have advised against the arrangement. As Myrtle remembers it, her sister's driving was the stuff of family legend. "She didn't always obey the rules of the road," said Myrtle. "Her mind would tend to wander. As a result, I don't ever remember being in the car with her when she was behind the wheel. It just wasn't a good idea."

Brother Vic concurs. "Dad taught all of us to drive." His sister Joél was, said Vic, "the toughest to teach." He should know, since he was in the backseat on many of those occasions. "She ran the car off the road a couple of times. She got distracted looking at the pretty fields, or the corn growing, or the trees and the woods." He attributed this to Joél's "artsy" personality. "She would say, 'This is so pretty. I should paint it.' My Dad was always sitting close to her when she drove so he could jerk the wheel if he had to." Unfortunately, neither Myrtle nor Vic were anywhere near Fort Dodge that day in 1966 to warn the others.

Decades later, Sister Toni Cusimano recalled the outing with great glee. "Joél was our designated driver," she said, "even though she didn't know how to drive stick. I did, but I didn't have a license." They worked out a plan whereby Toni would sit in the passenger seat and help Joél by telling her when to shift gears.

After a few fits and starts Joél seemed to get the hang of it and the women were finally out in the country breezing along with the windows rolled all the way down and enjoying a scenic drive. As anyone who has driven stick knows, once you get started it's a snap—until you have to stop, that is. About an hour into the drive the sisters had still not arrived at a desirable picnic spot and one cornfield began to look uncomfortably like another. "I think we'd better stop for directions," came a sensible suggestion from the back seat. "I see a farmhouse just up ahead."

The three passengers took the opportunity to stretch their legs while Joël headed to the door to knock. Unfortunately, no one answered, so back the quartet went to the car. Joël started the car, pushed in the clutch then shifted into first gear, but she goosed the gas pedal a bit too much. The car shot off towards a ditch at the side of the road. She stomped down on the brake just in time so that the car came to a stop perched over, but not yet in, the ditch. After a few Hail Mary's all around, Alvina got out to assess the damage and reported that the two rear wheels were still on the road, though mired in mud.

More than a little exasperated, Alvina and Flora climbed into the trench to push the car, while Joël worked the brake and clutch and Toni worked the accelerator. They finally managed to get all the tires once again on the road, but the picnic was forgotten. The morning's sunny optimism was damped down by the roadside muck clinging to Alvina's and Flora's skirts. The return trip home was made in near silence, except for the occasional command coming from the passenger side as Toni called out shifting instructions to a chastened Joël.

There would be more close calls for Sister Joël as a driver.

One infraction, passing a stopped school bus, even resulted in a six-month's suspension of her license. Somehow she was able to creatively finagle her way out of driving duties for those six months: always finding a good excuse not to drive and never letting on to her fellow sisters the real reason.

Many years later, when they were both stationed in Liberia, Toni would become an accomplished driver of many vehicles, confidently picking her way over rutted roads on her way to visit villages deep in the bush. Joél, on the other hand, would become the mission's designated passenger.

LIBERIA BOUND

After celebrating her twenty-fifth jubilee as an ASC sister, in July of 1982, Joél made a decision. She was ready for a new challenge and decided that she wanted to serve in Liberia. Her cousin, Shirley Kolmer, was now provincial in Ruma, so getting permission was a snap. Indeed, Shirley had encouraged Joél to go Liberia, having felt the value of her own experience there. Joél was so excited to take up this new phase of her life that her brother Vic said "she glowed like a new bride" when she was leaving. She arrived in the African country on Sept. 1, 1982.

At the time, Army Master Sergeant Samuel K. Doe was running Liberia, having overthrown the elected government two years earlier. But politics were of little concern to Joél (or really to any of the other missionary sisters living there at the time). What interested and excited the newly-minted missionary most were the people she met; especially the women.

In October, from the mission in Grand Cess, Joél writes about participating in a retreat for 10 Kru women. She found the ladies to be "fantastic pray-ers and beautiful at discussion. They inspire me to no end!" Clearly, Joél was experiencing the first flush of love for her new calling. She also filled-in at the mission school, teaching ninth-and-tenth-grade religion. She called the students "eager to learn," saying they really liked school. "It's a joy to teach them." In addition to teaching religion, Joél instructed all the students in music. "Do these kids love to sing!" she exclaimed.

While in Grand Cess, Joél lived with fellow ASC missionaries Sisters Rachel Lawler, Martha Wachtel, and Julia Lengerman. She was assigned teaching duties at Saint Patrick's School, participated in parish ministry, helped with the sacramental program, and visited the poor and shut-ins.

By 1985, Joél's cousin Shirley Kohler was back in Liberia, having completed her five-year term as Provincial in Ruma. Shirley was named coordinator of the three ASC missions, and it was in that capacity that she had Joél transferred to the Gardnersville mission, which Shirley believed would be "a better fit" for Joél. The transfer brought the cousins together once again. Joél was initially attached to the local parish, Saint Anthony's, where she helped with sacramental preparation for elementary students. She also taught religion part-time at Saint Michael's High School in nearby New Georgia.

By the following year, Joél was asked to establish and run a program for young Liberian girls wishing to explore becoming sisters. This program, called the "Aspirancy," would occupy the lion's share of Joél's spiritual and work life until her untimely death. It would bring her joy, as well as headaches. The girls, three total the first year and up to five later, lived in a wing of the convent that was separate from the one occupied by the sisters; though Joél, as their director, lived alongside them.

The Aspirancy program began on a high note for Joél, who relished the opportunity to help the girls develop spiritually. But she started to show ambivalence about her new assignment fairly early. A March 1986 letter reads: "Well, I'm breathing a sigh of relief with the girls (aspirants) going home today. I feel so foot loose and fancy free, but yet, in another way, kind of lost."

As some girls exited the program, new ones entered. Sometimes a girl was sent home because she did not seem mature enough, and in one case, when one of the girls was discovered to be pregnant, she too was sent back to her family. Yet Sister Joél tried to remain upbeat and put the best face possible forward: "My girls are back and things seem to be good." Then she adds as if surprised: "I'm enjoying them!" But she immediately adds the caution: "I'm sure we'll have some hard days yet."

1988 is a busy year for Joél because Shirley has taken ill

with hepatitis. For weeks, Joél helps nurse her cousin until she is well enough to travel to the United States, where she will recuperate. Shirley will be away from Liberia for about two months, her recovery complicated by a case of malaria that she apparently contracted just prior to leaving the country. It is clear that Joél misses her cousin dearly. In a May letter to her other cousin Elizabeth, she remarks that Elizabeth must be "pretty happy" to have Shirley home. Then she goes on to complain about the hot weather, about the inconsistency of their electric service. She pronounces herself "vexed." The remarks are atypical of Joél, but what comes next seems to get to the crux of the problem: "I'm hanging in there with the girls. I really find it difficult a lot of the times with them and I miss Shirley in that she was a good sounding board for me!"

When her two oldest aspirants "don't show as much promise as I think they could be showing by now," Joél reaches out to her cousin Shirley for advice and counsel. Her girls often worry her and wear her down. They are not as serious about their vocations as Joél had hoped they would be. The question is how does such a deeply pious person like Joél, who can feel God working within her as strongly as she can feel her own heartbeat, transfer that sensation to a group of only partially serious teenagers, especially those from another culture? It is a challenge, and we can almost hear Joél questioning her abilities again, as she once did at the Children's Home in Alton so many years earlier. But, as is her nature, Joél never gives in and never gives up.

A PAPER LIFELINE

In Sister Joél's earliest letters home, enthusiasm pours from the page, not just for the people she is meeting but for her surroundings as well. She remarks on the beautiful hibiscus bushes that line the walkway outside the convent in Grand Cess, saying how people "in good ole U.S.A would delight in having just a few of these bushes." She marvels at the moon, calling it "gorgeous" and exults when for the first time in her life she is able to make out the outline of the man in the moon. "Finally, I *did* see him!"

She remarks on the soothing sounds of the waves breaking onto shore from the mighty Atlantic Ocean. When a canoe man serenades her on a late-night ride across the river with "By the Light of the Silvery Moon" she is enthralled. Everything is new and of interest to her. "Greetings from the green, green country of Liberia...! Aren't we blessed with God's touch of freshness?" she writes enthusiastically.

What strikes me in reading these letters is how neat and readable her handwriting is; so beautifully flowing, unlike the hurried scrawl of her cousin Shirley. It is clear that Joél is an artist and is taking time with her words and their presentation on paper. Sometimes, in a fit of whimsy, she will add a sticker or a gold star to her letters. One can imagine her sitting at the oil-cloth-covered kitchen table rummaging through a box full of art supplies, carefully considering what kind of finishing touch to affix to one of her letters. As time went on, this ritual of writing letters became more and more important to Joél, and the letters from home became a life-line tethering her to loved ones she left behind. Especially when a bone-deep loneliness began to take hold of her.

As the years passed, Joél's tender nature began to feel the strain of being isolated from home. Letters from those she loved were essential to her well-being. When they were delayed, as they often were, she suffered great anxiety bordering on depression.

Sister Joyce Rupp, OSM, gave a retreat for the ASC missionaries in January of 1990 and spent considerable time with all of them. She saw firsthand the difficulty Joél was having: "I had some really good talks with Joél. She told me how lonely she was." While Joél didn't find the lifestyle in Liberia very difficult, the loneliness was sometimes depressing for her. "She missed family and friends and just longed to have letters from home, though sometimes letters took a long time" getting there Sister Joyce remembers. The sisters didn't have a phone so they only called home when necessary. Letters were Joél's sustenance, feeding her depleted spirit, but they didn't always arrive regularly. "Sometimes they got Christmas letters at Easter" and Joél "found that really, really hard," Joyce says.

Shirley understood this about her cousin, and would take pains to take care of her. In a letter home to Elizabeth, Shirley expresses concern about Joél, saying she is having a hard time with a particular situation and that "if I am not here she really has no one to talk to. She takes it all too seriously."

Joél could also be self-critical; holding herself to high standards. In a letter home in March of 1992 she writes: "I've got a lot to learn in patience...yet I can't tell you how hard it is to have patience...every time I think the things will go right, something comes up, whether it's the group who aren't there on time, or someone flubbs (sic) up, then I have to re-organize or re-adjust to something else again."

As Joél predicted, "something" again came up a few months after this self-assessment, which sorely tried her patience. A men's group at the parish was allowed to use the school for a meeting; in the aftermath, beer bottles and other debris were left in the school courtyard. Joél, who was then managing Saint Michael's School, was "incensed" and reported the group to the bishop. Her cousin Elizabeth assessed Joél's reaction this way: "When she was mad, she was mad. She knew how to fuss." The result of all the "fussing" was that the men's group was mildly disciplined. Joél's reaction to the punishment was a bit smug, yet refreshingly human: "I just smiled when I heard what the Bishop did in discontinuing them for a time."

SISTER AGNES MUELLER

Agnes was, in the terminology of her time, a bookworm. She loved learning, and learning for her was often found in books. Bookworms by nature are elusive. They defy easy categorization because they live interiorly, where it is harder for outsiders to grasp what they are all about. They can be brilliant yet often choose to keep it to themselves. As such, they are often overshadowed by those with whom they share an orbit.

Agnes was brilliant. But her star was situated so closely to the dual suns of Shirley and Barbara Ann that at times she seemed to be obscured. Yet from these suns she also drew strength with which to fortify and rejuvenate herself. The quintessential Greek chorus, she often served in a supporting role while others stepped into the limelight. It would be a role I might find comfort in myself; one less scrutinized yet none-the-less essential to the success of the whole.

Even in a death both valiant and tragic, Agnes has been overshadowed. A stamp, issued by the Liberian government claims to feature the five martyrs. Yet it is in error. The person *purported to be Sister Agnes Mueller is in fact Sister Elizabeth Kolmer, who in truth does bear a resemblance to the gray-haired, bespectacled Agnes.*

Perhaps the only way to see Agnes clearly is to turn our faces away, just a bit, from the tragedy of Liberia and begin our search elsewhere.

MEMORIES

Sister Mary Ann Mueller, ASC, sits in her kitchen leafing through a scrapbook that contains photos and mementos from the life of her long-dead younger sister, Agnes. There is a kind of serenity in sharing these images with another person, but also poignancy in remembering a loss still deeply felt.

Though close by nature of birth and by choice of vocation, Mary Ann and Agnes were in many ways opposites. Mary Ann, the older by two years, had entered the convent after her freshman year in high school, while Agnes, the more high-spirited and fun-loving of the two, waited until after her high school graduation to join the Adorers of the Blood of Christ in Ruma. Agnes was dark-haired and a middling 5 feet 4 inches, while Mary Ann was tall and fair. Agnes grabbed on to the precepts of feminism early on, while her sister embraced them more cautiously, though eventually just as fervently. Perhaps most telling—where Mary Ann was wary, Agnes craved adventure.

In Mary Ann's scrapbook, a teenage Agnes poses in a formal sepia-toned studio portrait. Perhaps it is her high school graduation photo? She looks, not at the camera, but to the left as if something interesting has caught her eye. She has an abundance of permed hair that blossoms out a full several inches from her face, until finally giving in to gravity. It flounces downward, just grazing her shoulders. Her coif is topped by a white flower pinned to one side. This is the hair of a girl who appreciates her looks. Her lips, colored in a deep shade, show just the slightest hint of a smile. She has a secret, the smile seems to say. Her dress is a modest satin affair, made all the more so by the strategic placement of a brooch that gathers the neckline higher than intended by the dressmaker. From all appearances, this is not a girl thinking of entering the convent in just a few short weeks. In fact, when Agnes finally did decide to join it caught Mary Ann completely by surprise.

AUTUMN 1947

Seventeen-year-old Agnes was finding it hard to concentrate as she sat at her desk trying to read while she waited to be called downstairs for her family visit. It was the third Sunday of the month; the one day a month allotted for mothers, fathers, and siblings to come to Ruma and see their daughters. It was always such a trial for Agnes to see her parents and then have them leave her. Of course, it was what she wanted, but it still hurt; when would she get over this homesickness?

The call finally came over the intercom, "Agnes Mueller, your family is here." Agnes ran her palms along the front of the modest black dress, then straightened the small black veil pinned to the back of her head and stepped out her door and ran down a set of stairs that led to the main floor and three large rooms set at the front of the red brick building. Here she would find her family among the many clusters of people who had come this visitation Sunday. She was determined not to let them see her cry, so she put on a smile and stepped over to the side of the room where the Muellers were gathered. She was happy to see that her older sister, Mary Ann, who was also preparing for sisterhood, was already seated with their parents and deep in conversation. For the next two hours, the girls shared small details of their lives and politely inquired about things at home. While Mary Ann at 20 was already beginning her seventh year in Ruma, Agnes was just a few months into her studies and still adjusting.

Agnes had spent her high school years like a typical 1940s teenager—there were her studies, a part-time job at the local bowling alley, and friends, lots of friends, who filled up her days with fun. But that was only part of the story, because Agnes was also a very introspective young woman who thought long and hard about her future. From her grammar school days at Saint Cecilia and her first encounters with the Precious Blood sisters, there had been an attraction to the kind of life the nuns led. And over the years the young Agnes had come to know well the sisters who lived just across the street from the Muellers in a house with a welcoming front porch that beckoned visitors to stop by and chat informally on quiet summer evenings. Best of all, Agnes loved hearing about the Precious Blood missionary sisters serving in China and decided that she, too, would do that one day.

In Ruma, years later, when the family small talk was finally exhausted, the Mueller clan would get up in unison and walked towards the doors and down the long concrete front steps. Outside they moved along the ground-stone pathway that led to the grotto and pond area just beyond the small garden of tomato and bean plants. Released from the indoor confines, the two youngest Mueller girls, Rose and Leona, skipped ahead a little, taking in the warm afternoon sun. The family stroll indicated that their visit was coming to a close and it would soon be time to go. When it was time, Agnes and Mary Ann walked their family back toward the large parking lot that fronted the main building. After hugs and promises to write often, their parents and siblings were off and the two young women stood momentarily watching the car drive down the winding path that would lead them off the grounds and onto the Great River Road on the first leg of the two-hour journey home to Bartelso, Illinois.

It was then that the tears often came long and hard

for Agnes. Mary Ann had seen this pattern now for several months and finally she sought to correct the situation. With a hint of exasperation that only a big sister can get away with she said: "Agnes, you are so miserable. Every time Mom and Dad leave you are homesick. I don't think you can go on like this. If you are not happy, go home."

"No. I'm not going home!" was her sister's defiant reply. Agnes was determined to become a nun. At that moment, she resolved not to let homesickness overwhelm her any longer, and she tried never to cry again at partings.

Agnes was indeed bookish and loved to read and study and challenge herself by learning something new. Hers was a most inquisitive mind. It was this love for learning that propelled her to help other women with their own educational pursuits, a desire that would come to full fruit with the women of Liberia, where she would conduct leadership and literacy classes.

Agnes was a fun-loving, people-oriented person who liked to play jokes and make bad puns. Yet she also had a deeply meditative side. "She was much more contemplative than me," said Mary Ann. "She loved to go on retreats and would often choose a hermitage for the solitude it offered. She had a full spiritual life. But she also loved to be among people and to do fun things and to travel."

Early on, Agnes developed a feminist viewpoint, one that

said it was easier for women to understand Jesus than it was for men. Needless to say, it was a stance not shared by most Church officials. She felt that women in the Church were not respected as much as the men were and was in the vanguard of pushing for women's equality. "It was in my future," said Sister Mary Ann, "but Agnes was already there." While other women religious were just waking up to the idea that their roles in the Church could expand, Agnes had already grabbed hold with both hands. "She was a pioneer," said Mary Ann.

During the years that Agnes worked in parishes in the United States, it was important to her that it was with a pastor who valued her as an equal. If she felt resistance from the priest, she would move on. Women's equality was a core value for her, and when she ran into others who did not share that value or appreciate the role of women in the Church, she could become frustrated, "to say the least," as Mary Ann put it.

While Agnes cherished the challenge of going into a new situation and meeting new people, once she had imparted what she had come to teach she would hand over the reins to others and move on, rarely staying more than a couple of years at one posting. It would only be later in life, when she was missioned to Liberia that some of her natural restlessness finally seemed to settle. Proof of this came when she volunteered to return to Africa for a second assignment in 1991 after having served almost three years there already. Finally, something snared her adventurous spirit; the "something" was embodied in the women she met in Liberia.

FAMILY LIFE

Agnes Mary Mueller was the fifth child of nine, and the second girl. The names read like a litany of the saints: Paul, Joseph, and Marcel, were the oldest, followed by Mary Ann and Agnes, and finally John, Rose, Leona, and Leonard. Born on November 18, 1929, in the 300-person farm town of Bartelso, Agnes would be the quintessential middle child: empathetic, independent, and devoted to principles like fairness and justice.

While her older sister, Mary Ann, was designated to be their mother Mary's main helper in the home and with the younger siblings, Agnes more often was asked to aid their father Joseph. When she was old enough, Agnes went to work with him at his job as postmaster in the small town. The trip to the post office was a short one, just two blocks from the family home. In typical small-town fashion, Joseph would walk home for lunch every day. When school was off for the summer Agnes would run to the post office early in the morning and help her father stamp and sort the mail that had arrived by train from far off places. They placed the letters in assigned post boxes, where the town folk could then pick up their mail during the day. As she got older, Agnes would also assist Joseph with the detailed record-keeping required of a government office.

She had a circle of friends and a spirit ready for fun. She loved going to ball games on Sunday afternoons. But when daughter number three, Leona, got old enough Agnes was often called upon to look after her. "I was called the tag-a-long," remembers Leona Beckman. "When Agnes went out with her friends in the evening, Mom would say to take me along." Five years younger, Leona remembers hanging out at the bowling alley with Agnes and her friends. Though her big sister never showed real annoyance with her babysitting task, Leona concedes "She probably was not too happy to have me tag along."

The bowling alley was not all fun and games for Agnes, who began setting pins there to earn a little extra cash. In those days, bowling pins were set by hand and the pin setter had to be quick on her feet. After the bowler rolled the first ball, the setter would place the ball on the return rail. Before the ball got back to the bowler, the setter had to pick up and place the pins in the rack. Too slow and the setter risked getting hit by a ball whizzing down the lane. The really good setters could pick up five bowling pins in each hand. Just how good a pin-setter Agnes was…is not recorded in the family history!

In the evenings at home, the Mueller children would often listen to the radio for entertainment. Mother would sit and listen as she worked on another hand-made quilt. Everybody in the family had a hand-made quilt. Agnes would most likely be curled up in hers with a book. An avid reader, she had eclectic tastes, though she "loved mysteries" as her sister Leona remembers.

As the postmaster in Bartelso, Joseph had a good job. So much so that the children hardly realized that they were growing up in the midst of the Great Depression. Unemployment in the U.S. had reached staggering proportions by 1933, when Agnes was only four, with nearly 20 percent of the population out of work. Bank failures, bread lines, soup kitchens, and homelessness were endemic. But for the Mueller children life was much more secure. A large yard to play in, a puppy to cuddle, and home-grown vegetables to eat were hallmarks of their childhood.

Another important element of childhood, especially for the girls, would be an attachment to the nuns who taught them in Saint Cecilia's Grammar School. Agnes would often find her way to their porch across the street for conversation, especially in the warm summer months. The women were all from the Ruma province of the Adorers. Both Agnes and Mary Ann were captivated by the sisters, with Agnes especially drawn to their stories about women religious who served as missionaries overseas, particularly those who were then serving in China. It lit a desire in the young girl's heart. Dreams, however, are often deferred and changed. It would not be until she was 59 years old that Agnes finally realized her dream of becoming an overseas missionary—though it was Africa, not Asia, where she ultimately served.

OBEDIENCE ABOVE ALL

In 1949, when she was a junior sister (called a "postulant"), the 19-year-old Agnes was given her first assignment. She would teach at Saint Elizabeth's School in East St. Louis. As a first-year teacher, Agnes gave it her all. She had fun and by all accounts was looking forward to continuing there. But fate had other plans for her. Or at least her superiors did. In those days, there was a propriety that was followed by the sisters, especially when in public: Always do things in twos. That meant home visits, shopping, and even attending school with a partner. So, when one of Sister Agnes' friends, Mary Maurice Loepker, was told that she would be sent to nursing school and needed a companion, Agnes was chosen to be that companion. One of the hard things for most people in life is to follow orders—especially those orders they would rather not follow. Most military people know the value of obedience, and so do most religious sisters. Agnes was one of them.

So she did not question her duty to accompany Mary Maurice to nursing school, even though it seemed obvious to everyone that she would have preferred to continue on in education or religious studies. Very soon, however, Agnes took up the challenge of learning something new and she excelled. It was just like her. As a life-long learner, she warmed to the task without complaint and earned her bachelor's degree in nursing in 1954 from St. Louis University.

She then worked in the healthcare field for 14 years,

attaining the directorship of nursing at Saint Vincent Memorial Hospital in Taylorville, Illinois. But she was always the educator at heart and relished teaching the LPN classes. When she became director of nursing, she made changes that benefitted her female staff. As a champion for women—albeit in what now seems commonplace—Agnes instituted a policy of giving her nurses every other weekend off so that they could spend time with their families. From this point on, women's causes, especially as they related to matters of the Church and female empowerment became central issues in Agnes' life.

After Vatican II in the late sixties, there was a more open attitude in allowing religious sisters to pursue careers that interested them. For Agnes, it would be religious studies. She would leave nursing and go on to become the first woman to earn a master's degree in theology from Aquinas Institute, then in Dubuque, Iowa, in 1971. Even that would be topped when she earned a second master's degree in theology from the Graduate Theological Union in Berkeley, California, in 1981. Over those years, Agnes worked in several parishes, but never more than a couple of years in one place. Though she liked pastoral work, it seemed she couldn't completely settle down anywhere. Some kind of restlessness was pushing her onward. In the various places she worked, Agnes is remembered as a dreamer, a true feminist, and a spiritual person. She is also remembered as a "sweet woman," as several put it, who prized family life above almost anything else and encouraged parents to make their children their top priority.

Agnes' vision of God was expansive. She talked of God as being any color, any gender. She did not tie her God to maleness, as traditional Catholics at the time did. She was a true feminist who sought a more equal footing for women in the male-dominated hierarchy of Catholicism. It is said that nothing bothers a well-educated female theologian more than being told to take a back seat solely because of her gender, and that was certainly true of Sister Agnes.

Agnes felt strongly that she had been called to do something to overcome injustice, particularly as it manifested itself in the lives of women. Poor education, poverty, unequal opportunities were wrongs—especially against women—that she sought to correct. She was presented with a grand opportunity to address these inequities in 1988 when she was invited to join the Adorers serving in the missions in Liberia. Finally, she would realize her childhood dream of becoming a missionary.

A LIFE IN PICTURES

It is probably early in the 1950s. Two women, Agnes and Mary Ann, garbed in the full regalia of the ASC sisters sit shoulder to shoulder and look into the camera. They wear black woolen capes with cloth-covered buttons that disappear under the gimp, a circular piece of white plastic that encircles their necks. A white cloth is wrapped under their chins and works its way around each wearer's face, framing her so tightly that not even a stray hair can be seen. The top of the sisters' heads appear flattened by the coronet, another bit of white plastic that goes around the forehead; a long black veil perched atop the coronet drapes down their backs. On hot days these "habits," as they are called, were exceedingly uncomfortable. While the cloth around the face would absorb some sweat, a good bit would just drip from the wearer. In the photo, the women's faces are magnified; taking on added importance since their faces are all I can see of them, covered as they are from the tops of their heads to the soles of their feet in yards of heavy black cloth. Though Sister Agnes looks content in the photo, I wonder what had become of the saucy young teen of just a few years earlier.

There are many treasurers like this in Sister Mary Ann Mueller's scrap book. Photos that are a virtual timeline of Sister Agnes' life. We see her young; and we see her old; and we see her in between. In a black-and-white family photo from the 1950s, we see four white-shirted young men wearing ties, standing to attention. Aligned in front of them are two figures covered from head to toe in swaths of black fabric. They are flanked by two younger girls. Completing the scene is an aging set of parents perched on outdoor chairs—their progeny to their backs. This is the Mueller family.

In a second photo, taken many years later, the four tall young men have begun to show signs of aging. Their hair is graying and, for some, thinning. The little girls are now full-bodied women. The parents are old. But the two black-clad figures look remarkably the same, as if caught in time. They are still swathed from head to toe, with just minor modifications to their habits. The photo is in color, so a red sash that falls from the women's waists is all the more striking against their black habits.

But with a turn of a page, there is a shocking transformation in Agnes, hinting at the startling transformation religious communities in the 1970s are undergoing. We can see the Agnes who was hidden for years. Here her hair is dark brown and bountiful, finally freed from its prison. Like a molting bird, she has seemingly shed her habit for sectarian dress. It is of course modest, colors subdued, but there is a big floppy bow on her flowered polyester blouse, and a heart, the symbol of the Adorers, hangs prominently from a silver chain around her neck. She shows off a quirky, half-turned smile, and her big blue eyes seem to shine behind round spectacles. There are more photos over the years that show Agnes experimenting with clothing—slacks and wildly printed tops. In one picture she appears to be at some kind of office party. Here she sports a comic pin—big red lips—affixed to her shirt.

And then there are the adventure photos. One is dated 1975 and shows Agnes clad in sweater and slacks with a paddle in her hand canoeing down the Elk River in Missouri. Another shows her treading through knee-deep snow, arms outstretched as she tries to stay upright. Here she is an astronaut standing in Chile's barren Valley of the Moon desert; there, in Bolivia, she poses near a child wearing a gaucho hat. Flash forward, a gray-haired Agnes tosses a coin over her shoulder into Rome's Trevi Fountain.

There is a final family photo, most likely taken during the summer of 1992 when Agnes made her final visit home. The four brothers, now considerably older, stand behind four seated women. Two have dark hair still, while Mary Ann's and Agnes' hair is completely gray. The parents are now gone. The most striking thing about the photo is that Agnes looks to be happiest among her siblings. Her smile is broad and content, even though she is destined to die soon.

Finally are the photos from Liberia. Agnes stands in the kitchen with Sisters Shirley and Joél. Shirley is centered between the two, smiling widely, proudly displaying her gap teeth. Joél is to her right, her smile just as broad, and it stands out all the more on a face that looks narrower than it should because she is so skinny. Agnes is holding some kind of paper. A letter from home? Or to home? Her hair, like Shirley's, has settled into a comfortable white shade, while Joél's still seems to be fighting to retain some of its old brown fervor. Agnes is smiling, too, but it is less brilliant than the Kolmer women's smiles. It is tentative, like she was just told by the photographer to "say cheese" and obediently complied. The photo was most likely taken in the time between 1991 and 1992 and would be one of the three missionaries' last. When viewed through this prism, one can project that Agnes might have been feeling some misgivings about their situation and been just a bit nervous. (Or perhaps she just didn't like having her picture taken.)

From about this same time, there is also a group photo of the five sisters gathered around their dinner table. The meal has apparently just finished. A bottle of some beverage, possibly gin, sits on the table, as does a tin of sugar cookies. The women beam at the camera. This time Agnes' smile seems genuine as she coquettishly rests her head on her hands folded under her chin. Sister Barbara Ann is obscured, only the top of her black hair visible behind a sideways-sitting Sister Kathleen. But there is a second photo that tells another part of what was going on that night. In this picture Joël is absent. She has switched places with a priest (obviously, the photographer of the first photo), who is clearly their dinner guest. But in this photo, the only one truly smiling is the priest. Shirley looks more resolute than happy. Barbara, clearly visible in this photo, looks uncomfortable, with her eyes turned just a bit off center. Kathleen looks caught off guard, as if Joël had snapped the picture before she was ready. Agnes clearly looks tired, worried even. Her eyes, still a brilliant blue, now have reddish circles under them. Less staged, this photo seems to capture the truth of the nuns' situation better than the first.

DOING GOD'S WORK FOR WOMEN

Sister Agnes arrived in Klay on April 21, 1988. She was 59 years old. Her hair, which she had colored up to now, would be allowed to go gray in short order. Vanity and creature comforts will have no place in her life anymore, that much is clear, when she sees her new home for the first time. It is a modest mud and stick affair with a leaky roof "really in need of repair," she says. Fellow Sister Adorers Barbara Ann Muttra and Antoinette Cusimano had called this their house for the last five years, but it was definitely showing its age. In a letter home Agnes reports on a large building project that is underway. One of the buildings is to be a new convent, along with a church, an education center, and an elementary school. Then she adds, "We are hoping to move soon. Will take a Liberian miracle, I guess." With those words of resignation, Agnes makes it clear that though she has been in Liberia but a few weeks, she is catching on to the rhythms of her new country, where "hurry" is just a verb, not a way life.

Sister Toni recalled that when Agnes first arrived in Klay she was "business-like" when it came to transitioning to their new home, though she was certainly not above providing the necessary elbow grease either. "She was on all fours scrubbing the floors and getting the house ready," Toni said.

In July, when Agnes has been in Klay three months, the sisters finally moved to their new home. It was not without its own problems, however. Agnes described it as "new and nice," but with leaking sinks, "shorts in the electrical sockets," and a well for water that was still uncompleted. "We still take bucket baths," she writes. "I'm looking forward to the day I can take a shower."

Agnes, however, quickly finds herself thriving in an environment where ecclesiastical oversight is more relaxed. Priests are spread thin in Liberia, so the women are often called upon to lead in prayer and religious gatherings. She talks of leading a service one Sunday that is attended by some Peace Corps volunteers. "After the service, they said I had a good homily," she reports proudly. Then she goes on to quote one young woman volunteer: "I loved it. I had to come to Liberia to see a woman officiating." Agnes glowed, "They all gave me a real boost."

In a November 1988 letter home, Agnes reflects on the strangeness of hearing familiar Christmas melodies sung in Gola, "a language I can't understand." She goes on to say that while Christmas will be a different experience, she wants to be open to this difference, "I hope I will learn some new ways to think about 'Emmanuel'—God among us."

Toni remembered that as the new arrival to the mission, Agnes was reticent to offer her views. If you wanted to know what Agnes was thinking or how she felt, "you really had to ask," Toni said. If someone had a problem, rather than stepping in to offer a solution, it had long been Agnes' practice to hang back and allow the person to work it out for herself. This is the attitude she brought with her to Klay, where she saw herself as the newcomer and Toni as the expert on the people and their customs. Agnes would learn from her. And even though Agnes had more experience with catechesis, she held back any critique or comment about Toni's way of doing things, "Though she thought," added Toni proudly, "I was doing a fine job."

Agnes' hesitance to offer direction or input would lead to occasional skirmishes later on when she and Sister Kathleen McGuire partnered on projects in Gardnersville. A mutual friend noted that Agnes would recognize a problem, but not offer a solution—and though she appreciated this about Agnes, it could be wearing on Kathleen, who believed in working through a process with others to find solutions. Kathleen's view was if you were going to point out a problem, you should offer a way to fix it, too.

Back in Klay, Agnes was finding herself plenty busy. She described the work she was doing with a group near to her heart—women. "I teach three literacy classes," she wrote. In addition, she taught Confirmation classes, instructed people wishing to become Catholic, and went to five villages a week for prayer service and Bible discussion. In the outlying villages, Agnes found that the people "are most welcoming." Though they had little themselves, she noted, people generously offer their guests "mangoes and whatever simple things they have." Their big-heartedness impressed Agnes, who had long eschewed the more material aspects of the West.

Sister Agnes also talked about the upcoming dedication

of the new church, which was almost finished. "It will be a big celebration. And, there will be rice and greens.... Many people will come for the food if nothing else. But they are so poor and have so little that no one will begrudge them a little food." Living among the poorest of the world's poor, Agnes determined to fulfill Jesus' directive: *Truly I tell you, whatever you did for one of the least of these brothers and sisters of mine, you did for me.*

In May 1989, Agnes is planning on moving to the less remote Gardnersville mission. She begins to wind down her various ministries in Klay. "There have been many good experiences in Klay and the villages," she reflects. "I'm sure I am not the same person who came a little over a year ago now. I feel my life is much richer for having spent time with these people." Despite differences in cultures and values, Agnes makes an acknowledgement, "They have given me every bit as much as I have shared with them."

In Gardnersville, Agnes blossomed in her leadership role even more. The pastor of Saint Anthony's, the local church, was new himself. Father Michael Moran, an American, had been serving in Africa for 10 years when he was assigned by the SMAs to the Gardnersville area. He lead Saint Anthony's for the next two years. In his previous mission in Tanzania, Father Mike had experienced what he called "basic Christian community groups." But in Liberia, this kind of community-centered church was not common. In the Precious Blood sisters, however, he found a team of willing allies, not least of whom was Agnes Mueller.

The principle of the basic Christian community is to break a parish into smaller groups of about 15 to 20 people. The groups meet weekly to reflect on scripture and then design an action for the week that would reflect the scripture reading. Best of all for Agnes, whenever members voted on their leaders, fully half of the ones chosen were women. Agnes was active with the groups, and later so was Sister Kathleen McGuire, another avowed supporter of women's empowerment. They would make a dynamic duo.

In 1990, Agnes wrote a short analysis of her time as a missionary. It was quite frank. She called it "the most difficult time in my life." Yet she also labeled it the most "growthful" (sic) period of her life as well. She talked of "learnings in pain, vulnerability, and suffering" and readily admitted that in other cultures and places she would never have allowed herself these experiences. She was seeing that her theology and approach to life were changing. And she was being challenged in another way too. "This is probably the first time in my life when I have not been in control of almost every area of my life." And though she wrote that this had helped her see her own "great inner strength," there would be times when she would be frustrated and downhearted when things did not go as she planned. Indeed, this would be a problem that would continue to fester until the end.

In a 1991 letter home, Kathleen McGuire addressed Agnes' moods obliquely. After agreeing to help Sister Joël Kolmer, who was "overwhelmed" by the administration of

Saint Michael's school, Agnes seems to regret it. In Kathleen's words, Agnes is "in a real twist with it." She does not go into detail, but apparently there must have been an emotional release of some kind. "I have to remember," wrote Kathleen, "that her periods of devastation are usually quite fleeting.... Agnes could well come home for lunch in high spirits today."

Agnes' frustration would continue to grow when a new priest, Father James Hickey, SMA, was assigned to replace Father Michael Moran as Saint Anthony's pastor. Her first mention of him is probably her most charitable. "Hickey is our new pastor now. First time I've met him. He is quite old and seems overwhelmed by all the activity in the parish." Eight months later she has had quite enough of him. "Our pastor is very conservative and tries to make our parish a white Irish or American parish. I used to do a lot of pastoral work and religious education and RCIA, but not anymore. So, I pray God will move him as the opportune moment presents itself." Once again Agnes found herself struggling for respect against the male-dominated Church hierarchy.

In truth, Agnes was not alone in this assessment. All of the Precious Blood sisters were chafing under what they viewed as Father Hickey's autocratic rule. Joël, who was administering Saint Michael's school, would boil over just shortly before her death when she learned that the priest had summarily closed the school in order to house refugees without even consulting her.

For Sister Agnes Mueller, the waning days of October

1992 would be fraught with worry. She, more than any of the others, seemed to be most aware of the growing danger around them. At the end, caught up in chaos, she became uncharacteristically quiet. She was truly afraid. Yet, and this is the amazing thing, she chose to stand with her sisters and remain in Liberia. Was she fortified by those around here? Most assuredly. She relied on their courage to help support her. She reminded herself that they were all following in Jesus' footsteps together.

In the end, though, Agnes had a choice. She could have called her Provincial weeks earlier and been assured of a warm welcome home to Ruma; no questions asked. But she didn't. For one final time, Agnes called upon her great inner strength. It would be enough to see her through to the end.

After Agnes' death, a friend of hers, Midge Biegler, commented, "I wish I could know her again." Her remark was made with a kind of wistful longing we associate with lost opportunities. "Sometimes," she said wisely, "people enter our lives and then leave again, and if you are not attentive or if you are preoccupied, you can miss something important."

Indeed, many people wish they could know Agnes again, if only to experience one more stimulating conversation, one more smile, one more photo for her sister Mary Ann's album. I am one of them.

CIVIL WAR, RETURN TO RUMA, AND BACK TO LIBERIA

In the Liberian civil war, there is no middle ground. Chance lets you survive, or soldiers kill you. Very few are wounded. There are no prisoners of war. The killings are random. You can be shot because of the color of your skin, because of your inability to speak a tribal dialect, or because your killer wants to use up a round of bullets.

THE SHADOW OF DEATH
BY HÉLÈNE COOPER

A KILLING FEVER

Nimba County, located in the north central region of Liberia, is a place replete with mountains and iron-ore mines. When viewed on a map, the county's long and oddly shaped configuration puts one in mind of a conch shell erupting from the main landmass, elbowing its way north between Guinea and Ivory Coast.

It was through Nimba County on Christmas Eve in 1989 that former Doe-loyalist-turned-rebel Charles Taylor and his fighters entered the Liberian border town of Butuo from Ivory Coast in the opening salvo of war. Taylor's fighters were a fairly small group at that time, numbering as few as 100 to 200, but they were eager and had been trained to fight in Libya, a smoldering cauldron where insurgents of all nationalities were being educated in the techniques of guerrilla warfare. The fighting between the rebels and government soldiers decimated Butuo and sent some residents fleeing over the border into Ivory Coast. In short order, Taylor's National Patriotic Front of Liberia (NPFL) army earned the support of the local population in Nimba County, particularly the Mano and Gio people, who were eager to throw off the cruel, heavy hand of President Samuel K. Doe. Doe, an ethnic Krahn, had supplanted the 150-year yoke of Amerio-Liberian rule with his own Krahn-heavy domination.

In fact, 10 years on, Doe's strong-man government had become unsustainable except through intimidation, brute force, and murderous repression of those who opposed his authority. For many Liberians, their president was little more than a despot who raided Liberia's natural resources for personal gain and installed people from his own ethnic background to positions of power at the expense of the 15 other indigenous cultures. Because of this repression, it was no surprise that people throughout Liberia, especially in the countryside, were quick to back Taylor's cause. It would not be long, however, before Taylor and his rebels began employing tactics every bit as despicable as Doe's. Some of the worst human rights atrocities during any war would be committed in Liberia in the cause of the status quo on one side and the promise of liberty on the other.

Doe quickly dispatched his African Forces of Liberia (AFL) troops to fight the NPFL incursion, and within months large scale massacres were being reported with alarming frequency. In February and March 1990 alone, there were three cases of mass murder reported in Nimba County. It was during this time that Doe's troops charged irretrievably into the abyss of depravity with the burning of 52 houses and the killing of 71 residents in the village of Yarsonnoh. With this action, it became evident that Doe was targeting specific ethnic groups, especially Mano and Gio people. Even civilians with no particular political allegiance became targets just by nature of their ethnic affiliation.

Later, members of Doe's own armed forces would become fair game for the president when he sought to purge his ranks of the two offending tribes. In June of 1990, 27 Gio and Mano members of the AFL, plus their families, were taken from the barracks where they lived in Monrovia and killed on the president's order; their bodies reportedly buried on the beach behind the barracks. Doe's troops may have been the first to engage in large scale murder, but they would not be the sole perpetrators; soon Taylor and his NPFL rebels were stirring up reciprocal hatred and targeting people not only from Doe's Krahn background but from other ethnic groups as well.

On July 12, 1990, proving that no area of the country was too isolated to suffer the scourge of war, Taylor's NPFL rebels carried out a particularly despicable crime when they murdered over 500 ethnic Mandingos, including an Iman, in Lofa County. Lofa, about 200 miles northwest of Nimba County, is the furthest northern district and one of the most remote areas in Liberia. It is believed that many of the rebels who carried out the murders in Lofa were child soldiers whose leaders intentionally stirred up the young, undisciplined soldiers' animosity towards other ethnic groups using ancient tribal rivalries, drugs, and fear to stoke the hatred. Mass murder frenzy was spreading, and by the end of July the Lofa massacre would trigger a response in Monrovia. This time, six hundred innocents would lose their lives at Saint Peter's Evangelical Lutheran Church, thereby setting the stage for an ever-growing, seemingly endless string of reprisals and atrocities.

It is clear that the warring factions purposely split the Liberian nation along ethnic lines to further their own political agendas without as much as a thought for the suffering they caused. A frenzied madness was descending upon Liberia. Those with guns lived as if in a fever-dream fueled by mystic beliefs and drugs. Spurred on by commanding officers who encouraged this depravity, teenage fighters carrying AK-47s dressed in women's wigs, prom dresses, and wedding gowns—voodoo bombast meant to mimic the rights of passage practiced by secret forest societies. Strutting young killers carried their infection to virtually every town and village, acting with impunity. When the fever finally broke 14 years later, a quarter of a million people had lost their lives.

For the first months of 1990, the five ASC sisters who were in Liberia at the time: Sisters Shirley Kolmer, Joél Kolmer, Antoinette "Toni" Cusimano, Martha Wachtel, and Rachel Lawler were not directly affected by the distant fighting to the north. But later, as refugees began making their way south, the sisters found their ministry increasingly transformed into one of feeding and sheltering the homeless and comforting the sick and wounded. Entries from the nuns' journals at the three mission sites they then occupied in different parts of the country indicate a growing concern for the safety of the ordinary people of Liberia. In reading the entries, it becomes clear that the precariousness of their own situation was also beginning to hit home, especially by July of

1990 when Taylor's troops (dubbed Freedom Fighters) began their quest to take Monrovia.

Veteran missionaries Sisters Agnes Mueller and Barbara Ann Muttra were not in Liberia at the time. Both were home in the U.S. for medical reasons: Agnes for cataract surgery and Barbara for treatment of ovarian cancer. They would watch developments from afar with great concern.

By this time, life in Gardnersville had taken a distinct turn for the worse. Utility companies were destroyed or damaged. Water had to be hand-carried from a distant well and electricity was mostly cut off, though when it did make an occasional fitful appearance in the evening it "really makes a difference in our outlook," according to the sisters, by dispelling some of the fear that surely accompanied sitting in dim candlelight and listening to the sounds of war closing in.

The journal kept in Gardnersville by Sister Joël describes increasing violence in the area throughout June. At first, she records more about lawless activity as rogues begin to take advantage of the unstable conditions in the area around Gardnersville. While everyone is on edge wondering when the rebels will make their advance, the thieves begin to target homes and businesses. On June 9 rogues "chucked" the convent's kitchen windows with rocks. Two days later, the sisters asked Charles Konneh, a teacher at Saint Michael's school, to stay in the recently evacuated Aspirancy wing of the house, since the girls had all been sent home to their families. When rogues once again struck, this time in the garage in an effort to siphon gas from the sisters' cars, the convent immediately hired a night watchman.

But by the next month, when the sound of rebel artillery and guns got "very close and very loud" the sisters put the safety of their watchman, James Vaawa, ahead of their own by telling him "to stay home for the weekend and not come anymore until all of this crisis is over." The sisters had tried to get James to stay away before, fearing he would be caught out during the 6 p.m. to 6 a.m. curfew and punished. To his credit, James had not listened to the nuns before, but this time he did. "Thank God!" wrote Joél. This would not be the last time that the sisters would put the welfare of the person who was supposed to be protecting them ahead of their own. The next time, however, the results would be tragic.

A July 12 entry talks of "plenty of real bad shooting and looting" that took place overnight. "The soldiers broke into the Lebanese store up the road from us. This is Abraham's store." The entry is poignant in that Abraham Nassar will be killed along with three of the sisters just two years later.

By July 20, Joél and Shirley have invited another young Liberian, Andrew Tuley, an 18-year-old seminarian, to join Konneh in the Aspirancy wing of their home. Now there are five, the two men living on one end and Shirley, Joél, and Ramona Chebli, an ASC Affiliate, living on the other end of the convent. The men offer some protection for the women, not just by their presence but by accompanying them when they venture out of the house to attend Mass or go to the nearest market. By now, someone—including one of the men—always stays at the house in an effort to limit rogue activity.

As their world continues to devolve from a society capable of governing itself into one increasingly ruled by thugs, there are more and more mentions by the sisters of armed men looting and killing and artillery fire creeping closer to Gardnersville. Accompanying these reports, there are also a number of editorial comments on food. It seems a curious juxtaposition until you realize the increasing importance that just having enough to eat has taken on. People are growing hungry. Many farmers are unwilling to chance tending their rice crops due to the fighting. Prices for scarce commodities are getting higher. Cooking itself, without proper accommodations, is getting more difficult. So, when the convent actually has success in obtaining supplies, it is celebrated in the face of all the difficulties. Here are some of the sisters' entries:

> *July 10: Another day of trial.* (There is not elaboration as to these difficulties, instead the tone becomes light.) *Joél baked bread today and Shirley made cookies.* (Without electricity, the sisters had to be creative.) *We placed hot coals...in low pans in the oven and baked.... It worked very well. The cookies were very good.*

But very soon, the mood of the journal turns much more somber.

July 25: We've heard that the Freedom Fighters are in the market, so we think the whole area will be soon taken.

July 26: Around 11 a.m., a ring of shots exploded in the air and we all ran for safety and lay on the floor for about 20 minutes, waiting for the silence in the area. Around 4 o'clock another ring of shots resounded in our ears. Approximately at 6 p.m....a group of neighborhood folks ran cheering up to the road where they saw some Freedom Fighters running along the freeway.

The next few days were relatively quiet with artillery fire only heard in the distance; even so, the fighting was beginning to wear on the residents of the Gardnersville convent. And while Shirley and Joël tried to project strength for the sake of their three young houseguests, Sister Joël relates that as they are surrounded by the sounds of artillery fire growing closer, "a very powerful prayer comes to mind.... The light of God surrounds us, the love of God enfolds us, the presence of God watches over us, the power of God protects us, where we are, God is!"

And then on July 28: Charles Taylor was broadcasting the news that he was now the president of the National Patriotic Reconstruction Assembly.

Taylor had, in effect, proclaimed himself the leader of the country. But Samuel Doe still held the capital, and he wasn't backing down. Fighting among the various rebel and government troops intensified, while innocent civilians paid the price. Nowhere would the cost be higher than at Saint Peter's Lutheran Church in the Sinkor district of Monrovia.

MASSACRE AT SAINT PETER'S

With the July 29 attack on the refugees sheltering on the grounds of Saint Peter's, the veneer of religious reverence that had been so carefully cultivated for over 150 years in Liberia cracked. It was part of an epic collapse that would take down religious institutions, schools, businesses, government offices, and virtually every aspect of civilized society throughout the country.

What small pockets of compassion may still have existed in Liberia fled in the nighttime hours of Sunday, July 29, 1990. That night as many as two hundred government soldiers loyal to President Doe raped, shot, stabbed, and hacked to death over 600 men, women, children, and babies who had sought sanctuary on the church grounds. It was estimated that at the time 2,000 Mano and Gio people were sheltering there. One of the refugees was Charles Taylor's own father, Nelson. It was later suggested that Doe's soldiers may have known of

Taylor's presence and targeted the church as a result. It was also likely payback for the NPFL attacks on Khran supporters of President Doe. With each new killing and atrocity, the ties that had once bound indigenous groups frayed even further. With the overthrow in 1980 of the Americo-Liberian elites, the sense of shared injury among the 16 native tribes lost its focus. The elevation of a particular ethnic group or groups over the others set up a new paradigm of haves and have-nots and encouraged animosity. Unscrupulous leaders and warlords capitalized on these feelings, turning them into hard-core hatred.

The mass killings in Nimba County was the logical outcome of this ethnic hatred. The survivors of these murderous incursions fled their homes with whatever they could carry and migrated towards their country's capital. Men, women, and children made the 150-mile trek to Monrovia, where 2,000 of them finally found sanctuary on the grounds of Saint Peter's Lutheran Church. People had been encamped there for about three weeks, believing they would be safe and at least minimally cared for. It was not an unrealistic expectation in the nominally Christian Liberia, where church institutions were generally respected. But Samuel Doe's Armed Forces of Liberia would shred the people's expectation in truly evil fashion, and in doing so would sweep away the last vestige of legitimacy of his government.

The attack began around 7 p.m., so it is likely that while people were finishing their meager suppers of donated rice and vegetables heavily armed soldiers were surrounding the mission compound. Doe's particularly vicious Chief of Staff, Brigadier General Charles Julu, was reported to have told his soldiers to have no mercy on the refugees. Survivors have spoken of the church's sanctuary running with blood, the floor slippery with gore; little children's bodies strewn across the altar as in some macabre sacrifice. They talk of seeing mothers with babies on their backs or in their arms lying on the floor where they fell, ripped by bullets.

Years after the end of the war, in testimony before Liberia's Truth and Reconciliation Commission, people spoke in hushed voices about what they witnessed. One woman, Winifred Kemo, who survived the bloodbath sobbed all through her testimony as she described how soldiers used guns and cutlasses and knives to kill their victims. "After they had killed and killed," she testified, "then some of the soldiers said they were tired of killing. So they decided to collect money from the few of us there in order to allow us to leave the compound."

Another survivor, James Dogolea, described how soldiers raped and killed the women even after they had paid a ransom. And another survivor who lost his father that night, Peterson Sonjah, was quoted as testifying that President Samuel K. Doe and some of his top advisors were present that night to watch the carnage. He said that Doe and his associates chanted slogans and encouraged the soldiers in their murderous onslaught.

A Catholic order serving in the area at the time, the

School Sisters of Notre Dame (SSND), recorded the events as it affected their circumstances. Two of their sisters were living just a few blocks from Saint Peter's in Sinkor, on the campus of the Arthur Barclay Business College, having evacuated their own convent on Tubman Boulevard after it was damaged by shelling. The two Notre Dame sisters spent "every day" in the Arthur Barclay campus compound, "which had become a refugee camp during July when classes had ceased."

The sisters worked with the refugees by "distributing rice, entertaining the children, caring for the sick, and doing all they could to protect the people." On the very evening of the Saint Peter's massacre, AFL soldiers came to the gate of the Barclay campus to demand vehicles. But three Salesian priests who were present at the time were successful in turning the soldiers away, first pleading and then demanding that "they respect the Red Cross flag flying over the gate."

It is likely that those same soldiers then went on to take part in the murderous rampage a few blocks away at Saint Peter's. After that attack, the sisters and priests at the Barclay compound became convinced that it was their duty to disperse those taking refuge with them "since there was now no safety for them in groups." They distributed all the available rice to the people and "sent them away." Because "it seemed safer for the people to walk the streets alone or in groups" than to remain on the enclosed campus where they would be easy targets for mass murder.

On August 11, the SSND sisters joined a large convoy fleeing Liberia for Ivory Coast. The convoy of 75 cars left from Catholic Hospital in Monrovia, carrying all its patients away to safety. Taylor's men intended to make the hospital its headquarters in the capital. The rebels provided an escort out of the area to the convoy before eventually commandeering all of the vehicles and placing the evacuees on buses.

"Everywhere alongside the road they saw dead bodies and destroyed, devastated, empty villages," according to a report written by Sister Kay O'Connell. The last leg of the SSND's journey in Liberia was completed courtesy of Doctors without Borders (MSF), who loaded the evacuees onto an open truck for an hour-long ride to the border as they shivered in the evening cold. "The sisters remember how strange it was to feel cold in Liberia," she wrote. Very soon, all international Catholic missionaries would be out of Liberia.

This was the state of Liberia in 1990. And as bad as it was then, it was destined to get even worse. While Liberia's Truth and Reconciliation Commission lists 200 massacres between 1989 and 2003, some sources believe there may have been as many as 70 more, bringing the total to 270 cases of mass murder committed in the span of 14 years.

Though the Gardnersville ASC sisters' journal does not record the Saint Peter's killings, news would surely have reached them through missionary contacts and word of mouth. The massacre of so many innocents on hallowed ground mere miles from their own home must have made the blood of the Kolmer cousins, Sisters Joël and Shirley, run cold and emphasized the precariousness of their own situation. For days, they and their Gardnersville neighbors had been caught in the continuous cross-fire between rebel and government soldiers. By the grace of God, they had been unharmed, but as the following entries demonstrate, they understood that their luck was not going to hold forever.

> *July 30:* *It's Monday, and loud shooting in the area began around 7:45 a.m. Gun fire, machine guns and explosives were going on all this time.* (Joël goes on to say in the journal that NPFL rebels came to their gate to see if they were harboring any government soldiers. Satisfied that the nuns were not, the Freedom Fighters went away, only to return a couple of hours later to engage in a frightening battle with government troops virtually on the nuns' doorstep.) *During the time of the shooting we stayed low near the floor because there was so much gunfire going on that it was very frightening…. By 7:15 p.m. we very quietly got ourselves something to eat and then prepared for bed.*

Things were just as bad in Klay, where Sister Toni Cusimano recorded the following account in the mission journal:

*July 31: Bomi is now in the process of being taken....
When rebels came they marched us all, hands up, to the
center of the town by the main road and held us there
for about four hours. Two AFL soldiers were tied up
and lying on the ground stripped to their briefs. The
local harmless 'crazy man' was shot to death before our
eyes when he got up from the ground to talk to the rebels
in his usual rambling way.*

TIME TO LEAVE

Back in Gardnersville, Shirley and Joél decided to leave the
country. Sister Joél recorded the following:

*July 31: We were the only people left in the neighborhood
and when we checked around the house we saw all the
damage that had been done by the gunfire around us—
bullets riddling our house and many holes in our roof.*

Early the next morning as Joél packed, Shirley got on the
mission radio to warn her fellow ASCs in Klay and Grand
Cess that they should strongly consider leaving the country.
Indeed, most Americans in Liberia had already evacuated.
Sister Rachel, who with Sister Martha was far to the south-
east along the Kru coast, recorded in the Grand Cess journal:

August 1: We were shocked, because there is no trouble here. But she (Shirley) said its coming and we might be blocked in and can't get out later.

The morning of August 1 saw Sisters Shirley and Joél, as well as three young Liberians, Ramona Chebli, Charles Konneh, and Andrew Tuleh, shoulder their few belongings that included a packed tub of food plus several barnyard chickens crammed into sacks. Giving their home a final goodbye, Joél locked the door, hid the key by burying it in the ground, and then she and her small contingent began walking towards the city of Kakata, over 40 miles to the north of Gardnersville. From there, they hoped to get safe passage out of Liberia.

As the five moved inland putting physical distance between themselves and their home they would bear witness to the many obscenities of war and the collapse of all that was once familiar. All along their route, dead bodies littered the road and burned-out homes spoke of the fierceness of the carnage that had driven everyone into hiding for the last three days. The small group had planned to walk the 40-plus miles to Kakata, figuring it would take two to three days. The Catholic Bishop of Gbarnga, Benedict Sekey, had alerted the NPFL rebels to be on the lookout for the refugees. At this early point in the war, the rebels had yet to degenerate completely and many still had respect for missionaries and the religious who had taught some of them in school.

Ramona Chebli, the young ASC affiliate who accompanied the sisters, recounts how after they had walked about two and a half hours a young commando spotted them and offered a ride. The roads were bad and the young soldier was new to driving which combined for a "rough ride." Still, the group was happy for the lift. But when the driver announced he was running out of gas, the group was once again left on foot. Ultimately, they were picked up by another rebel Freedom Fighter, this one driving a commandeered forestry department bus. They reached Kakata in the early afternoon. Though their journey had been an unexpectedly easy one, their reception in Kakata would be anything but.

All refugees who arrived in Kakata were directed by Charles Taylor's rebels to the campus of the Booker T. Washington Institute, where they were to be interrogated before being issued passes. The Gardnersville group would receive especially harsh treatment. The three Liberians were accused of being supporters of President Doe, while the two sisters were accused of being CIA spies. Andrew was said to be of the Krahn tribe—that marked him for execution. Whether the rebels actually believed these charges or if this was just bluster is not certain. The group was separated, Americans taken to one spot and the Liberians to another, which was still within eyesight. In typical style, Joël tried to keep up the young people's spirits. Looking away from her own interrogators, she sought out Ramona and with a smile, doffed her red and white baseball cap and with a big smile, waved it in her direction.

Into this highly charged atmosphere, three people, unknown to the Gardnersville group, stepped in to assist. According to Joél's account of the situation, the three, two women and a man, helped convince the interrogators to let the entire group go. Two and a half hours after they entered the school they were issued passes and a voucher for rice.

Sister Shirley never mentions anything of these tense moments in her written account of their 1990 escape. Some things were just not for public consumption, she probably concluded, especially if you wanted to return to Liberia as soon as possible.

For the next several days the refugees stayed with some Catholic sisters in Kakata as they worked on trying to get bus tickets to Ivory Coast. The city was crowded with people and food was in short supply. The vouchers they had been given were almost useless since there was no rice to be had. The Kakata missionaries shared what little food they had with their visitors. Finally, on August 6 the group was able to secure passage on a bus leaving for Ivory Coast.

Refugees crowded on to the bus. "It was a difficult journey," recounted Joél. Ramona recalled the bus was packed with an assortment of Lebanese, Chinese, Liberians, and the two American sisters. There were about 50 people onboard all told. The ride to the border town of Danane in Ivory Coast took about seven and a half hours. Along the way, the bus became mired in the mud and all the men had to get out and push. Their route took them through Nimba County where the fighting had originally begun on Christmas Eve 1989. Ramona wrote: "It was such a pity to see houses that were burnt down to the ground by government soldiers. The old people and those who could not escape when the soldiers came were in these houses when they were burnt down."

When the bus reached Danane, it was nighttime and raining. The Gardnerville group opted to sleep on the bus, though some of the passengers, who were apparently members of the Freedom Fighters, chose to spend the night in noisy conversation making sleep almost impossible for the rest. The next day, the sisters and their companions were welcomed at the convent of the Sisters of the Assumption, where they rested and ate before obtaining bus tickets for Abidjan, Ivory Coast. Once there, the two Liberian men, Andrew and Charles, were granted visas for Freetown, Sierra Leone, and Ramona was granted a visa for the United States. Ramona, Joël, and Shirley's long journey to the U.S. would finally end on August 17 when they landed in St. Louis, Missouri, at 8:30 p.m. local time.

Sister Toni Cusimano had initially demurred when Shirley advised her to evacuate Klay in early August. Sisters Barbara Ann Muttra and Agnes Mueller had returned to the States earlier in the year to receive medical treatment, so the decision of when to leave would be Toni's to make. But the decision was complicated. During the previous weeks, hundreds of refugees had taken shelter at her mission, and Toni was loath to leave them on their own. On August 2, she wrote in the Klay annals: "We now have over 800 on the mission. Every room in the center and the school is packed, even the church."

In good times, Toni's mission in Klay was just a half hour drive from Gardnersville where Shirley and Joël lived. She would visit the Gardnersville missionaries frequently and they her. But now her friends had left, and traveling the roads in Bomi County was becoming a very dangerous proposition.

Years later, Toni recalled driving the back roads at the time and seeing cars burned out and overturned. "I was scared," she said, but that did not stop her and Father Garry Jenkins, the SMA priest who had first invited her and Barbara to the Klay area, from doing what they had to do to help the refugees. Fifteen miles away, Garry's mission in Bomi Hills was the closest in proximity to Klay.

"Father Garry and I would each take a load of refugees from Klay in our cars and move them out of harm's way," said Toni. "He would drive them up the road to Bomi Hills and I would drive them towards the border with Sierra Leone." Their ad hoc underground railway was necessary to relieve overcrowding at the Klay mission, where more and more people crowded in each day. On the drive out Toni would have the companionship of as many people as she could fit in her car, but on the way home she travelled alone, alert for potential danger and battling fear the whole time. "Yes," she said, "I was afraid, but we had to keep people moving along in order to free up space at the mission for others who could not travel any further."

Each morning Toni and another sister who lived at the mission, a Claretian nun, would tend to the refugees as best they could, cooking up Cream of Wheat for the babies and ministering to the physical and spiritual needs of the refugees. Then Toni would make her daily run to the border. But by August their supplies were running perilously low, constricted as they were by warring soldiers, and it was becoming increasingly clear to Toni that she was in growing danger. On August 6, she fled Liberia never thinking that it would be the last she would ever see of her beloved mission at Klay or its beautiful people. Decades later, when I interviewed the then 80-year-old nun at her home in Ruma, Illinois, she still referred to the mission in Klay as "her mission." For the rest of her life, it would always be so.

By August 18, with war reaching even far-flung Grand Cess, ACS Sisters Rachel Lawler and Martha Wachtel, and a young German volunteer named Bergita would also begin their flight from Liberia. Sister Rachel recalled the harrowing evacuation:

The day before we left was a Sunday, and at our communion service that morning with the local people we told them we had to leave the country the next day. We didn't want to, but our bishop, Boniface Dalieh, insisted we go because there had been a missionary priest killed up the coast in Sinoe County a month earlier and the bishop was worried for our safety. All that afternoon people kept coming by the convent saying, 'sorry you have to leave'; it was like a funeral.

On Monday, Popu our yard man gave us a ride to the edge of the Grand Cess River. We had to get out and cross by foot because there was only a small bridge, so we told Popu to take the car back home and put it in the garage and lock the door. We had every intention of coming back.

Once across the river, Bishop Dalieh had arranged the escape route for the trio. Their course, however, would not be a direct one out of the country. First the women travelled south to the very tip of Liberia where another order of Catholic nuns, the Bernardine Franciscan Sisters, had a mission in Cape Palmas. The Grand Cess women would spend the night under the aegis of one of the OSF sisters, Sister Caroline, who, with several local Liberian girls in her care, was in residence at the mission.

Rachel described a troubling night spent walking the convent hallways waving a flashlight about and praying. "As it got dark, Sister Caroline grew worried because of the rebel activity in the area and the increasing lawlessness that accompanied it. She directed each of us to walk up and down the hallways of the building with flashlights hoping that any potential intruders might be put off by what appeared to be a large group of people walking around. She also played the radio loudly." It was near midnight when Caroline gave the all clear and said it was "probably safe to go to bed," recalled Rachel. Caroline's fears had been well-founded. Though the convent and its residents escaped the night unscathed, the mission clinic just a few hundred yards away was not as lucky. Under cover of darkness, thieves scaled the compound's walls and broke into the pharmacy, stealing precious medicine while smashing vials they did not want. "There were two night watchmen, but one ran away and another hid in a tree," recounted Sister Rachel.

Into to the clinic, the most vulnerable residents of the compound huddled together with their protector, an American Bernardine Franciscan named Sister Sponsa Beltran. (This was the self-same Sister Sponsa who had aided in the 1971 Grand Cess cholera epidemic.) On more than one occasion, Sponsa proved to be a strong-willed, deeply prayerful woman who had found her true calling in Africa. Now, as the thieves ravaged the small pharmacy, she kept vigilant watch over a score of crippled children, quieting their fears with songs and prayer. There would be no way that she would let anyone, armed or not, harm any of the little ones in her care.

Sister Sponsa was a friend to the ASC missionaries, especially Sister Barbara Ann Muttra, who like Sponsa was a nurse with two decades of service in Liberia. In 1970, the

45-year-old Sponsa had come to set up a clinic for the general population in Cape Palmas, but much like Barbara she had been drawn in by the overwhelming needs of the children. Though she had not intended to create a medical center for the crippled and outcast children of the country, it would not take long for her work to go in that direction. "The Liberian people thought that a crippled child was witched," she told me in an interview years later. "They were often ill-cared-for by their families, who considered them shameful burdens."

It would become Sponsa's life's work to change the culture of superstition surrounding handicapped children and provide them a caring place to live. As word of the nun's work spread, her clinic was transformed into a rehab center where youngsters could receive therapy, affection, a safe place to live, and a tireless advocate. She would not leave them alone now or ever, even in the face of armed invaders.

The next morning after the attack, the bishop sent a car, a truck, and a bus to pick up the whole contingent—and everyone was more than ready to leave. They were driven to the Cavalla River, which forms a natural border between Liberia and Ivory Coast. Two men with dug-out canoes, little more than hallowed out trees, awaited the group to ferry them across the river and into Ivory Coast.

The logistics of ferrying two dozen handicapped children, along with their leg braces, across the river were daunting, but after many hours it was finally accomplished. On the Ivory Coast side of the river, arrangements had been made for the refugees to stay in an old seminary. The day after their arrival in Ivory Coast, Rachel, Martha and Bergita were driven to Abidjan, where Bergita caught a flight to Germany and the two sister Adorers, by this time showing the ill-effects of recently contracted malaria, flew to Spain, then to New York, and then on to St. Louis before finally reaching their Provincial home in Ruma.

Sister Sponsa, meanwhile, refused to evacuate to the U.S. She would remain in Ivory Coast for several years with her young charges, opening a make-shift school in the old seminary where they had taken refuge. The school would not just serve her children but would ultimately draw in scores of other displaced youngsters hungry for education. When it was once again safe to return to Liberia, Sponsa would settle with her dependents on the outskirts of Monrovia and establish a rehabilitation center for disabled children and adults. She would run the center until 2007 when, at the age of 82, she finally returned to the United States for good.

Mostly blind and confined to a wheelchair which she would push through the hallways with a kind of paddling foot motion, Sister Sponsa spent her retirement quietly in the hill country of Pennsylvania at a home run by the Bernardine Franciscans. There she would occasionally hold court with others who had served in Liberia and share stories. In 2016 she died at the age of 91, a world away from her beloved African adopted home.

Meanwhile, the Precious Blood sisters who had been

recalled to the United States would spend the fall and winter of 1990 and the spring of 1991 watching the dreadful news of fighting in Liberia. They prayed for those they had left behind and prepared for the day when they could return. To no one's surprise, the most vocal among the group was Sister Shirley Kolmer. But standing right alongside her was Sister Barbara Ann Muttra.

IN LIMBO

The Precious Blood sisters were safely back in the United States—though it was the last place they wanted to be. They felt displaced. They were home, yet not at home. After being away for so long, it was hard to readjust to life in the United States. They felt "temporary" and longed to get back to their mission where people needed their help.

Reports of mass starvation in Liberia began reaching them in Ruma. A news release from the Catholic Relief Services dated January 3, 1991, detailed the agency's efforts to feed 500,000 starving refugees in Liberia as well as those now staying in places like Sierra Leone, Ivory Coast, and Ghana. Using a network of church and other voluntary organizations, CRS had distributed over 30,000 metric tons of food donated through the United States government. It was reported that 600,000 displaced people still living inside Liberia and

750,000 refugees outside the country were in need of food assistance.

The United Nations reported on the dismal conditions inside the country, saying that due to extremes of "malnutrition and...starvation, many thousands of children are by now frail skeletons barely able to hold themselves up." Adults as well as children were in such weakened physical conditions that many were succumbing to malaria and infections. Violence plagued the capital where children "are found wandering aimlessly and sleeping on the pavements."

In a February 1991 report, the administrator of the Ganta Leprosy Center in Nimba County, Sister Bridget Murphy, a Medical Missionary of Mary, painted a truly desperate picture. Nimba was where Charles Taylor's NPFL originally entered Liberia on Christmas Eve of 1989. The leprosy center had become a refuge for local residents displaced from Ganta City and neighboring villages; about 700 people sheltered there, where they received food, work, and stability. It was the only institution in Nimba to stay open during the early part of the war. In addition, the center had 110 leprosy patients and 44 tuberculosis patients in its care.

The report states: "The Sisters and workers stayed during the terrifying days when the fighters entered the Leprosy Center on May 14, 1990. There was a lot of shooting in the Center, several people were wounded, and 32 patients lost their lives."

To make matters worse, rebels stole the center's livestock,

including 143 chickens, 159 pigs, 27 ducks, 11 sheep and rabbits: "...all gone," said the report. To complete the devastation, the NPFL looted the crops from the farms, and stole all of the center's vehicles. In plain words, Taylor's people left over 700 souls to starve in veritable isolation. "The suffering of displaced people within Liberia is beyond description," wrote Sister Bridget.

For Sister Barbara Ann, who had seen conditions of war very like these in Vietnam, the reports made her want to speed her return. Barbara's lobbying was all the more astonishing because she had been given a rather devastating cancer diagnosis in early 1990 when she underwent an operation to remove a six-pound tumor on her ovaries. Repeated malaria and hepatitis exposure had weakened her immune system, making follow-up treatments of radiation and chemotherapy impossible. In spite of everything, Barbara did improve. She pronounced it a "miracle." Now, almost a year into her recovery, she was itching to get back to Liberia, so she proclaimed herself cured and ready to go.

Sister Shirley Kolmer was of the same mind as Barbara, and as a former Provincial her opinion held some sway. She and the other missionaries had found it hard to reacclimate themselves to living in the U.S. Not that their lives were extravagant; after all, they were living in a religious community. Even so, they felt out of place, or "temporary" as described by Sister Mildred (Millie) Gross, who was Provincial at the time. Shirley especially lobbied hard for their return, thinking Millie "too cautious" on the matter. "Shirley told people to work on me," Milllie told me with a sigh.

While Millie could not put aside her misgivings about the nuns returning to Liberia, she did agree to be open-minded. A facilitator was brought in in early 1991 to help moderate the conversation on what to do. There were meetings with family members and with the Archbishop of Monrovia, Michael Francis, who journeyed to the U.S. There was then a cease-fire in place, and the archbishop was eager to get Catholic missionaries back in the country. He wanted their help in reopening the schools.

As anyone who knew her would admit, when Shirley made up her mind it was awfully hard to go against her. Her adamancy was backed up by a firm trio in Sisters Agnes Mueller, Mary Joél Kolmer, and Barbara Ann Muttra. All felt the pain of those they had known and loved and ultimately left behind. Other sisters who had served in the missions were less inclined to return to the tumult; some were pulled by familial and other commitments at home. But a newcomer stepped up in ACS Sister Kathleen McGuire. She was a close friend of Sister Shirley, and when Shirley asked her to join the mission group, Kathleen didn't hesitate. Kathleen still hoped to be sent to a mission in Latin America, but in the interim she was willing to serve where the need appeared greatest, and that was Liberia.

A little reluctantly, the ASC leadership team drew up a set of guidelines that the sisters would have to follow if they wanted to return to Liberia. Among the guidelines was a directive for regular phone calls back to Ruma to report on conditions in the country. But before the group could return in force, a scouting party of two—Shirley and Joël—was dispatched to assess the situation in March of 1991.

Other missionary organizations, as well as international relief agencies, were also weighing the consequences of returning to Liberia. For some, the time was not quite right. Things in the country were still a little too unsettled. But as the year wore on without major outbreaks of violence, people began to have a quiet hopefulness. Some put their faith in the various peace agreements being struck among the warring parties. The School Sisters of Notre Dame (SSND) had operated out of Cape Palmas and were friends with their ASC counterparts in Grand Cess. Four SSNDs had been granted permission to return to their mission in the spring of 1992 after "months of prayer and consideration." Their decision was not made lightly. They realized that conditions in Liberia were neither "stable or predictable," but much like the ASC sisters (who would precede their return by over a year) the SSNDs "wanted to assist in the healing process and to try to reestablish the educational system in this devastated country." Missionaries, it seems, speak a common language.

Shirley spent much of her time waiting for some sign that the time was right for her to return to Liberia. When Archbishop Michael Francis wrote saying a cease fire was holding and inviting the sisters to come back so they could reopen the schools, Shirley jumped at the chance, as did Joël, Barbara, and Agnes.

When the decision was made to return to Liberia in 1991, Agnes decided to give away a number of her personal items. She felt she didn't need so many "things" anymore. It had been a hard transition for Agnes to come back to a country with such abundance after living in a place of so much want. Some in her family tried to talk her out of going back. They were worried about the danger, but Agnes shrugged it off. "She was grown up enough to know what she wanted," said her sister Leona Beckman.

But not all of the sisters who had fled Liberia in 1990 were ready to go back, and one, Sister Rachel Lawler, seems haunted by that decision. "Shirley begged me to go back," she said. But Rachel's mother was 96 years old and Rachel feared that if "something" happened to her in Liberia, her mother would die of grief. So, she stayed in the U.S. and Sister Kathleen McGuire went in her place. "I've always felt guilty" about that decision Rachel told me. "I feel she took a bullet instead of me."

RETURN TO LIBERIA

In March of 1991, Shirley and Joël returned to the Gardnersville convent. What they found was shocking. Their home was badly damaged by bullet and mortar holes. The roof leaked.

Their furniture was gone. The bathroom was bloodstained. Worse still, it was common knowledge that people had been tortured and killed inside the home. In light of all that, the SMA fathers, who were providing temporary housing for Shirley and Joél, questioned whether they even wanted to go back there. Perhaps they should start fresh somewhere else? But the women were determined to reclaim their former home, so in short order repairs were underway.

The convent annals from that time, which were kept by Sister Joél, make small mention of the shameful acts that took place there. In fact, the March 17, 1991, entry records the sisters' first view of their convent. Joél's most disturbing assessment was, "It was a mess." She goes on to cite an almost mundane litany of items present and missing from their home: "We found five bunk beds in the whole house, two tables on the aspirants' side, and one divider cupboard.... No chair in the whole place." The omission of the more worrying aspects was obviously intentional.

It was not until they returned to Illinois several weeks later that more horrific facts came out. Shirley and Joél confided in person to others what they were hesitant to put down on paper. The story they told was "gruesome," recalled their sister and cousin Elizabeth Kolmer. She remembered Shirley recounting to her that the ASC convent had been used as a headquarters by soldiers, and one of the bathrooms had been used for executions. A charge that was borne out by bullet-riddled walls and a bloody bathtub. "Shirley said that one of the priests had told her that they had taken two heads out from behind the door," added Elizabeth.

A few days after their arrival in Gardnersville, Shirley prepared a written report of conditions as they found them: "We have been and will be quite busy now." Indeed, virtually all of the books at their convent and in the schools had either disappeared or been destroyed. While schools throughout the country were still closed, the sisters wanted to be prepared for the students when they finally returned. So, in addition to supervising the restoration of their living quarters, the women had to rebuild the stores of necessary educational materials and supplies taken from the schools where they worked. "We are embarking on a project of writing books for school," she said. A printing press that "hardly got hurt" was to be used to help print the new books. Shirley wrote, "If I can find a set of elementary mathematics books I can put together some workbooks."

By April, Shirley and Joël were eager to get some kind of school up and running. "We are trying to get an emergency school together for grades 1-6," Shirley reported. The children required lots of remedial work, having not attended classes in almost a year; they also needed "a good meal and plenty of time to play and have fun." Of course, counselling would also be part of the program: "The kids need to talk about their experiences. Some of them know the person who killed some of their family." But the older children will be problematic, wrote Shirley, "as many of them carried guns themselves."

Saint Patrick's High School, where Shirley was principal,

was described as "badly hit." The walls were pockmarked from bullets and the administration wing needed to be rebuilt. Saint Michael's School, where Joël taught, was described as faring better damage-wise. It was, however, currently being used as a feeding center. "There must be a couple of hundred kids there being fed in various stages," Shirley explained. Many of the children were "near starvation." The most severe were sitting on mats on classroom floors where volunteers fed them in small amounts and often; those in less dire straits were placed in an intermediate feeding program at a different end of the building, which Shirley now referred to as "the clinic."

The task of rebuilding that lay before the women was daunting. The world they had known before 1990 had been torn to bits, and many of their friends and former neighbors were missing; some were dead. "We visited Ramona's family," they wrote. They were fine, but one of their other daughters was missing. "They think she is in Gbarnga.... It seems many people were killed in the war.... Josephine's sister Celestine is helping with the feeding program...her son Doe died of cholera.... Helene Howard...thinks she lost her Sylvester...the rebels took him." On and on, the sisters named those they had found and those they had lost. And they marveled at the fickleness that condemned some while preserving others. "So many were close to being killed but were spared. Agatha said they were ready to kill her husband...when one of them said the man (Agatha's husband) was a doctor who had helped them, so they let him live." In another letter, Shirley wrote: "We know...

of a few of our students and parishioners who were shot."

Meanwhile, other missionaries began to trickle back into Liberia. The nuns wrote: "About a week after we came, Suzanne, Tripola and Elfrieda came to stay.... They decided to try to live at STC 'til after Easter.... The Sister of Charity (M. Teresa) came about a week after we did.... Brother Thomas came in January. He is working hard at Saint Pat's as the administration section got blown up."

Scenes of destruction were everywhere, as were reminders of the recent period of starvation people endured: "One hardly sees a cat, a dog, or a chicken in Liberia." But with the cease-fire holding, people were getting food aid from the United Nations and Catholic Relief Services and some local churches; they began to look less emaciated. The feeding programs for children and the elderly showed progress, too. "I am so happy the people have enough to eat," wrote a relieved Shirley. "I am so amazed at them. They ask for nothing from us in that way. They are so happy we are here." And the people's resolve seems to infect Shirley, too. One man from their village ran to another town during the fighting in 1990. On his return, he discovered he had lost everything. The man, though, told Shirley, "it doesn't matter." He felt "blessed" to be alive. Another young man Shirley knew recounted how he and his parents had defied the rebels and remained in their own home during the intense fighting. The man told the fighters that they would have to kill them, or leave them alone. They left them alone, not even daring to take a "handkerchief."

Shirley was impressed. "I imagine that kind of strength and faith was too much for the soldiers."

Even the smallest things were difficult, "We did not bring a can opener. I say it was something to find one," wrote Shirley to Elizabeth. "All our electrical appliances we bought were in vain. Electricity and water are on the other side of town." Still she tried to find a bit of humor in their situation. "We've done all right without the celery salt. We use onion and garlic salt and salt and pepper.... And of course gin."

Finding the everyday items needed to set up their household became a kind of scavenger hunt. A few stores reopened, but many remained closed; so when they found something they could use, Joél and Shirley reacted with excitement: "We bought some dishes at a market nearby.... We actually got 5 plates that match." When they found a grocery with "fresh lettuce, tomatoes, radishes, and frozen chicken," it was worth noting. "We came home and had sandwiches.... That day was like heaven."

Meanwhile, an interim government is trying to hold the country together and make accommodations with the rebels. Shirley mentions "the voting meeting" that is scheduled for April 18, the next day. While "It all looks good on paper, no one knows if C. Taylor will cooperate." The warlord, reports Shirley, "is starting trouble in Sierra Leone now. They are fighting on the border." Unknown to Shirley, of course, was that Taylor's involvement in the neighboring country would mushroom. His support of a rebel group there would lead to the brutal humanitarian crimes for which he will be tried in the International Criminal Court in The Hague 25 years later. It will be this foray into Sierra Leone—reported on here so briefly by Shirley—that would ultimately lead to a 50-year prison sentence for Taylor. But before that happened, Taylor woud lead his own country into hell.

In May, Joél and Shirley return to Ruma to report on the state of affairs in Gardnersville. In person, with those they trust, they are honest about the horrors they have seen. But they are confident that the worst of the war is behind them. They are convinced that the nuns are needed in Liberia and will be safe.

They gather up all the supplies they can carry, and on July 17, Shirley, Joél, Agnes, and Barbara leave St. Louis. Five days later, after a stop in Sierra Leone, they arrive in Liberia. By the time they get to their house in Gardnersville it is already dark and they unload their luggage by lantern light. The next day they get serious about cleaning up their newly remodeled house. It takes two weeks before the place is up to the standards "for a sisters' convent," as they put it in a report home.

Two days after their return, Joél came down with malaria. She records it as a "real disappointment" but with the kindly ministrations of her fellow sisters, she is on her feet again in a matter of days. The annals record many similar incidents of sickness among the sisters at this time, ranging from malaria to hepatitis. All are taken in stride.

ALL TOGETHER NOW

On August 6, 1991, the full complement of the ASCs is realized with the arrival of Sister Kathleen McGuire. Now they are the five who would die in service to their faith and the people of Liberia. For the remainder of the year, Shirley and Joél would be occupied with readying their schools, Saint Patrick's and Saint Michael's, for their reopening. Kathleen would assist wherever she was needed as a teacher, healer, or cook. Agnes once again worked in parish outreach. Barbara began working on ministering to the displaced. But even with five of them, their workload was strenuous. Not only were they busy locating school supplies and furnishings, they also had to rebuild their entire educational curriculum and write their own workbooks for the students; something that Shirley and Joél had started earlier in the year. And in some cases, they would also have to locate the students and teachers who fled their neighborhoods during the fighting.

The sisters' annals record some of their early activities: Agnes goes to Saint Michael's School and their local parish to do whatever she can to help. Barbara and Shirley head to Monrovia daily, Barbara to help with the Archdiocesan Rehabilitation Committee and Shirley to prepare for the reopening of Saint Patrick's High School. Joél is putting together an English workbook for the students. In addition, Agnes and

Joél begin serving on the parish Social Concerns Committee. The newcomer, Kathleen, is laid up with a serious reaction to numerous ant and spider bites. But before long, her skills as an educator and homemaker will be put to good use.

By mid-September, the schools are set to reopen. Saint Patrick's is first and begins with a three-day faculty workshop. Kathleen is called upon to work with the returning teachers and students to help overcome their trauma by facilitating healing-transformation workshops. A few days later, Saint Michael's School holds its faculty in-service days. But conditions here are more unorganized; there is frustration with the high school program. Adding to the problems, the "trusted financial manager of the school had decided to return to his seminary studies almost immediately," Joél reports. The books are summarily handed over to her and she is left to figure things out on her own. When it becomes too much for Joél alone, Agnes is called upon to assist her. In the meantime, though, Agnes continues to work with students, both as a teacher and in directing healing workshops. By the end of September both Agnes and Barbara begin to feel the ill-effects of malaria. Troopers that they are, however, the two women rebound after just a few day's rest.

SISTER KATHLEEN McGUIRE

I am intent upon finding ministry which answers an urgent need and is commensurate with my faith and commitment, hoping to place whatever education and experience I have at the service of the dispossessed.... It is what I need to do about it that has taken me off guard.... This realization is quite contrary to my own expectations. I have always expected some day to experience a call to Latin America—I keep studying Spanish to be ready for such a call. Shirley and Antoinette had often urged me to come to Liberia, but never before have I felt I was supposed to be there. Now I believe I am supposed to go.

SISTER KATHLEEN McGUIRE, 1991

Sister Kathleen McGuire, ASC, began her service in Liberia after the start of the war years there. She, unlike the other four Precious Blood sisters, would only know it as a country that had failed its own people. In spite of that reality, Sister Kathleen was willing to follow her sisters to a place that was soon to be labeled "the most dangerous country in the world."

PLAIN FOLK

Norma Katherine was a late Christmas present for Pauline and John McGuire. Born on December 28, 1937, baby Kay (as she was called) would be the proverbial "middle child" between her older brother, Robert, and sister, Carol Ann, both already on the scene, and younger brothers, Charles and Frederick, in the offing. The place where Kay made her debut wasn't a city; it wasn't even a town, but a small, close-knit Catholic community named Pond Settlement. It is located in the southeastern part of Illinois in Gallatin County near the confluence of Indiana and Kentucky and just north of the Shawnee National Forest. Pond Settlement was established by Irish emigres in 1819, the year after Illinois achieved statehood. Soon, more immigrants would follow, as would settlers from the eastern parts of the country who were seeking to homestead on Illinois' vast prairies.

At the time of Kay's birth, the whole county had a population of about 11,000; today it is less than half that number. The closest "big" town is Ridgway, with a population of around 1,000 souls. Once home to a popcorn factory, the town playfully dubbed itself the "Popcorn Capital of the World."

Charles (Chuck) McGuire and his wife Linda still live in Ridgway. Not much has changed in the decades since his sister Kay left as a 13-year-old girl, eager to enter the convent high school in Ruma. Chuck describes his hometown as a "nice community where everybody pitches in." A case in point, Chuck said, was when the Catholic Church in town, Saint Joseph's, was destroyed by a tornado in February 2012 and everybody who was able helped with clean-up, regardless of what religious denomination they professed. Growing up, Chuck remembers his older sister (by two years) Kay as a bit of a tattletale. In the early days of their schooling in Pond Settlement, three grades shared a room, meaning he and Kay were in the same classroom. As a result, "anything I did," said Chuck, "Mom and Dad knew about that night." By the time he was in the third grade and Kay was in fifth, they transferred to the larger Saint Joseph's Catholic School in Ridgeway.

Family played a key role in the development of the McGuire children. Sundays would usually find John and Pauline's brood at grandma and grandpa McGuire's house after Mass, along with assorted aunts, uncles, and cousins who lived nearby. A typical Sunday dinner would find at least 30 relatives gathered to eat fried chicken with gravy, ham, and homemade ice cream. "Everybody went to grandma's," said Chuck fondly.

Kay's first encounter with religious sisters came when she was six years old, during a two-week summer program held in Pond Settlement for Catholic children who were attending public school. The nuns who taught the religion classes were members of the Adorers of the Blood of Christ. Kay loved them. Chuck remembers, "She told Mom, 'That's what I want to be!' Our mother, Pauline, thought it was great that Kay wanted to become a nun. She was so proud of her."

Professing a vocation to the vowed religious life at that time and in those circumstances was hardly a foreign concept for a young Catholic girl. Lots of girls were still entering the convent in the 1950s. Often sisters and cousins followed aunts and other family members into community life, with some families having two, three, or even four daughters pledged to the sisterhood; perhaps even in the same religious community. In Kay's case, she would join the community of ASCs where her cousins, Linda Lou (Alicia) and Marilyn (Raphael Ann) Drone, would also profess their vows a few years later.

During the years when Kay attended Precious Blood High School, she lived at the Provincial House in Ruma like the other high school girls and came home only at Christmas and for summer vacation. In 1955, upon graduation, six months shy of her eighteenth birthday, Kay entered the novitiate of the Adorers of the Blood of Christ. Donning the long black habit and white veil of a novice, she chose a new name: Kathleen, which fit her Irish heritage. While advancing through formation, Kathleen began teaching third graders. On July 1, 1961, Sister Kathleen McGuire professed her final vows as a member of the ASC religious community. Over the next dozen years, she would both teach at various schools run by the ASCs in Illinois and Iowa, as well as continue her own studies. She would earn her undergraduate and a master's degree from St. Louis University, and finally a doctorate in education from the University of Massachusetts in 1973.

Physically Kathleen was of short-to-average stature, standing just 5 feet 3 inches tall and weighing 120 pounds. Her most impressive feature was a shock of short, prematurely white hair that sat above a pair of jet black eyebrows. The contrast made an arresting visual impression, especially on the boys at Assumption High School in East St. Louis, Illinois, where she assumed the office of vice principal in 1973. The boys nicknamed Sister Kathleen "the silver fox."

"She had an easy smile but she could also be quite stern," said Sister Kate Reid, ASC, who was a teacher at nearby Saint Theresa's Academy for girls at the time. Kathleen was also exceptionally bright and intuitive. Though she eschewed hugs and was not particularly demonstrative, if she sensed someone was uncomfortable she had a way of putting them at ease. Her perceptive nature sized up new people fairly quickly. Kathleen also had a fun-loving side and enjoyed hosting gatherings of friends and colleagues. "We threw some great parties in Carbondale," said Sister Kate, who worked at Southern Illinois University in campus ministry with Kathleen in the 1980s.

One of Kathleen's greatest skills was her ability to build consensus. This talent was put to the test when she was chosen for the task of helping facilitate the closure of Saint Theresa's Academy in East St. Louis. Precious Blood sisters had built and staffed the historic school since the 1890s but could no longer afford to run it. The closing was emotional for the generations of women, many of them minorities, who had received their educations at the school and still held the institution in high regard. At the time, East St. Louis was in the grip of decline. Railroads, which had attracted industry to the area, began to fail in the 1960s, and businesses that had once flourished in the city left, taking jobs and middle-class residents with them. Newly built interstate highways callously dissected neighborhoods and contributed further to urban blight. Poverty, a changing demographic, and a declining population created a nexus of instability and loss from which East St. Louis has yet to recover.

Against this delicate canvas, Sister Kathleen gently and with great consideration helped to create opportunities for dialogue within the community, where people could come to terms with their loss at the school closing. Eventually she helped facilitate the welcoming of the female students and teachers from Saint Theresa's into the formerly "all-boys" Assumption High School. It was, said her friend Sister Cecelia Hellmann, ASC, the way Kathleen operated: "She would stay with a problem until there was a graceful resolution." After the transition, Kathleen was named Director of Academics and remained at Assumption High School until 1980. Her cousin Sister Alicia Drone believes that the time spent in East St. Louis in the midst of "real poverty" may have been the genesis of Kathleen's social justice activism.

Sister Kathleen has been described as a feminist and a crusader, which she was, but she was also a processer and a deep thinker. Her sense of independence often drove her to puzzle through problems on her own. Because the pursuit of social justice was a central creed for her, she would drill down on the causes of injustice, always asking the key question: Who benefits from this wrong? "Justice," said her brother Chuck, "was her big thing." When people were treated unfairly, whether in the courts or through some other form of mistreatment, Kathleen would become upset. She longed to correct the situation, and when she could she not only spoke up—she stood up. Harkening back to the lessons of her mother Pauline, Kathleen always sought to align her actions with her prayer life.

"For me," Kathleen wrote in an autobiographical reflection, "where my prayer and peace converge, there is the reign of God."

LIVING HONESTLY

Sister Kathleen's mother, Pauline, was one of the most influential people in her life. "For Mom," Kathleen reflected, "the practice of religion, the art of prayer, all had to be grounded honestly in the experience we lived with. She would never admit to two different realities and try to balance them or move between them. Her God was as much interested in what she did outside of 'prayer time' as in her prayer—and in fact was not at all interested in her prayer if she didn't do right at other times.... I never forgot the need to live in such a way that my words and my actions gave witness to each other, and this need has made the search for integrity a life project for me."

Pauline's rooted-to-the-earth kind of faith was complemented by, and occasionally at odds with, her husband John's more transcendent, unquestioning view of the Almighty. Kathleen wrote of a particularly humorous incident that brought her parents' approaches to living out their faith into sharp relief when the family was in the market to buy a new car.

"Dad felt that it was evidently God's will that we suffer from the heat—that's why God made summers hot—so, he thought we had no business getting a car with air-conditioning. Mom, who has always suffered much more from the heat than from the cold, said well, if that was true, then it follows that in the winter God must want us to suffer from the cold and what business do we have to have heat in our homes and in our cars. So, she would agree to do without the air-conditioned car if we would also have the heater taken out. So, we got our first air-conditioned car!"

Anyone who knew the two women well could see that Kay was her mother's daughter—down-to-earth, spunky, and outspoken. Though she valued her father's spiritual outlook, Kathleen, like her mother, was more concerned with putting faith to work in the here-and-now. In an undated written reflection, Kathleen admitted, "The 'otherworldliness' of my dad's faith, although I reveled in it at different times during my years of initial formation in religious life...never had the authenticity that could stand up very well in good times and bad, during hard teaching days and discouraging human relationships."

INTEGRITY

Kathleen's quest to live her life with integrity, combined with an inquisitive mind and an impressive intellect, made it impossible for her to be satisfied with superficial improvements and half-measures in the quest for social justice. She needed to dig deep into the nature of an inequity once she identified it. She would ask questions about why people were in the situations they were in as she sought to discover who was profiting on the backs of the oppressed or suffering. "She was doing social analysis and theological reflection before people had a name for it," said Sister Kate.

It seems natural that Kathleen's sense of social justice led her to oppose the Vietnam War. Back in Pond Settlement, that led to many heated discussions between Kathleen and her younger brother Fred, a helicopter pilot, who served in the conflict. Sometimes their disagreements over matters of war and peace could be contentious, and their mother would have to step in to "call time out," according to Sister Marie Clare Boehmer, ASC. Still, the siblings loved one another dearly. When Kathleen went to Washington to take part in protest marches in the 1960s and 1970s, she would invariably stay at her brother Fred's house.

In the 1990s, when the United States went to war in the Persian Gulf, Kathleen again took a stand. In a draft of a talk she hoped her local bishop would deliver, she wrote that being Catholic meant that we are challenged "to be more than U.S. citizens." She said that Catholics needed to pray and study and reflect so that they could make correct and responsible moral judgments on matters of war and peace.

"We have to realize," she wrote for the bishop, "that we are citizens of a nation which readily uses military force to secure its national interests.... We are tempted to assume that our 'national interests' are God's interests, that God fights on our side. When we strive for a return to 'business as usual' for ourselves, then we are really helping to deepen the despair of the poor...because it sustains unjust social situations." It is not clear if or how much of this talk the bishop actually gave, but that is not the point. This was what Sister Kathleen thought he should say.

After studied reflection, Kathleen would ready for battle on whatever ground necessary, even the hallowed ground of Holy Mother Church. For her, God and Church were not the sole province of men. Women, she felt, were men's equal partners, or at least they should be. In her writings, she referred to God in the feminine form when she spoke of looking at her life experience through faith and there finding "God revealing herself most intimately to me." She also looked forward to the day when women could offer Mass.

Not everyone was as forward thinking as she was, however. Kathleen's tendency to constantly ask the hard questions on women's and social justice issues would prove to be problematic for her because it made some of the more conservative members of her own religious community uncomfortable. Nominated for leadership several times, she was never elected to office and finally gave up seeking it. She became unsure of where she stood with some of the other sisters. This seemed to be an echo of earlier doubts she had during here initial formation as a nun. "I used a lot of energy worrying about whether I was going to meet someone's standards and be admitted to final vows," she wrote. But then she concluded that she did indeed "like this life" and that she was the only one to judge whether or not she had the understanding and insight "with which to live this life, and so I am the only one responsible for fidelity to that grace." She resolved to "show how I intend to live and give folks a chance to send me packing before I stay too long." She called this decision "one of the major choices for integrity I made."

Kathleen would always be responsible for her "graces" and not rely on someone else "to decide right and wrong for me." She would, in all things, remain true to herself. Eventually, her personal integrity and leadership skills would be recognized and put to good use when she was asked to coordinate the ASC's Justice and Peace Commission in 1984. She would devote herself full-time to the coordination of the social concerns efforts of the Ruma sisters. It proved to be a momentous opportunity that would last until 1990. During this time, there was a growing effort among U.S. churches to provide safe havens for people fleeing the violence taking place in Central America. At the time, federal immigration policy was very restrictive in offering asylum to these refugees, in spite of the terrible conflicts in their home countries, especially Guatemala and El Salvador. Many churches of different denominations—as many as 500 across the country—stepped in to offer shelter to the refugees in defiance of U.S. law. This became known as the "Sanctuary Movement."

When Kathleen became Justice and Peace coordinator for the Precious Blood sisters, she picked up the cause of the Sanctuary Movement. Her approach in convincing the members of her order to join the movement, which they had resisted earlier, was persistent and methodical. It took the sisters a year to prepare for a vote on giving sanctuary to refugees, during which time people were given the opportunity to voice what they needed to help them make a decision. Forums were held for the sisters to hear personal stories of refugees. Many sisters traveled to Concordia, Kansas, to visit with nuns there who were already part of the movement. Under Kathleen's leadership, support was built brick by brick. In the end, the vote was 95 percent in favor of joining the Sanctuary Movement.

Over a two-year period, the sisters of Ruma housed a succession of three refugee families, one for a year. During that time, the family's children went to school and their parents helped out by working on the farm that surrounded the convent. Eventually the families went on to Canada, where they were given legal status.

Sister Cecilia Hellmann was a direct participant in the movement and remembers it with a wry humor: "At the time I was a principal and very busy, but I volunteered to be one of the 'up front' people." It was in large part, she said, because Kathleen was a close friend and used gentle persuasion and "even a bit of manipulation" to get her to agree to help the cause. "I was living in East St. Louis at the time and the airport was in St. Louis, so I would get the call from Kathleen to go to the airport and pick up the people who were arriving. I remember we communicated by telephone and we were very careful, referring to 'our friends' coming in. It was all cloak and dagger." Transporting the refugees from the airport to Ruma for the first time, a 60-mile drive, was nerve-racking because Cecilia knew she was acting in direct violation of the law and subject to arrest.

The ASCs' lawyer had told the community as much, advising them strongly to give up on the idea of participating in Sanctuary. "Our lawyer told us our tax-exempt status was at risk and she told us that we could jeopardize all of our other charitable works," says Sister Kate. But when the lawyer said something like 'you don't have the right' to go against government policy, that irritated the sisters. "People thought, 'I don't have the right to live out the gospel?'" The lawyer "overplayed her hand," Kate insists.

Kathleen awaited the refugees' arrival in Ruma, at which point she, too, would be in jeopardy for harboring the exiles, as would all of the sisters who were present at the time. Kathleen developed a close relationship with the first family from Central America to come through—a mother, father, and their four-year-old son. They stayed about a year with the sisters. Later, when it was time to move on safely, Cecilia drove them to Canada. Kathleen stayed behind in Ruma. "She did come along on the second trip though," Cecilia recalls.

The memory of how her good friend Kathleen, "the strategist," could get others onboard to do the heavy lifting makes Cecilia chuckle. "She was so convinced in her heart and her soul that she could bring other people along and then get them to do the work. She had the courage and she had a way of expanding the field in a way that let others show their courage, too. She convinced people, but she did it delicately."

A LIGHTER SIDE

Though Sister Kathleen was a serious person, she also had a fun side that she shared with close friends. One of her favorite pastimes was camping; a love of the outdoors having been instilled growing up in rural Pond Settlement.

Cecelia recalls the first time they camped together. At the time, the two were living in East St. Louis. "Kathleen suggested we should take a vacation and go camping because she had gotten a new tent from her family." She pulled out a big map of the country and placed it on the dining room table, asking "Where do you want to go?" On a whim, Cecilia pointed to Acadia National Park in Maine. It was a long drive from southern Illinois, but Kathleen agreed. A third housemate, an older nun named Sister Carina Vetter, a Sister of Loretto, asked if she could go along and Kathleen, always gracious and eager to share her interests, agreed.

The first day, the trio made it to Pennsylvania. It was midnight when they found a campground and closer to one in the morning before they finally pitched their tent. Exhausted, they fell asleep. And then the rain started. And it was no small shower but a real cloudburst. It was then that they discovered that Kathleen's brand-new tent leaked. Bundling up the now useless tent, the women gathered their sopping belongings and piled into their car in search of a motel. They finally found one in the wee hours that had a single small room. When at last they settled in, Kathleen, wet but unbowed, pulled out a bottle of schnapps that she had the foresight to pack. "The three of us shared the bottle to ward off pneumonia," laughed Cecilia. "It was an unforgettable trip."

LATIN AMERICA CALLS FIRST

Kathleen had never intended to go to Liberia. It had always been Central America that had a hold on her heart. In February of 1989, while living and ministering in Carbondale, Illinois, Kathleen filled out the ASCs' annual Action Sheet/ Placement Form. In answer to a question of what her ministry plans for the next two to three years were she wrote in part: "I hope to continue to ready myself for involvement with our Latin American sisters (& brothers) should I see the way to do that after these next years in Carbondale." Yet she seemed unsure of her direction because she also wrote in answer to the same question, "There is no clarity for me at this time."

The following year found Kathleen still struggling. While she wrote that it seemed "a little too early to move away" from her student ministry in Carbondale, she began entertaining the idea of mission work in Liberia. "Sister Shirley has asked me to come to Liberia for a few years." The seed of her destiny, now planted, would continue to germinate for the next year. Still, Kathleen never gave up on her love of Latin America: "Eventually, of course, I think of South or Central America," she wrote.

But even the idea of serving with her fellow ASCs in Liberia had to be put on hold when in the summer of 1990 all of the Adorers on mission in Liberia at that time were called back home because of the deepening civil war in that country. After their escapes, Sisters Shirley Kolmer, Joél Kolmer, Antoinette Cusimano, Martha Wachtel, and Rachel Lawler were all settled back in Ruma by August of 1990. Though "settled" is perhaps the wrong word to use; if anything, the missionaries were "unsettled" and restless as they lobbied for a return "home" to Africa. Eventually Shirley and Joél would go back to Liberia, but Toni and Martha would never again set foot on their beloved Liberian soil and Rachel would return only once as a visitor.

Kathleen's decision to go to Liberia came as a surprise to those who knew her. In truth, she even surprised herself. She had always sought to be of service to others, to "finding a ministry which answers an urgent need" where she could put her talents to use for the dispossessed. "I feel that discernment was accurate," she wrote in a letter to Sister Fran Schumer, ASC, in February of 1991, "but it was what I need to do about it that has taken me off guard.... This realization is quite contrary to my own expectations.... Shirley and Antoinette had often urged me to come to Liberia, but never before have I felt I was supposed to be there. Now I believe I am supposed to go."

The dispossessed of Liberia had presented themselves in all their aching need to Kathleen. Whatever the impetus, once she had comprehended their plight, she was incapable of looking away or turning back. In her time in Liberia she would minister to those who had been emotionally scarred by the war, especially the school children. And she would tend to the mundane household needs of her fellow sisters with generosity and grace. No task that had honor would be too small for Sister Kathleen McGuire, whether it be baking bread over an open fire, or keeping the convent floor swept.

ALWAYS SEARCHING

Kathleen thought deeply about how to live as truthfully and with as much integrity as she could. She pondered the mysterious life of Jesus for indications of how to model her own. She saw Jesus as a searcher who first had to discover and then grow into his ministry. Jesus, she wrote, had to make "personal sense of the God he came to know from Joseph, from Mary, from the community of believers, from his own listening to the Hebrew Scriptures." Finally, when he felt the call to public ministry, he understood "he had to speak." She talks of Jesus "getting his head and heart straight about how to do the mission he had received...learning to be faithful rather than successful." Jesus' faithfulness led him to a realization: he must go "up to Jerusalem" to face the authorities.

In her understanding, Jesus "was faced with the temptation to keep on keeping on." His work was deeply appreciated and needed after all. Still, the reign of God could come about only when he made the choice to face his adversaries in Jerusalem, knowing full well this would most likely mean his own death.

Her following words have a chill of foreshadowing: "But, if I choose like Jesus to be totally faithful, even when that fidelity brings me into life and death conflict with religious leaders and with political leaders as it did for Jesus, the reign of God is present fully in my life and the rest I let go." In a battered world, Kathleen put her faith in the power of "one space-time bound human life given over completely to the reign of God" to be able to make limitless changes for good. Her last act in life as a "space-time bound human" would be a courageous walk of but a few yards in the face of armed killers. That would be Kathleen's going up to Jerusalem moment, and it was about to be upon her.

Kathleen had always found inspiration in the lives of those who freely gave over their very human lives completely to the reign of God. In Oscar Romero, the Archbishop of San Salvador who was assassinated in 1980 while saying Mass, and Father Stan Rother, an American priest killed in Guatemala the following year by government troops, she found personal examples worth honoring. Each man had chosen to accompany Jesus on the "road to Jerusalem" by standing up to injustice, poverty, and torture being inflicted upon the poor by those in power, she wrote. She had visited the tombs of each man (in the case of Father Rother, only his heart is buried in Guatemala) in 1988 while on a visit to Central America.

Kathleen described the journey to the site of the American priest's church in Santiago Atitlan, where he had ministered to the indigenous Tzutuhil people. The account begins almost idyllically. She speaks of having an early breakfast at a local café then buying a ticket for the "lancha." It was a boat that would take her and her companions across Lake Atitlan to "the site of Stan Rother's ministry and death." She described the hour-long crossing as "lovely" and mentioned the "havoc" that cool breezes and sun reflecting off the water caused on their "winter skins." At the church, she describes seeing a funeral for a young man who had been killed the night before by the military. She writes of seeing "soldiers, guns in hands, spilling all over the town" as the funeral procession got underway. The sisters did not dawdle but returned to the shore for the boat ride back across the lake.

Sister Kris Shrader, ASC, was on that trip with Kathleen. She remembers seeing the bullet holes in the wall where Father Rother was gunned down by armed soldiers. "You can still see the blood stains," she said. Kris' voice is wobbly, like Katherine Hepburn's in her later years. When she talks of her own experiences in Central America, it is as if she is reading from a screen play. In the mid-1980s, while on a visit to Guatemala, she was recruited by a human rights organization, Peace Brigades International, to accompany leaders of the families of the "disappeared" as they moved about during the day.

Guatemala was the first Latin American state to use forced disappearances against those who opposed the government. It is estimated that over 40,000 citizens were "disappeared" during the civil war. "You went with these people hoping that your presence...would be a deterrent" from their being shot or killed, Kris explained to me. The expectation was that being in the company of a U.S. citizen would cause the authorities to hesitate before acting. Kris described the experience as being horrible and frightening. "We'd be followed. Chased. It was like a bad B movie," she said. The nun accompanied people on their daily rounds for two weeks. As she was leaving the country, she noticed her name in the newspaper. For simply escorting those the government deemed worrisome, she and her companions had been placed on a list of personae non-grata.

Like Kris, Sister Kathleen had also experienced some of the turbulence and danger of life in Latin America. In 1986, she took part in a Christmas delegation to El Salvador. She wrote of leaving Ruma for El Salvador on Christmas morning with messages, toys, and school supplies for children there. The trip, she wrote, was also an effort to show solidarity "with our suffering sisters and brothers" who were enduring a devastating civil war and recent earthquake. She said the hope was that the presence of U.S. citizens might "help protect... those whom the Salvadoran government might otherwise find it politically convenient to disappear."

Kathleen had come to El Salvador bearing assistance

courtesy of her home communities in southern Illinois. From the many towns where she had served—from Waterloo, to Shawneetown, to Belleville, to East St. Louis, to Pond Settlement—she gathered toys and messages for the children in the refugee camp of Calle Real. A local American bishop sent her off with a generous financial donation on behalf of his diocese, and her community in Ruma and family supported her with their prayers.

The trip would be eye-opening for Kathleen. She saw first-hand the people's suffering. A suffering she said "that is caused in large measure because our government makes it possible for their government to continue to wage this war against its own people." She spoke of military and paramilitary groups terrorizing those who sought to aid earthquake victims and of those who had "received death threats for aiding or organizing the poor."

She and some companions made an unscheduled trip to pray at the tombs of "the martyred Church women of Chelatenano." The women—three Catholic nuns, Maura Clarke, Ita Ford, and Dorothy Kazel, and a lay missionary, Jean Donovan—were raped and killed in 1980 by El Salvadorian security forces. (Ironically, in later years, many people would often confuse the murders of these four women in El Salvador with the killings of the five ASC sisters in Liberia.)

Kathleen describes the trip in some chilling detail: "Twelve miles from the town, we were stopped at the site of the country's largest military base, questioned, ordered onto the base, separated from our Salvadoran escorts, told to hand over our passports and visas one by one, lectured about the ingratitude of foreign visitors, and finally allowed to proceed under military escort." She goes on to describe the intimidating presence of soldiers who accompanied them to the site. "Not only did the soldiers ride facing us with their rifles aimed in our direction, but they surrounded us in the small cemetery and followed us again until we were well out of that 'department.'"

Though disturbed by this experience, Kathleen closes her report on an upbeat note, saying that in El Salvador she had experienced a "popular church" that is both "fruit and promise" of the spirit of Jesus, a church that goes beyond "doctrinal and creedal divisions" to minister to the "suffering body of Christ."

It is clear this is where Kathleen saw the hope for her Church. She believed, and paid for that belief with her life, that only in ministering to those who suffer and in standing up in the face of tyranny is the Church fulfilling its promise to its founder, Jesus, by walking by his side on the road to Jerusalem. When Kathleen McGuire left for Liberia in August of 1991, it was with full knowledge that she, too, was putting her feet on that same path.

FINAL DAYS

It might be said that action defined Sister Barbara Ann Muttra nearly as much as her religious calling did. Nursing had given her the opportunity to serve others in a material way that suited her dynamic personality. And when she found a place where she could contribute, she did so unstintingly and with her whole heart.

"Barbara loved wherever she was," said Sister Mildred Gross. But she always, "loved the people more than the place." Former lay missionary Theresa Hicks agreed, "Barbara totally loved the people. No one was excluded from her care. She was a woman of justice, faith, strength, and conviction."

Nowhere would her love of those denied justice be more prominently on display than in the tiny village of Klay, where in 1991, hundreds of refugees were living on the mission that she and Sister Antoinette Cusimano had started in 1982. And nowhere would her faith in human nature and strength of character be tested more often than when she came face to face with armed men, often boys, at the numerous checkpoints she had to pass through to get there. For though Barbara was back in Liberia, she was not permitted to live in Klay, which was now in rebel hands. She and the other sisters all lived in the Gardnersville convent in an area that, at the time, was considered safer due to its proximity to Monrovia and ECO-MOG peacekeepers.

Stuck in Gardnersville, Barbara longed to get back to Klay. Letters home reflected this longing: "I have not been able to settle down as yet in my own mission as Taylor keeps sending different rebels in our area," she wrote. But within weeks of her return, she was behind the wheel of a donated truck and ferrying supplies behind rebel lines to Klay, which lay cut off from most other assistance.

"On August 20, CRS (Catholic Relief Services) got me a pass to travel to Bomi." Her relief work, she wrote, granted her rare access to travel into occupied territories. "I have an open pass from the General in Command of the Bomi, Lofa, and Cape Mount areas." When Barbara finally saw her old mission for the first time in a year and a half she could hardly contain her joy: "My, I had to cry at all the hugs and kisses and welcomes I received. It was almost like a different place. The people (refugees) now around 400 had built 33 thatch huts across the school playground and almost to the very tall palm tree. They also made gardens beyond the huts." Barbara went on to say that her former convent now housed seven children and one adult and that Sister Agnes' old room had been converted into a storeroom for food for a special feeding program. The school also housed refugees with seven families to a classroom. "They make their beds from school benches and desks."

Barbara's old clinic was still operating under the guidance of a licensed practical nurse and two physician's assistants. However, they saw only 40 patients a day. For Barbara, who had operated her clinic until the last patient of the day was seen and treated, this was a hard pill to swallow. "I don't like that," she complained, "but can't control it from this side. They hardly get enough intake to pay their salaries."

Open pass or not, travel between Monrovia and Klay was far from worry-free. "There were 14 checkpoints between the Po River bridge and Klay," she wrote. "ECOMOG ends at the beginning of the bridge and rebels start at the end of the bridge. It was really heart rending to see so many young kids at the check-point with guns over their shoulders." Later, Barbara had this assessment of the soldiers who manned the checkpoints: "The soldiers are nice to me and call me the 'ole Ma' and I preach to them about love and peace and we get along fine."

This diminutive, grandmotherly figure, nearing her 70th birthday, dared to stand toe to toe with soldiers, some barely more than boys armed with guns and machetes, and preach to them about love and peace. The older ones may have remembered what love and peace were like, but for the youngest ones, these were probably just abstract concepts they barely grasped. They had been fed a steady diet of fear and violence and encouraged to allow their hatreds to run wild. Still, Sister Barbara would offer the young ones a stick of gum and a kind word. And most of the time that would do the trick.

But as time wore on, those seemingly cordial relations would wear thin as the rebels became more suspicious of white people and of Catholic missionaries in particular. And since they were often hungry, because Charles Taylor did not always provide food for his troops, they became more belligerent. In May of 1992 Barbara writes that at one of the many checkpoints she passed through, rebel soldiers "took 3 bags of rice out of the 8 bags I had for the people." When soldiers at a later checkpoint also demanded rice, "I refused.... I could only carry enough for the people who did not have access to food." As a punishment, she was forced to unload and reload the heavy bags of rice in her car. That trip took her four hours to cover the 20 miles from Monrovia to Klay. Yet the increasing harassment did nothing to deter the nun's weekly supply runs. While the roads remained closed to ordinary travel, "I still go every week with CRS to take food supplies, clothes, and drugs to the mission. Presently their (sic) are 304 displaced on the mission and 116 on the Peace Corps campus." Though she did concede, "What an ordeal to go through those 14 checkpoints from the Po River to Klay!"

Towards the end of 1991, Barbara's letters revealed how the NPFL's attitude towards foreign missionaries was beginning to sour. She explained that anyone possessing a car in rebel territory was a target and in danger of having it confiscated by the soldiers. She recounted how Father Garry Jenkins, pastor of the mission in Bomi Hills, received a note from Nelson Taylor requesting the use of his car for military purposes. At midnight the next day, four men came to the mission and at gunpoint took the car and all the cash the priest had on hand, threatening not only Father Garry but the 16 people who were sheltering in the rectory.

While the incident may have given Barbara momentary pause, it did not deter her efforts to shuttle needed supplies to the refugees in Klay. Indeed, she began transporting Garry, too, as she explained: "...still a lot of harrassment (sic) at the check point (rebels) wanting some food or medicine. When we were taking Gary (sic) to Monrovia they made Gary take everything out of his suitcase suspicioning (sic) him to be a spy. He had letters to mail and they read most of them—took about 1 hr. It made me weak! They wouldn't let Gary go until he dashed (bribed) them."

Sister Kathleen McGuire's assessment of the rebel-held checkpoints is equally as bleak. In an October 1991 entry in the Gardnersville annals she talks of the harassment that Barbara and other Catholic Relief Service volunteers undergo as they ferry needed supplies to the Bomi area, citing the constant "questionings, the lectures, the searching of vehicles, bags and persons, the hostile attitude, and the forced delays" that she says "frustrate the CRS personnel almost beyond endurance." By Christmas of 1991, the roads had gotten much more dangerous. Relief agencies were no longer heading into the territory controlled by Taylor's forces and Barbara was warned not to try a run to Klay, a warning she summarily ignored.

Since Barbara would not be deterred, the rest of the sisters and the aspirants decided to lend a hand in packing up gift bags for the children by forming an impromptu assembly line, bagging up small trinkets for the displaced children that could be handed out at Christmas. But there was genuine concern for Barbara's safety. On December 23, Sister Kathleen recorded: "Barbara Ann left for Klay with Christmas dinner supplies for the displaced. We are concerned since she went alone. Rebels have begun confiscating NGO vehicles again and so no agency will allow their cars to cross behind the lines just now."

Of course, a little rebel insurgency was not going to keep Barbara from her mission. Kathleen's next lines express both admiration and exasperation: "Barbara roused the bishop from bed, demanding a car! She got a truck and packed it and headed out." In a letter from that time, Barbara recorded her trip this way: "As we had planned over 600 people to feed since our village people come to Mass Christmas Day, I went with $500 candy, $300 fish and pigs feet, and gifts for Father and the children 2 days before Christmas. It took me three and a half hours to go 19 miles through 14 check points, but what a joy it was to see how happy the people were to see me."

Then, in February of 1992, Barbara would became a victim of the NPFL's policy of commandeering vehicles. It was a particular embarrassment for her since the truck she was driving was the one she borrowed from the bishop. "On Feb. 11, my weekly trip to Klay to take food and medicines," she related, "6 soldiers came to take the pick-up truck I was using. They promised they would try to return it after the fighting ceased on the border. The Colonel who sent them refused to return it, so after one and a half weeks waiting in the mission, I went to their headquarters 15 miles up the road from our mission, since we were out of food. After many trips to the general's office, I finally met him and he was very nice to me and said he would tell the colonel to return the car. Well the colonel refused, since he said I gave him the car."

Back in Gardnersville, the other sisters nervously awaited Barbara's return from Klay during each of her trips. Sister Kathleen recorded their concerns this way:

Feb. 10: Barbara goes to Klay with food.

Feb. 11: Barbara was to have returned this afternoon. She does not come.

Feb. 12: In the afternoon a Baptist relief minister Ed Laughferty stopped to tell us he had just come from Klay and brought word that Barbara is OK but without her truck. The NPFL sent a 6-man contingent to demand the use of the truck for 24 hours. Some of them were armed. They assured her they would not drive the truck out of the area.... Eventually she handed over the keys. She waits in Klay for the truck's return at 4 PM today.

Feb. 13: Barbara does not return.

Feb. 14: Barbara does not return.

Feb. 17: A woman from Klay stops at SPHS (Saint Patrick's High School) to bring word from Barbara that she's fine but stays "behind the lines" working to get the truck back.

Apparently satisfied that Sister Barbara Ann was temporarily safe, the succeeding days of the annals continue to record the everyday activities of the sisters with no further mention of Barbara's quest until these entries:

Mar. 3: Barbara returned from Klay overnite (sic). She has not given up on getting the truck back. Meanwhile she received a cool welcome from the bishop and the diocesan bursar!

Mar. 6: Shirley makes the monthly call to Ruma. There's not a lot of news exchanged. We make little of the fact that the NPFL took the truck Barbara drove into the territory.

That same day, Barbara recorded in a letter that she, "finally met the 'Chief of Staff,' Taylor's assistant, and he personally took me to the colonel and so returned the pick-up." Two days later she arrives in Gardnersville, and the convent log reports:

> *Mar. 8: Barbara Ann arrives, driving the orange truck! Fathers Garry Jenkins and Balaswami were with her, Garry loudly and continuously proclaiming how terrific Barbara had been in her confidence and persistence. The truck was somewhat abused but still runs. Barbara insists she felt the support of our prayers.*

But a further entry in the convent annals a few days later strikes a more ominous note:

> *Mar. 11: Barbara Ann's birthday. She and Shirley carry supplies to Klay and return. There's tension "behind the lines."*

Indeed, tension was building, and from then on, every trip to Klay would be even more of an ordeal. "So all went well," Barbara recorded, "until the last weekend, when I was supposed to return with the supply of rice, oil, and beans for our 250 refugees when another incursion started which then put an embargo on food and supplies coming into the area. The people will be all right this week, but next week with

God's power, I will have to chance it again."

In mid-April, a Catholic missionary priest assigned to Kakata, Father Serophino Dolpont, was arrested by Taylor's NPFL on suspicion of espionage. Sister Kathleen wrote that the accusation was based on an article in a Catholic magazine that criticized Taylor and the NPFL. In spite of the increasing threats, Barbara was undaunted. She packed up the bishop's Korando with food and picked up Father Garry so they could deliver the provisions to Klay, which had been cut off from supplies for weeks. Despite encountering increased harassment from rebels, they made it through.

By May, Sister Barbara's health may have begun to decline under the continued stress. She offers a clue in a May 6, 1992, letter that states, "We are all now in that age of having health problems, but that is to be expected." But that is as far as she would go in acknowledging that her cancer may have returned. In spite of how she felt, she continued to bring food and supplies to the refugees living on the campus in Klay.

Far more concerned about the state of others than in her own health, Barbara reflected sadly on life in Liberia: "Many people are still being killed, tortured, or starved because of their tribes." Then she adds, "I'm so glad to be here to assist the people when I can and be a support to them in their suffering. War is just so terrible."

She concludes her letter with a request: "Please continue your prayers for peace, as so many people are still being killed, tortured, and starved. It's a terrible guerilla war!" Very soon, she will be completely cut off from Klay; not even her pass to travel the roads will be honored. In her very last letter, dated October 4, 1992, just 16 days before her death, Barbara admits to the growing desperation of the people and her inability to help them. "And now Liberia is again on the brink of another war. How sad it is that people cannot meet and settle their differences, but just continue fighting and killing innocent civilians." Her letter goes on to explain that many of the people in Bomi County fled to Monrovia when ULIMO fighters (soldiers who had once served in Samuel K. Doe's army), began crossing into Liberia from Sierra Leone and attacking Bomi. "The soldiers have taken over our mission. The commander is living in the convent and soldiers in Father's house and around the campus."

Now confined to Gardnersville and the area around Monrovia Barbara writes: "There are over 40,000 displaced and refugees now here in Monrovia, and it's just overwhelming as to know what and where to go to help, as everyone is in dire need...and many are suffering."

Though suffering herself, Barbara hid it well. Most, including Father Michael Moran, one of the last people to see her alive, did not even know she was dealing with cancer. "I never saw her weaken," he said. Barbara's only thoughts were for others: "And so God continues to bless us all and has spared my life from the gun, so I know God wants me to continue to be courage and strength for these people. It may take a while to rebuild lives, but praise God I will be here to help when the time is ripe, even though it may take months for peace to come." She closes as she has every letter for decades: "Love you, Sister Barbara Ann."

ROGUES

By late 1991, not even Gardnersville was safe anymore. Emboldened by the lawless nature of a country at war with itself, roving bands of armed thieves preyed upon their fellow citizens with impunity, robbing and terrorizing businesses as well as private homes. The only recourse ordinary people had to protect themselves was either to hire private security guards or to surround their property with high walls and fencing. The Precious Blood sisters did both, albeit somewhat unwillingly.

The convent had previously been secured with a 6-foot-high wall, but the increase in "rogue" activity (as Liberians are wont to call the marauders) convinced the sisters to raise their protective wall to 10 feet and top it with shards of glass. Entry to their property was secured by a locked metal gate. Security guards were on duty at night and, later, even during the daylight hours as well.

The convent journal kept by Sister Kathleen for September 12, 1991, reads: "Most of us were awakened when a commotion outside climaxed in shouts of 'Rogue! Rogue!' and the sound of shattering glass." She goes on to say that night guards employed by the sisters succeeded in chasing off the intruders, but only after they had successfully scaled the compound's wall. The journal continues: "The Bishop and others have been telling us to raise our 6-foot wall.... We are very reluctant, yet all predictions are that in the aftermath of such a violent and bloody civil war, armed robberies and violent crimes will increase dramatically. Our present alternatives seem to be 1) moving, but we are not sure we would find safe housing; 2) leaving the country; or 3) raising the wall. So, we'll raise the wall." Apparently, options one and two were never seriously considered.

Not to be put off by a danger they could deal with, the sisters went about the jobs of helping their Liberian neighbors. When Sister Elizabeth Kolmer visited Liberia in the summer of 1992, what she saw was a veritable beehive of activity. On a typical day, she said, the sisters would get up and Joël would have a breakfast of oatmeal ready for everyone. Then Shirley would head to Saint Patrick's for several hours of work, heading home around 2 p.m. for lunch and, during the hot dry season, a nap. A bit later, she would head back to school for a few more hours. "When I was there," said Elizabeth, "I went to the office with Shirley and helped out with odd jobs. I would hear the staff people interact with Shirley and I could tell they held her in high regard. They often referred to her as 'Old Ma' which was a compliment."

The other sisters would be busy with their own particular work. Barbara Ann, said Elizabeth, was single-focused on taking care of the people in Klay who she felt "were in her charge." Elizabeth describes accompanying Barbara on one of her supply runs. "When the children saw her car drive into the yard, all the little kids came running up and yelling, 'Barbara Ann, Barbara Ann!'"

Elizabeth also witnessed firsthand the difficulties of attempting to restock the necessary supplies for the schools the sisters were running. On the streets of Monrovia, people would set up stands to sell items that had been, most likely, looted. "It was like a national swap meet," she said. Since all of the books from Saint Patrick's High School were stolen, Shirley was impelled to locate books. She found a seller just outside the Ministry of Education building offering a number, many stamped *Property of Saint Patrick's*. With a shrug, as if to say there was no sense in protesting, she bought them back.

OPERATION OCTOPUS

On October 15, 1992, while peace negotiations among the Economic Community of West African States (ECOWAS), the Interim Government of National Unity (IGNU), and various rebel factions were taking place in Cotonou, Benin, Charles Taylor's soldiers launched a well-coordinated attack on Monrovia. The multi-pronged push, called "Operation Octopus," was designed to capture the Liberian capital and unseat Amos Sawyer, the interim president, so that Taylor could wrest control of the government for himself. Though Taylor's National Patriotic Front of Liberia (NPFL) rebels controlled an estimated 90 percent of the countryside, where they had set up a parallel, quasi-government, the seat of internationally-recognized legitimate power remained in Monrovia.

As designed, Operation Octopus would surprise the West African peacekeepers and the other forces guarding the capital. But the defenders would quickly regain their footing and push back against Octopus, causing it to devolve into a bloody 120-day siege of Monrovia. In 1993, Human Rights Watch reported: "The situation exploded on October 15, when Taylor launched 'Operation Octopus,' attacking ECO-MOG positions around Monrovia, and even striking at the AFL, which was encamped at its Schiefflin barracks on the outskirts of the city."

The assault continued for months, as ECOMOG soldiers struggled to repel the several thousand-strong rebel army's advance. Suburban areas around Monrovia like Gardnersville, Barnersville, New Georgia, and Caldwell were especially vulnerable due to their proximity to the capital but lack of government protection, and therefore they suffered greatly from the fighting. The report states that about 200,000 people were displaced during the onslaught and fled either towards the center of Monrovia or were pushed into the interior, which put them behind NPFL lines. Many civilians, however, never made it and would be summarily executed by the rebels. The Human Rights Watch report goes on to say:

> As in the past, the NPFL often used young boys and teenagers, many of whom were intoxicated, to attack Monrovia. Some of these children belonged to the Small Boys Unit (SBU), which has become one of Taylor's most trusted divisions. Scores, and probably hundreds, of these boys died in the swamps surrounding Monrovia. Since the NPFL fighters are not paid, they were promised the loot of Monrovia, often including a house. Indeed, many of the houses that were not destroyed were "claimed" by NPFL fighters, who wrote their names or units on the outside walls, hoping to return to claim the homes after the fighting.

The World Health Organization (WHO) estimated that approximately 3,000 civilians and combatants died in the 4-month siege. Various groups of fighters besides the NPFL, including the AFL and ULIMO, engaged in ethnic "score-settling," which resulted in high civilian casualties. The WHO went on to state that between December of 1992 and February of 1993 "scores of human skulls and decomposed bodies" were discovered in Gardnersville, as well as 300 more bodies found in a nearby suburb and a mass grave discovered on the Firestone Plantation. In a 2013 article, the Coalition for Justice in Liberia described Operation Octopus this way:

Verifiable and documented reports, including revelations made at the public hearings of Liberia's Truth and Reconciliation Commission (TRC) a few years ago, uncovered that the Operation Octopus was conceived with the purpose of implementing a pogrom to ensure that the NPFL exerted full and total control over the City of Monrovia and its environs. This would become the NPFL's scorched-earth policy and template for prosecuting its senseless war throughout the 1990s, making the city unsafe and unlivable for its inhabitants, and meting out unspeakable crimes to instill fear and submission in the populace.

General Christopher "Mosquito" Vambo was identified as the general who, acting on orders from NPFL leader Taylor, spearheaded the operation. He has also been named by survivors and others as the man who orchestrated the murders of Sisters Shirley Kolmer, Agnes Mueller, and Kathleen McGuire at their Gardnersville convent. He has denied this accusation. Following is an eyewitness account of the early stages of Operation Octopus. It was related in conversation several years after the war and recorded in Jerome Cabeen's *Memoirs of a Reluctant Servant*:

I was living in Monrovia at the time the rebels launched the Octopus attack. I lived in a residential area off the Capitol-Bypass Road. Around 2 or 3 in the morning I heard a shrill whistle and I thought it was a teapot or something outside. Then I heard another and they got louder and closer. I jumped up and found a huge cement barrel to hide in out back of where I was staying. That bomb blew up stores and houses a block from where I was. The ground shook terribly and already I could hear people screaming.

Cabeen then went on to describe a horrific scene in which numerous child-soldiers became entrapped in the swamps surrounding Monrovia. Sitting on sandbars, the boys huddled together and waved white flags of surrender as alligators attacked them. By all accounts, the children, some as young as 10, were expendable. Taylor's pursuit of victory was so single-focused that the fate of the Small Boys' Unit was inconsequential. They were but chum on the water, intended to draw out the soldiers defending the capital. The boys, in thrall to a deadly combination of drugs (mostly "brown-brown," a concoction of gunpowder and cocaine), sex, and mysticism, were told that the city had already fallen and that they could claim the spoils. That one lie would cost hundreds of them their lives.

Many of the young boys fighting this ungodly war had been taken from their families against their wills and pressed into service. Some were drawn to the fight as a way to avenge the death of a father or mother. Almost all were driven by a desire for food, protection, and companionship. Without parental guidance to help set their moral course, the youngsters sought recognition and approval from soulless commanding officers who promised them great rewards. Members of the Small Boys Unit, estimated in 1992 to number around 570, were even assigned to Taylor's personal security detail. The children became calloused killers. They committed unspeakable acts in the name of their leaders.

In 1994, Human Rights Watch examined the phenomenon of using children to fight in wars with its September 8 report titled *Easy Prey: Child Soldiers in Liberia*. The agency interviewed child soldiers, social workers, rebel commanders, and many more in its April 1994 fact-finding mission to Liberia that provided the basis for the report. Below are some excerpts from *Easy Prey*:

> *Some children were the most vicious, brutal fighters of all. I once saw a nine-year-old kill someone at a checkpoint. Children learn by imitation; they saw killings and then when their commanding officers ordered them to kill, they did. Some of the kids killed out of fear; they were told they would be killed if they didn't carry out orders to kill.*—child care worker

> *They gave me pills that made me crazy. When the craziness got in my head, I beat people on their heads and hurt them until they bled.*—13-year-old soldier

Kids have told us that they were actually forced to witness the execution of members of their family or their friends. If they screamed or cried, they were killed. Boys have told us of being lined up to watch executions and being forced to applaud. If you didn't applaud, you could be next.—counselor for former child soldiers

It's a children's war. Kids get promoted in rank for committing an atrocity; they can cut off someone's head without thinking. The troops move into a village; they take everything and kill and rape. They stay there a couple of weeks and then move on. The children are all part of this. There's almost never a real attack against the other side. It's civilians who are attacked; it's not soldiers against soldiers. Relatively few soldiers have been killed. But thousands of people have been displaced and turned into refugees.—ULIMO's Chief Operations Officer, Colonel Winkler

In a tortured explanation that defies logic, Taylor explained to a reporter that arming the children was a "means of control." He is quoted in a 1992 Atlantic magazine article as saying, "We keep them armed as a means of keeping them out of trouble." If keeping the children out of trouble was Taylor's true aim, his methods were a miserable failure.

After the final fall of Charles Taylor's government, an American missionary serving in Liberia, Jerome Cabeen, encountered some grown-up child soldiers on the streets of Monrovia. Pariahs for their part in the murderous civil war, missing limbs and unemployed, many of these young men were forced to beg on the streets for survival. In his personal memoir, Cabeen recounted his meeting with five former child soldiers.

> *"Hey my man, white man, my good friend I beg you please hear me-o." The speaker was a man of about 25. He was missing a leg and supported himself with a single crutch. Soon he was joined by four more men. All had missing legs; all were dressed in cast-off clothing. They had come to share a common story. Each had been a soldier during the war serving one rebel band or another. One of the group, called Little General, began his story by saying, "My man, we had guns, drugs, sex, and death all before we were sixteen."*

Another of the young men described how he had been forced at age 14 to shoot his own brother by a commander in the Movement for Democracy in Liberia (MODEL), a rebel group that sprang up in the later years of the civil war. Then yet another told his story. He said their unit often played a game called "Guess of Death" where two youngsters were blindfolded and a third was given a gun. Prisoners of the rebels would be lined up in front of a freshly dug trench, then shot. The object of the game was for the blindfolded boys to identify by sound the kind of gun used to murder the prisoners. The winner of the contest would get to have a hot meal and sex with one of the euphemistically called "teaching mamas" who accompanied the soldiers. The loser would bury the bodies.

Undoubtedly the most egregious "game" the bored child soldiers indulged in targeted pregnant women, where the object was to guess the sex of her unborn child. One of the men explained to Cabeen:

> After the bet was placed one of the children would come out of the bush and shoot the expectant mother through the back of the head. The other child soldier would open up the mother's womb with a knife and remove the unborn baby to determine the winner.

It was obvious that the young man had played this game himself and was ashamed. When asked what the winner of the bet won, he quietly replied, "a pack of cigarettes or a beer."

When Charles Taylor uttered his nonsensical statement about giving AK47s to 10-year-olds "as a means of keeping them out of trouble," everyone knew he didn't care about the cost of this decision to the children or to their victims. All Taylor wanted was fighters, and if his fighters were small an automatic weapon was a great equalizer.

FIRESTONE'S BLOODY HANDS

Besides being a great manipulator of children, Charles Taylor was also astute at deception. His persuasive personality would fool former U.S. President Jimmy Carter, a devout Baptist, into thinking Taylor was a true believer who only had the best interest of the Liberian people at heart. When Taylor met with Carter on a visit to Liberia, Taylor showcased his religious devotion by intentionally displaying a Bible on his desk. The warlord was also a master of turning human greed to his benefit.

In 2014, *ProPublica* released the first of several articles concerning the October 1992 Operation Octopus offensive. In the series, they carefully examined the relationship between Charles Taylor and Firestone, lessee of a 220-square mile rubber plantation in the heart of Liberia. One of the articles described how "killers launched from the plantation" one night in October 1992. This was the beginning of the deadly assault on Monrovia. The series exposes Firestone, which is owned and operated by an American subsidiary of the Bridgestone Corporation of Japan, as culpable in Operation Octopus. For a year and a half before Octopus, Firestone had supported the NPFL, perhaps less than wholeheartedly, as Taylor "built his army of butchers and believers in part with the resources of one of America's most iconic businesses: Firestone." In return for housing, funding, and other considerations, Taylor's rebels provided security to the plantation and enabled it to resume operations previously halted by the war. While other international businesses closed up shop in Liberia, Firestone chose to continue running its business there, thereby encouraging the company to make deals with the NPFL that are now viewed as reprehensible by all civilized nations.

The *ProPublica/Frontline* story described the well-coordinated Operation Octopus attack pressed by the NPFL as it sought to capture Monrovia. Four prongs, or arms of the octopus, began advancing on the capital in a pincer movement on Friday night, October 15. One point of attack originated in Caldwell, which lies to the north and west of Monrovia; a second line came from Bomi Hills and pushed south. But two points of the rebel attack originated some 50 miles east of Monrovia, from within the Firestone Rubber Plantation, where several thousand NPFL troops had been living for over a year. While General Christopher Vambo's attack came from the northern region of the Firestone plantation, a simultaneous attack was being launched from its southern region near the city of Harbel (a town originally named for Harvey Firestone and his wife Idabelle). All four prongs of Octopus were designed to meet on the outskirts of the capital and then overwhelm it. Fortunately for Liberia's interim government, though they had been caught by surprise, West African soldiers and others guarding Monrovia were able to fend off the rebels.

"Liberia: Firestone and the Warlord" outlined a host of shameful connections and concessions made by Firestone to Taylor to keep their plantation running during the early war years. The company denies having had "a collaborative relationship with Charles Taylor," yet concedes that Taylor's rebels had been allowed to use Firestone's machinery, food, and other supplies, but only, it said, under "obvious threat."

Motivations may be murky for Firestone's complicity with the rebels, but what is crystal clear is that the plantation was the headquarters from which General Vambo led 2,000 troops in the Octopus assault. This would be the strike force to capture Gardnersville. And Vambo, under his war name of "General Mosquito," would be the man identified by survivors as the leader of the attack on the Gardnersville convent that resulted in the murder and violation of three American missionary sisters, Agnes Mueller, Kathleen McGuire, and Shirley Kolmer on Friday, October 23, 1992.

ProPublica was not the first to condemn Firestone for its complicity in the Liberian Civil War and the deaths of the sisters. The United Steelworkers of America, in September of 1996, prepared an extensive report on the company's sins in the war and labeled the Firestone Plantation the "command and control center" for Operation Octopus. However, the 43-page paper, titled *Preliminary Report: Bridgestone/Firestone's Role in the Liberian Civil War*, was buried for almost two decades. The Steelworkers' report is detailed and highly sourced. It is clear that their investigators went to considerable trouble to discover Firestone's involvement in the Liberian Civil War. Following are some excerpts:

> *The Liberian warlords, including Taylor, have utilized foreign commercial partners to gain access to hard currency that arms their soldiers and sustains their alternative governments. Firestone's agreement with Charles Taylor did just that, providing Taylor with the means to resist peace and launch attacks on other warring factions and peacekeeping troops.... Bridgestone/Firestone's role in the Liberian civil war is a stunning example of a transnational arrogance in pursuit of profit, heedless of the human cost of its actions.*

> *"Octopus" is perhaps the cruelest result of collaboration between Firestone and the NPFL. The Interim Government and ECOMOG have credibly accused Firestone of helping Taylor's army by allowing it to stockpile weapons on its property and use its communications equipment to direct the offensive. Moreover, during this period of intense bloodshed, Firestone continued to ship its product out of Liberia through Buchanan, a port controlled by the NPFL.*

> *NPFL atrocities also reached new heights during "Operation Octopus." In late October 1992—the month when Firestone produced 4.7 million pounds of latex and*

block rubber in Harbel and exported 600,000 pounds of block rubber through Buchanan—five American nuns were murdered by NPFL soldiers in Gardnersville, a suburb of Monrovia. On October 23, the rebels came to the nuns' convent and shot Sister Kathleen McGuire, a Lebanese businessman seeking refuge for his family, Sister Agnes Mueller, and Sister Shirley Kilmer (sic). The killers mutilated their bodies, hacking at their dead flesh and limbs with machetes. A few days earlier, two other nuns were killed by NPFL soldiers in ambush.

The report went on to call the deaths of innocent civilians "a direct and terrible consequence of Firestone's collaboration with Taylor." It documented payments made by the company to the warlord and said that Taylor used those payments "to buy arms and maintain his opposition to the internationally recognized Interim Government of Liberia and the peacekeeping force sent in by ECOWAS, which was supported by the United States and the United Nations." Indeed, Charles Taylor himself testified in his war-crimes trial at The Hague over a decade and a half later that Firestone's cooperation was vital to his success.

Page five of the Steelworkers report states: "The goal of this investigation is to make Firestone fully accountable to the Liberian people and to the world, in the hope that its exposure will prevent it from happening again." The reality, though, was that the union's motives were less altruistic than represented in the report. Two weeks after the paper was finished, a new labor deal was approved that ended a bitter standoff between Firestone and striking workers represented by the United Steelworkers of America. The paper was buried. It would be 18 long years before it finally saw the light of day.

THE OCTOPUS TIGHTENS ITS GRIP

Father Michael Moran, SMA, knew Gardnersville well. He had been the pastor of Saint Anthony's Catholic Church in the town prior to being appointed provincial of his order for Liberia and Sierra Leone. It was during his tenure at Saint Anthony's that he became friends with the ASC sisters living in Gardnersville. They all attended daily Mass at Saint Anthony's and were active in and around the church community.

Early on Monday, October 19, 1992, Father Michael made the 14-mile trip inland from the coast, where he was living in the SMA fathers' beach house, a consequence of his administrative role as provincial. His intent was to stop at Saint Anthony's parish to check on fellow SMA, Father James Hickey, the current pastor, and then look in on the Precious Blood sisters. That morning, Michael passed through several ECOMOG checkpoints on his drive to Gardnersville without incident. He remembered the drive as "easy." It was probably about this same time that Sisters Shirley and Joél

Kolmer were also on the road. Their destination was the campus of Saint Teresa's convent in downtown Monrovia where Sister Barbara Brillant, FMM, lived. They carried with them a malfunctioning short-wave radio.

Though it was the fourth day of Operation Octopus, people were still moving about freely and were more or less going about their business. A growing number of refugees were pouring in from the countryside, passing through Gardnersville on their way to the capital. Some stopped to take temporary shelter at churches and schools where they could rest and with luck get a bowl of hot rice. But most would not dawdle too long. Taylor's rebels, the NPFL, coaxed them onward with artillery blasts and rocket launchers at their backs.

The more seasoned missionaries like Father Michael and the Precious Blood nuns had seen this before in 1990, so they tried to remain calm and stay the course, hoping the situation would not become untenable for them. What they could not know, however, was that they were at the tip of a spear and that within just a day that spear would strike with ruthless vigor, stabbing any and all with intentional brutality.

Michael, now long returned from Liberia, lives in the United States in community with other SMAs, also retired from the mission fields, in Tenafly, N.J. He serves as the American Provincial for the Society of African Missions. He shared some of his memories of those chaotic last days with me. "I had lunch with the sisters on October 19," he said. "But first I went to see Father Hickey."

"I knew there was fighting in the area." But, he admits to being "able to go into that great world of denial." The fighting, Michael said, "seemed far off." And though shelling could be heard in the distance, he felt confident in the ECOMOG troops and their ability to hold off the rebels.

Michael spent the morning with Father James, who had begun to open the grounds of Saint Anthony's to refugees. While there were just a few people taking shelter that morning, by the next day the situation would grow increasingly severe.

After completing his visit with James, Michael traveled the short distance down the Gardnersville Road to check on the ASC sisters. All five were home. While there was some unease in the group, there was also a resolve to stay the course. "We sat around and talked a bit about what they would do. The three (Agnes, Kathleen, and Joél) were a little bit frightened. But it was obvious that Shirley and Barbara knew what they were going to do." Kathleen and Agnes, he said, were "very, very quiet."

It was Michael's belief that the five had already talked things through together and made the decision to stay for the time being. The undeniable leaders of the little ASC community were Shirley and Barbara. "They knew from the inside what had to be done," the priest said. But being good leaders, they also consulted the others. Such an important decision as this would have been made with much reflection and input from each person. Indeed, in all likelihood the group would have prayed long and hard over their decision to remain in Gardnersville rather than retreat to Monrovia. Calling on their 1990 experience, the women would also have been pragmatic and had a contingency escape plan. In fact, in a lengthy profile of the sisters printed after their deaths, *The St. Louis Post Dispatch* reported that if they were forced to flee, the sisters had decided they would stay on the continent and not return to the U.S. Sister Joël is quoted as saying, "I love Liberia. I don't want to leave."

Father Michael said the Gardnersville ASC community functioned well under the guidance of Sisters Shirley and Barbara, dynamic women who had the "maturity and humility to recognize what was right." The other three, he thought, needed that leadership and as a group, "they complemented one another." Understanding their group dynamic, the sisters' decision to remain in Gardnersville, at least for the time being, came as no surprise to the priest, especially since "things weren't that bad that day (the 19th), so I understood why they said they would stay." Then, ruefully, he added, "I thought I could check on them the next day, but by then everything changed."

The night of October 19, five rockets fell on Monrovia. Many people were killed, though none of the rockets hit their intended target, which was the Ducor Hotel where Interim Liberian President Amos Sawyer was lodging. For the wounded, there were no ambulances, let alone open hospitals. People bled to death where they fell. An ECOMOG contingent of Guinean soldiers was sent out to meet the rebels on the roads around Gardnersville, where the ASC sisters were sheltering in their convent. Other ECOMOG soldiers, reported to be Senegalese, were deployed toward the swamps and the airfield.

It was reported that defending interim government soldiers were able to hold back the waves of child fighters that night, but at great emotional cost. Grown men were called upon to fire into hordes of advancing child soldiers. Hundreds of the boys died; many who were trapped in the swamps drowned or were killed by alligators.

The five ASC missionaries would have likely heard the bombardment of Monrovia. The journal kept by the sisters may have recorded how they spent the night of October 19, perhaps taking shelter under tables or beds, but that journal was lost or destroyed in the aftermath of their murders. So, we have no firsthand account from them. But we do have eyewitness testimony that states the next morning the sisters were up and about, apparently unbowed by the rocket attack and ready to tackle the day by teaching at Saint Michael's School, ministering to the sick and injured, or doing whatever they could in service of the Liberian people.

FINAL HOURS

NPFL forces had been advancing through the countryside from several different approaches for days, raping, burning, and murdering their way towards the prize that Taylor coveted the most: Monrovia. As rebels swept their way through the country towards the capital, innocent people were caught up in the push. They were forced to abandon their homes and run for their lives taking what belongings they could carry. Not all of them would survive.

The soldiers had already proven that they would just as soon slaughter their fellow citizens as look at them. Decomposing bodies strewn along footpaths and roads bore this out. Newspaper reports written around this time describe a humanitarian crisis, as displaced people with their belongings on their heads and babies on their backs made their way by the thousands towards Monrovia and the hoped-for protection of the African peacekeepers who guarded it.

Realistically, theirs was a watery kind of hope. Too many

of their fellow citizens had already been butchered; victims of obscene violence. Too many villages had already been burned and people massacred for there to be anything resembling any optimism that once in Monrovia they would be safe. They had opened their eyes to the harshest of realities: Ordinary lives mattered very little to the warring parties that were now tearing their country apart. But they had no better option; they did the only thing they could. They marched on blistered, bleeding feet towards Monrovia, where they just might find refuge.

On Tuesday morning October 20, an ever-growing stream of people passed through Gardnersville. Several hundred, who were just too spent, took refuge down the road in Saint Michael's School. Reports in *The Los Angeles Times* and *St. Louis Post-Dispatch* mention the fact that upon seeing the crowds, the good ASC sisters rushed out with buckets of water to offer drinks to the weary refugees. One can imagine the great care and reverence the women would have taken as they dipped their plastic cups into the buckets of water at their feet and then placed them into grasping hands. As much care, perhaps, as they would have taken when passing the chalice at Mass. No doubt they would have realized that theirs was a holy task: an act of charity that rang out all the more clearly when placed in stark opposition to the cruelty that had driven these people to pass their door in the first place.

Agony must have shrouded the faces of those trudging along the Gardnersville Road that day. A growing viciousness and disregard for life was a plague spreading across the country and dogging ordinary people. So much so that by the end of the war, the charges of inhuman behavior on the part of those with power would grow legion and require the establishment of a Truth and Reconciliation Commission so people could at least have their own stories heard and begin the process of healing.

Many years after the war, I had the occasion to speak to a young Liberian girl about her own experience. I thought I was being kind by showing an interest but it quickly became clear to me that I was tramping in an area where I had no expertise. The girl was about 15 at the time we met. In what I now see as an effort to please me she began to recite her painful family history. Word had come to the village where the young girl and her family lived that soldiers were in the area. The girl, about 7 at the time, remembered that all of their neighbors fled rather than await the coming soldiers. But her father was very sick with malaria and confined to bed. Her mother bravely decided that she and her two daughters would stay and tend her husband. Perhaps she felt that they would be spared because of their tribal affiliation.

The soldiers came in the evening as the mother was bathing her fever-ravaged husband. They took what little rice the family had; then they set fire to the home with the girl's father still inside. A young soldier, perhaps only 16, took the mother into the tall grass and raped her while two others raped her oldest daughter. The screams from inside the home mingled with those from outside so that an observer could not distinguish among them. When they were done, only the woman and her youngest daughter would walk away alive.

As the 15-year-old sitting in front of me recited these horrors, her voice took on a flat quality and her gaze became unfocused. And I felt ashamed, like a voyeur who had seen something she had no right to see. I put my hand on the girl's and told her to stop. I had no right to ask her to go on. It was clear to me that she was not yet ready to relive these events. How this youngster came to live at the orphanage where I met her, and what became of her mother, were questions I left unasked.

My interview did have one positive outcome though. I could now put one young Liberian face to those many who had suffered incalculable agonies during the war, and in doing that I could understand a bit better why the good ASC sisters stayed as long as they did among their friends in Liberia. And now maybe you can understand as well.

The St. Louis Post-Dispatch reported that when a woman who passed on the road urged the sisters to flee the area on October 20, she was told by Sister Mary Joël with a shake of her head, "We're here to serve you."

It was stated by those who were present at the time that the increasing violence in the Gardnersville area was beginning to cause growing anxiety among local community members. Shelling by rebel forces had people in the neighborhood talking about joining the flow of refugees toward Monrovia. But the ASC missionaries were hesitant to abandon their mission. It may have been that their memories of fleeing Liberia in 1990 discomfited them. Also, the presence of nearby ECOMOG troops tasked with stopping the rebel advance may have provided a veneer of security for those still in Gardnersville. Even so, the sisters weren't foolhardy. They realized that if the fighting got too intense they would have to leave the area. If it became necessary, the sisters had decided that they would go to Ghana to wait out the fighting. When it was safe, they would return home to Liberia. By most accounts, Liberia had become home in the truest sense for the four veteran missionaries: Barbara, Shirley, Agnes, and Joël. Where Kathleen was concerned, Latin America was where her heart still lay, even at the end, but she would pay the ultimate cost of compassion, along with her four sisters, there in Africa.

The St. Louis Post Dispatch quoted a promise Sister Joël

made to a young Liberian man, Richard Sumo, whom the sisters had looked after for a number of years. If they had to flee, she told him, it would be to nearby Ghana. "I'll take you with me," she told Richard. That was on Thursday, October 15, the first day of Operation Octopus. Joél was not able to keep that promise.

By October 20, with mortars falling ever closer to Gardnersville, fear began to weigh heavily on the townspeople as they realized that, just as in 1990, they would have to flee their homes and become refugees in their own land. Unlike at that time, however, there would be no cheering crowds now welcoming the NPFL rebels. Over the last two years, the former champions of the people had morphed from a small group of Freedom Fighters into a large and uncontrolled army of indiscriminate killers. With danger increasing by the hour around them, the Precious Blood sisters continued to minister to others. These faith-full missionaries had long ago pledged their lives in service to their Lord and the Lord's people. That was a sacred promise they would not give up on easily. So, they stayed; each one's courage sustained by that of her sisters.

BARBARA AND JOÉL

After their deaths, most people honored their sacrifice, but a few critics called the nuns naïve for remaining in Liberia, as if to blame them for their own murders. There is a natural inclination to question whether the women really had a sense of the threat they faced and to believe that they would have bolted the country had they realized their true predicament. Perhaps. But friends and family who knew the sisters best say they were well aware that Liberia was a dangerous place and that they might die there.

Vic Weltig, half-brother of Sister Joél said he was "very aware" as other members of his family were that when the sisters went back to Liberia in 1991 "they were never coming back." Joél had told her family that if trouble resumed they would not come home as they had in 1990. "She kept saying there was no danger," said Weltig, but Joél also said that if "it got the way it had last time," she and Shirley would stay— even if they were ordered to leave.

It was a remarkable stand for someone as blithely esthetic as Joél to take. It would be easier to believe that a person with her temperament would find the reality of life in a war zone too terrifying to endure. But to believe that about Joél would do her an injustice, because deep inside that sensitive artist was an unyielding faith so pure that she could stare straight into the eye of a storm and recognize within its awful power the presence of a loving God.

By October 20, the storm was bearing down upon the sisters. It would unleash such a terrible destructive force that even God seemed to give it a wide birth and allow it to claim Joél as well as her dear friend Barbara. It would be an act of kindness that would be their undoing.

Father Michael was able to get to Father James in Gardnersville on Tuesday morning October 20 with little trouble, but within 30 minutes of his arrival everything was chaos as the Sierra Leonean contingent of ECOMOG defenses started to fall back under heavy pressure from Taylor's rebels. "There was no order and I realized that this was not a small thing. I got to Father Hickey's and I saw he had a lot of people taking refuge with him." It was at this point that Michael advised the priest not to keep the refugees at the mission, because they could become a magnet for trouble. Churches could no longer be considered safe sanctuaries for refugees. The massacre of 600 innocent civilians by troops loyal to President Samuel Doe on the grounds of Saint Peter's Lutheran Church in Monrovia in July of 1990 had put an end to that fantasy. "I gave him money and told him to give it to the people and send them on their way," said Michael.

Then a mortar exploded nearby and a boy was hit. "He had shrapnel in his stomach and I was asked to take him to the hospital in Monrovia." That effectively cut Michael's visit short, making it impossible for him to check on the ASC sisters that day. With a shake of his head, Michael recalled to me just how quickly things fell apart, "On my way out (to Gardnersville) I

saw cars on the road, but on the way back there were none."
What the priest did see were hordes of people running from
the fighting. In 30 short minutes, everything had changed.

Father Michael did not make another trip into the
Gardnersville area because, he said, another missionary,
Sister Barbara Brillant, FMM, volunteered to check on the
five sisters. Sister Barbara had become concerned when none
of the Precious Blood sisters had returned to Monrovia to
pick up their repaired short-wave radio. It was she who would
make three aborted attempts to rescue the ASC missionaries.

By October 22, Father James would evacuate Gardnersville. By that time, two of the ASCs were missing and the
remaining three, closer to the front of the rebel advance, were
trapped. All Michael could do was to pray that his friends
would make it out safely.

4 PM

In some respects, Sister Barbara Ann Mutter was a marked
contrast to the rail-thin, lanky, 58-year-old Sister Joël whose
gentle nature, ready smile, and expansive spirit, evident even
as a child, earned her the nickname "Honey." Former SMA
priest Jim McHale remembers Joël as "the opposite of the
driven Barbara. She was a joy, an animated spirit. The kids

loved her wonderful, playful spirit." Indeed, mention Joél's name even today to those who knew her and you will likely see a lightening of demeanor, followed by a knowing smile. Former missionary Theresa Hicks concurs, "I see her face and her smile. Everyone felt welcome with her; felt at home with her. You know when you are with someone holy because they make you feel so good."

Though improbably matched on the surface, inside both Joél and Barbara were women of a deep faith that often propelled them to act while others were still deliberating. Doing, not debating, was their primary mode of operation. Because we know this about them, it becomes easier to understand that when, at 4 p.m., Peter, their security guard, asked for a ride home to Barnersville, Joél and Barbara would offer to perform that fateful act without hesitation. Word had come that Barnersville, just a few miles up the road, was in the process of being taken by rebels, and Peter was worried about his family. Very little is known of Peter or his relationship with the sisters. Even his last name is a mystery, apparently lost in the scrum of war. Yet the tie must have been strong enough or the perceived need great enough to impel the two women to brave the increasingly dangerous roads around them in an effort to get Peter home to his family.

Father Patrick Kelly, SMA, knew Sister Barbara. He said it was no surprise to him that she would be willing to give the young man a ride home even in the face of increased fighting. "Barbara would say, 'whatever the Lord wants.'" Though Father Pat finds it painful today to think about what happened to Sister Barbara Ann and the others, he told me, "Knowing her faith, I think that's ok." Because, the priest went on, missionaries undertake their work knowing the risks they might face. Missionaries, he said, "have been promised we would be persecuted" for the sake of the Gospel. Though, he added, "martyrdom is nothing we seek."

Father Mike knew the situation that day all too well. "I'm sure they (Barbara and Joél) felt for the guy and were concerned for his safety," he said. "They wanted to help him." But, and here the priest shook his head sadly, "There was a naiveness in wanting to carry the security guy home. Taking your car out, it is a target. Why would you?" he asks. The result of that ill-fated decision still bothers him over two decades later.

Early in the war, explained Michael, having white skin offered a kind of protection for missionaries. White people were generally respected by Liberians and had not yet fallen under suspicion by rebels. But as the war raged on, white skin became more liability than asset; especially if one was perceived to be an American. Rebels, and in particular Taylor's National Patriotic Front of Liberia, were feeling much less charitable towards Americans, whom they perceived as favoring the Interim National Government of Unity (IGNU) and were often accused of being spies. In addition, the situation was growing more precarious for Catholic missionaries in particular because the Archbishop of Monrovia, Liberian Michael Kpakala Francis, was a vociferous critic of Taylor. While the archbishop, who habitually spoke out against Taylor and the injustices of war, was revered by many ordinary Liberians for his courage in taking on the murderous warlord, his outspokenness made him a target and, by extension, tainted all Catholic missionaries. There was little love lost between Taylor and the Catholic Church in Liberia.

As an example, Father Mike shared his own close calls with the rebels during the long years of fighting. "At one point, it was safe to travel with a white guy, but then it became unsafe for a Liberian to travel with me. I was arrested a couple of times and interrogated." He said in one incident he was arrested by rebels and made to stand for several hours in front of their fighters. "I was put on display," he said. "Finally, I said to the CO, 'Decide what you are going to do. Either kill me or let me go.' Because the CO was a Catholic, he eventually let me go. But from that day on I was marked as a spy when they saw me on the road. I presume they thought I was spying for the government."

It would be just before supper when Barbara slid behind the wheel of the Toyota 4x4 while Joél claimed the passenger seat and Peter took the back. They would not be long they told the others. It was such a short trip. Joél would have smiled and waved at the assorted friends standing at the gate in a small effort to reassure them. Though they may not have said it with words, their somber faces must have pleaded, "Be careful. Come back safe." As Barbara turned the car onto the Barnersville Road, those watching reassured themselves. It was only a four-mile drive. The sisters would be home in no time.

It was more than natural that it was the 69-year-old Barbara behind the wheel of the huffing, temperamental old truck that day. After all, she could handle cars, vans, trucks, and motor bikes with the skilled confidence of a teamster. For over two decades she had conquered every kind of challenging terrain that the Liberian countryside could throw at her in every kind of weather. She had driven her trucks full of medical supplies and food stuffs to some of the most forsaken outposts in the bush, often over bone-jarring, flooded dirt paths that passed for roads and over narrow wooden bridges so bedraggled that they threatened imminent collapse into the rushing river below. And she had readily faced down armed men on more than one occasion.

Yes Barbara, cool and calm behind the wheel, would be the driver for their dangerous dash to Barnersville. It probably never even occurred to her companion Joél to question this arrangement. After all, if truth be told, Joél had her own share of driving misadventures in the past, so it was just as well that she was in the passenger seat. This way she could make small-talk and try to keep Peter's mind occupied without the distraction of having to concentrate on the road. Joél's skills were people-oriented, not machine-oriented.

As their friends watched the three of them depart, they reported that still within eyesight of the convent gate they saw the car slow as it approached the checkpoint at the Barnersville Junction, which was manned by ECOMOG soldiers. They saw the car stop and two armed peacekeepers jump into the back seat with Peter. Later they would say this made them uneasy. Barbara resumed her driving and made a left turn onto the Barnersville Road.

Exactly what happened next is open to speculation, though the deadly results were clear enough when State Department representatives and peacekeepers were finally allowed into the rebel-controlled area two months later. What they found was an overturned, bullet-riddled, burned out shell that had once been the convent's vehicle, with human remains scattered in and around it. Exactly why the two nuns, who were well-known in the area and in their familiar car, had become targets that day is not clear; some people say that when the two ECOMOG soldiers got in the sisters' vehicle, it—and all the souls inside—became a target for the NPFL rebels lying in wait along the final curve in the road just outside Barnersville. To the rebels it was immaterial whether or not the sisters had willingly given the peacekeepers a ride. To them it would have looked like the nuns were taking sides against them and, worse, were spies for the government.

Father Michael offered another theory for the killings; referencing the incident six months earlier when Barbara had doggedly pursued a rebel commander for the return of the bishop's truck that he had commandeered. Michael wondered if the rebel CO might have been embarrassed when he was eventually ordered by a higher-up to return the truck to the pesky nun. Could revenge have played a part in the fatal attack? We will never know for sure, but what we can know is that at the time of these killings there was a total breakdown in social norms—so much so that the murder of white religious women, who had previously been a protected and respected class—could not only be directed, but then repeated in an even more brutal fashion three days later.

SHIRLEY, AGNES, AND KATHLEEN

The pounding on the front gate was frenzied and impossible to ignore. The young men doing the pounding were armed with assault rifles. One could almost feel the menace oozing from their whip-cord solid bodies. These were war-hardened rebel soldiers belonging to Charles Taylor's NPFL. They had come for cars and cash; it was rumored that the sisters kept U.S. money from school tuition and clinic fees in the house—but they did not. Watching out the front door of the large whitewashed convent building, Sister Kathleen could see that the security wall that surrounded their home would not withstand an onslaught from these men. It had been built to keep out thieves, not soldiers. She glanced over at Sister Shirley. But Shirley, the de facto leader of this small community of nuns, had her hands full with Agnes, who was shaking uncontrollably and beginning to cry. It would be up to Kathleen to open the gate. Grabbing up the key, the nun started toward the door.

Accompanying her was Abraham Nassar, a shopkeeper and neighbor who had been taking shelter with the sisters for the last day along with his wife and driver and the driver's family. Together Abraham and Kathleen started toward the gate. The others in the house, including four teenage Liberian girls, followed Kathleen and Abraham into the front yard but then stopped, obeying the orders being shouted from the men on the road.

Kathleen, trailed by Abraham, continued to move slowly towards the gate, knowing that every step brought them closer to danger. But what could she do? If she refused to open the gate the men would undoubtedly spray the compound with automatic fire. She knew this because she had seen how the rebels operated in the last few days. For Kathleen to put one foot in front of the other must have taken a supreme effort as the 30-foot dirt path from house to fence transformed into her personal Via Dolorosa. With each agonizing footstep, she was almost certainly searching for a way out and asking Jesus for help. Perhaps she even thought about this as the moment she was called upon to accompany him on the road "up to Jerusalem."

A personal reflection Kathleen wrote before going to Liberia bears repeating in light of what happened: "...if I choose like Jesus to be totally faithful even when that fidelity brings me into life and death conflict with religious leaders and with political leaders as it did for Jesus, the reign of God is present fully in my life and the rest I let go." Like a skydiver jumping from a plane, this would be Kathleen's ultimate moment of letting go.

Each painful step Kathleen took was a prayerful acceptance of what was to come. At least that is what her good friend Sister Kate Reid, ASC, believes. "I think Kathleen had spent enough time, just her and God, that she could walk those steps, because I don't know how anybody's legs would carry them otherwise."

The precariousness of the nuns' situation had been growing for days; from the minute Barbara and Joël had driven off on their errand of mercy on Tuesday afternoon. Now, three days later, the two had not returned. And the fighting, heavier and closer than ever before, was at the sisters' front gate. ECOMOG, the African peacekeepers assigned to defend Gardnersville, were no match for the heavy artillery bombarding them from the advancing NPFL troops.

For days Kathleen had prayed long and hard in solitude over their circumstances. Those who knew her say she would have done her praying alone in her room. They weren't surprised to learn that when Shirley and Agnes decided to go to Mass at Saint Anthony's Church on Thursday, the day before their deaths, Kathleen chose not to join them, claiming to be unwell. "She would have done much better with just her and God," said Sister Kate. "By then, I think she was pretty sure the other two sisters were dead."

In a letter dated December 26, 1992, one of the aspirants gave an account of events leading up to the murders. On October 20 she said, "Sister Agnes cooked the chicken soup that day and Sister Shirley and myself cooked the rice. Sister Joél was happy that day." She went on to describe Joél as working on a bulletin board in the house shortly before agreeing to accompany Sister Barbara and their security guard on the ill-fated ride to Barnersville. When the women did not return, the aspirants were frightened. "Sister Shirley was very brave," she continued. "She and Sister Kathleen tried to comfort us in the house." On Thursday, two days after Barbara and Joél disappeared, the sisters wanted to go to Monrovia to see if the women had somehow become stranded there. "ECOMOG said the place was not safe...they don't know what was going to happen to us...so we were afraid and we stayed in the house."

There would be more attempts to leave the area by the group, but intense fighting prevented them. It was during this same time that Sister Barbara Brillant would make her initial attempt to reach Gardnersville from Monrovia, but she was turned back by rebel shelling. Eyewitnesses say that on Friday, October 23, at three o'clock in the afternoon, there would be a final attempt by the group to flee with the help of ECOMOG soldiers (who had been alerted by the U.S. Embassy to the sisters' plight). They gathered the townspeople, and the three Adorers, with the intention of conducting them to safety. However, heavy barrages of rebel weaponry prevented their departure. People were advised to return to their homes for shelter. Another attempt was promised for the next day. Two hours later, at five o'clock, a small contingent of heavily armed NPFL rebels were at the sisters' gate, demanding entrance.

When Kathleen reached the gate, she was shot in the arm by one of the soldiers, identified as "CO Devil." The bullet went through her and into Abraham Nassar, who was killed instantly. The rebel then shot Kathleen in the neck, killing her as well. Eyewitnesses say that at this point the rebels divided up the rest of their victims, separating Sisters Agnes and Shirley from the others. They demanded money and the keys to their cars. Agnes was terrified and crying, while Shirley attempted to console her and begged for their lives. Agnes was shot first, and then Shirley was shot in the head. The sisters' bodies were then mutilated. The killers, not content to chop them to pieces with machetes, also violated them with sticks.

The four aspirants, along with the other survivors, were taken captive by the killers. Later, they would escape and give testimony of what they had witnessed. One of the teenage Liberian girls who survived the rebel attack on the convent said the nuns were, "foolish not to have left earlier." Indeed, Liberian friends and neighbors had been warning the sisters to evacuate even before Joël and Barbara's disappearance. In the end, uncertainty about the fate of these two held the other three in place too long. When they finally did try to flee on Thursday, the sisters were driven back by heavy fighting in the area. It was the same on Friday. And then it was too late.

OCTOBER 31

There is a press conference being held. Sister Mildred Gross, ASC Provincial, is reading from a prepared statement. She is seated at a table with Sister Meg Kopish, Provincial councilor for Liberia, and Sisters Elizabeth Kolmer and Mary Ann Mueller—natural sisters of two of the slain nuns. As Sister Mildred gives brief biographical statements to the press about each sister; Mary Ann and Elizabeth begin to weep silently. Mildred stops to gain her composure. She can barely bring herself to talk about the festivities that had been planned for the next July to celebrate Sister Barbara Ann Muttra's 50th jubilee as a Precious Blood Sister.

The leadership in Ruma had last spoken to their sisters in Liberia on October 15. The call had been routine, with no hint of the trouble to come. The first word that something was wrong initially came from a radio report on a St. Louis station that claimed the sisters were missing. That was October 29. When the ASCs in Ruma inquired, they were informed by the United States Department of State that the five sisters were safe and under house arrest. It would not be until two days later, October 31, that their deaths were confirmed.

In a press release dated October 31, Sister Mildred stated: "At 2:35 a.m. today we received a call from the Society of Missionaries of Africa, a congregation of religious priests in Tenafly, New Jersey, who work with our sisters in Liberia. They had received information from Bishop Sekey, Bishop of Gbarnga in Liberia, via the mission radio that the five Adorers in Gardnersville are dead."

POST SCRIPTS

HOME AT LAST

The evening sky presented itself in full darkness reflecting the general mood of the small company that waited in solemn silence at Dover Air Force Base in Deleware. It was December 7, 1992. Three metal caskets, each covered in a blue and white African cloth, containing the earthly remains of American missionary sisters, lay side-by-side almost touching in the hold of a United States Air Force C-141 cargo plane that had been dispatched from Germany to Liberia to the United States. Waiting on the tarmac were representatives of the Adorers of the Blood of Christ. As the cargo door opened, the finality of the moment with its accompanying sense of loss was visceral. The sight of three regimentally aligned coffins cradling the remains of Shirley Kolmer, Agnes Mueller, and Kathleen McGuire was enough to cause several onlookers to break down in sobs.

With their hands folded in prayer, Sisters Mildred Gross and Meg Copish, members of the Ruma Province leadership team, huddled quietly in dark winter coats near a military honor guard standing at rigid attention. Also nearby were representatives of the U.S. State Department and family members of the three slain nuns. The mourners surely must have asked themselves: How had it come to this? Everyone there on the tarmac that day knew that Liberia was a dangerous place; still it was where the sisters chose to be, danger or not. They had risked all and paid the ultimate price.

Since first learning of the sisters' murders on October 31, Sister Mildred, as provincial head, had waged a non-stop battle to recover their bodies. Packed into the caskets were mainly a collection of the bones of the three nuns. For weeks the bodies of Sisters Shirley, Agnes, and Kathleen had lain next to their convent in Gardnersville. Mutilated and left to bake in the African sun, the bodies had been subject to wild, roaming creatures for six weeks. It was not until a lull in the fighting in December that the American Embassy was able to send a contingent to Gardnersville on a recovery mission. Father Michael Moran was among the group. "The embassy asked me to go because they did not know where the sisters lived," he said. And since the priest was about the only missionary left who knew his way around, he agreed to help. "If you weren't from these areas you wouldn't know where they were." Towns with names like Smell No Taste, Chocolate City, or Daybreak Mouth Open weren't usually on the map. "As soon as we got word that it was safe, we mounted up like the cavalry." Michael described the group as consisting of ECOMOG soldiers, security personnel from the American Embassy, "a marine or two, myself, and a whole bunch of press." Kathleen's body lay just outside the gate and was mostly intact according to Father Michael, but the rest was "just bones, scattered." Fire ants and roaming dogs may have contributed to the damage, but there was no hiding that something more had gone on. "It was very brutal from the way it looked."

Getting the sisters' bodies home was "an interesting negotiation," according to Michael. When a staffer at the U.S. embassy in Monrovia asked what was to be done with the bodies "I said the community wants them to be sent home. He said, 'That's going to be expensive.'" Michael took this to mean that the U.S. government was not going to help out. But by the next day Michael received a call: "I don't know who you people know, but these bodies are going home at the expense of the State Department," the man said. Then he dropped a few names: Senator Ted Kennedy, Senator Paul Simon, and Cardinal Bernard Law of Boston. From then on it was, "Anything you want."

After a short prayer service in the hold of the plane, each casket was wheeled slowly down a ramp where eight young airmen grasped the metal handholds and slowly, with a deliberate cadence to match the solemnity of the moment, marched the caskets one by one towards a line of waiting black hearses; one for Shirley, one for Agnes, and one for Kathleen. The flight crew that had brought the sisters home at long last, stood at attention as a mark of respect. The remains of the three women of God were headed to Johns Hopkins for forensic examination. After that they would be released to the Adorers for burial in Ruma.

Lambert Airport, St. Louis, Missouri
December 11, 1992

Four days later Sisters Elizabeth Kolmer, ASC, and Mary Ann Mueller, ASC, natural sisters of Shirley and Agnes, stood solemnly among a small band of mourners on hand to accompany their loved ones on their final journey home. Mercifully, the cargo plane had landed in a special section of Lambert Airport in St. Louis, affording those gathered a few moments of privacy.

Lambert was the airfield the sisters had used regularly as the jumping off and returning point for their international travels. It was the one Agnes and Kathleen, full-bodied and vibrant, had flown out of scarcely three months earlier for their return trip to Liberia after a state-side visit with family and friends. This was not the homecoming anyone had envisioned when they left.

In an especially cruel twist, it was Elizabeth's 61st birthday, and four days hence would have been her sister Shirley's 62nd. Elizabeth told no one, preferring to mark the anniversary in private.

It would be two more weeks before the charred bones of Barbara Ann Muttra and Mary Joél Kolmer would be recovered. Though they lay just a few miles from the convent along the Barnersville Road, no one was certain of the location and intense fighting kept would-be rescuers from retrieving them. The remains would lie beside the torched, overturned wreckage of what once had been the convent's truck for 61 days.

December 21, 1992

Once again Father Michael Moran was called upon to assist. There had been several reports that the bodies of Barbara and Joél had been found; all had proved false. So Michael was understandably cautious when the message came. Bodies of the dead lay everywhere—on the roads, in ditches, outside of homes—and snipers were continuously adding to the count. But on December 21 it was the American Embassy that contacted the priest, and he knew their intelligence was more reliable. Michael put on body armor and, in the company of a U.S. army officer, headed towards the town of Barnersville. At first there was confusion. Reports had the bodies within sight of their convent at the Barnersville Junction. But in truth, the grisly scene was a few miles north of the intersection. There the team discovered the truck overturned in the Barnersville Road. It had been torched. Nearby lay two skulls, one Barbara's and one Joél's. They also found remnants of a soldier's body close by.

A photo taken later and printed in *The St. Louis Post-Dispatch* the following spring shows Father Michael and fellow SMA Father Doug Gilbert at the site of the wreckage. They are standing next to the truck Barbara and Joél had driven off in months earlier. All that is left of the vehicle is an empty hull lying on its hood. Burned and black, it was merely shoved off the road. An overturned turtle. A mute witness to atrocity.

REST NOW

Shirley is buried in the middle of the five graves. Her stone is raised while the other four are flat to the ground. That's because she was superior of the Ruma province from 1978-83. She is buried with her fellow martyrs, though she could have been buried in the section reserved for former provincial heads. To her immediate right lies her cousin Joël and next to her is Barbara. To Shirley's left are Agnes and then Kathleen. Their stones are plain, bearing only their names and dates—except in Shirley's case the dates of her service as superior are also inscribed. The five are set apart from the uniform rows of their fellow sisters. They rest on a small rise with a concrete ledge at their backs, red brick at the opening with three steps up to a large crucifix bearing the likeness of Jesus. Behind is a copse of trees that in summer provides the only relief in the flat expanse covered in regimented rows by hundreds of grave markers. The graves of the five women are separate from those of their fellow ASCs. They have been honored by this separation, but the honor is not ostentatious; it is subtle.

Perhaps the more noticeable monument to the five is a large sleek bronze sculpture that stands several hundred yards away, in front of the main campus building. It is a striking statue of five female figures forming a circle, hands linked, arms raised heavenward. The women look as if they have just completed a graceful dance move. Placed high upon a pedestal, they are clothed in simple shifts and wear short veils at the back of their heads. They are barefooted. Their faces look heavenward with eyes closed and lips slightly parted; perhaps in ecstatic prayer, though I think it is just as likely that they are pleading to God (as Jesus did in the Garden of Gethsemane) to have the cross of impending martyrdom lifted from their shoulders. The piece, by American sculptor Rudolph Torrini, seems a fitting memorial to five vibrant women religious who gave their lives for love.

WHAT REALLY HAPPENED?

The viciousness of the murders would be confirmed in the 2008 testimony of former NPFL rebel Morris A. Padmore before Liberia's Truth and Reconciliation Commission (TRC). Padmore was a 17-year-old soldier at the time of the killings and under the command of General Christopher Vambo, director of Operation Octopus for Charles Taylor.

Padmore described the attack: "Taylor called General Mosquito (Vambo) to launch the attack. We first took over Barnersville early morning hours and there is a house across the road going down to a big white upstairs building with white people, and General Mosquito and the late Achieboy, we all went there and started to question them and that they were supplying information and General Christopher Vambo known as Mosquito ordered Town Dable, the death squad at the time, and we rape and killed them and even inserted sticks in them." Later in his testimony when asked about whether he had known that these were Catholic nuns Padmore said, "I actually didn't know they were nuns." He claimed it was not until later when he heard a report on the BBC that he understood whom he had helped murder.

Inexplicably, neither Padmore nor those he named in his statement were ever punished for their crimes. However, it has been reported that the Center for Justice and Accountability, a U.S.-based organization that employs judicial and policy remedies in cases of human rights abuses, war crimes, torture, and crimes against humanity, has been investigating the murders for years.

In addition, *Pro Publica* has been investigating the murders since 2014. They interviewed Christopher Vambo in late 2014. He denied taking part in the killings. This is in direct opposition to statements made by eyewitnesses at the Gardnersville convent.

Charles Taylor has also denied complicity in the sisters' deaths from the beginning. A few days after their deaths were confirmed, a man telephoned the Ruma Province and spoke to Sister Mildred Gross, then superior of the ASCs. Momulu V. Sackor Sirleaf identified himself as a representative of Taylor, claiming to be an officer of the Ministry of Foreign Affairs. He said that the sisters were still alive, and that "his people would not kill a nun." He wanted Sister Mildred to offer him some response. "I told him I was in mourning. That I didn't have a response," wrote Mildred.

She knew the man was lying because other, more credible sources in Liberia, including the Archbishop of Monrovia, were reporting that the sisters were dead. A formal letter dated October 31, 1992, sent from Archbishop Michael K. Francis reads in part: "It is my sad duty to inform you and all the Adorers of the Ruma Province of the brutal murder of our dear Sisters: Shirley, Joél, Agnes, Barbara Ann and Kathleen in Gardnersville last week."

The Archbishop had received word via radio earlier that day from Gbarnga, where two of the four aspirants who had witnessed the murders at the convent had made their way and were under the protection of the local bishop, Benjamin Sekey. Later, the other two aspirant-eyewitnesses would also seek the help of Bishop Sekey and the Catholic Church. The Church would keep them hidden in Liberia until the girls could be relocated out of the country for their own safety. Eventually, they would all immigrate to the United States, where the sisters in Ruma would help them transition. Even today, the former aspirants remain in contact with members of the ASC community. They do not speak publicly about their ordeal for fear of reprisals against family members living in Liberia, where Taylor still has friends.

During his trial at The Hague for crimes committed in Sierra Leone, Taylor was asked about the murder of the sisters. He continued to deny NPFL involvement saying, "It could not be said with any certainty that the NPFL killed those nuns." He contended that they must have died from "crossfire." The statement is absurd given the traumatized state of the recovered bodies and the fact that the women died in two separate instances.

A LASTING LEGACY

Beatrice Sawa was just 10 years old when she met the Kolmer cousins living in Gardnersville. It was 1990 and her parents had been killed by Charles Taylor's rebels a few months earlier in their home city of Gbarnga. Beatrice and her older brother and sister were not at home at the time.

Her brother Martin was a seminarian and could not care for a child by himself. A sister, Marie, was already being helped by another friend, but what to do about Beatrice? Martin knew of Shirley and Joël Kolmer from church, so he approached them about helping his little sister. They accepted the challenge wholeheartedly. They found her a place to live with the assistant principal of Saint Michael's school. Then they paid for her school fees. "They were my guardians," said a grown Beatrice. Shirley even took it upon herself to visit Beatrice's siblings to bring them food.

"As a child," she said, "without your parents you become

hopeless and helpless. But then the sisters came into my life. I knew they were there and they had my back and it gave me inner strength." Without the help of the sisters Beatrice feels she would not have gone to school, and perhaps even been homeless. Because of their intervention, she now lives in the U.S. and has a career in criminal justice.

Beatrice describes the sisters as "down to earth." She said, "They were happy people with an inner joy.... Everybody in the community loved them." That makes it all the harder for her to understand why the sisters were killed. "It should never have happened. They were not involved in politics. Their mission was to help restore hope to people." She said they gave hope and love freely and described them as peace-loving people. They were, "very, very loving."

Ramona Chebli, the young Liberian woman who fled to the U.S. in 1990 with Sisters Shirley and Joël concurs. She did not become a religious sister, but married and had a family. Still, the time spent with the sisters was truly impactful: "My life was enriched from knowing and living with the sisters." She said that she has even, unconsciously, taken on some of their characteristics. She lives in the U.S. now and, like Sisters Barbara Ann and Agnes, she became a nurse, earning an advanced degree. "My love and gratitude to them," she said, "is immeasurable."

Gabriel Sawyer was an eighth grader at Saint Patrick's School in 1987. That was the year that Sister Shirley Kolmer took over as principal. "She was the first female mathematician in our school," he remembers. "She was very brilliant. Because of her, some of us grew to love math." Gabriel counts himself among that group. He says Shirley was a "big woman with a big laugh" who brought a "flair" to mathematics. She made it simple and so interesting that "you went home and wanted to do mathematics all day." She inspired all those she taught, he said. When she was killed it was a "shock" and a "disappointment." The disappointment was, in part, that such a woman as Sister Shirley, who could light the imaginations of her students with her own energy, was now lost to future generations. The shock was that a woman such as Sister Shirley "had to suffer such a painful death." Gabriel is now the Reverend Gabriel Sawyer. He serves in the Archdiocese of Monrovia. And he still loves mathematics.

Tony Borwah was just a young seminarian when he met the ASC sisters in the early 1990s. His older brother, Peter, had just been killed by Charles Taylor's rebels and his death left orphaned several children with no source of support beyond their aging grandmother. The family was living on the Firestone Plantation, which at the time was in the hands of the NPFL rebels. Though Tony's vocation was solid, his concentration began to falter as the critical needs of his family began to occupy his thoughts. "What kind of a priest would I have been to leave them languishing?" he asked during a 2017 interview.

Tony asked his Archbishop, Michael Francis, for a year off from his seminary studies in order to take care of his family. The request was graciously granted. But that was just the first step, the young man needed to find a job. Very soon, Tony's quest found him in Gardnersville, where he obtained a job teaching Christian doctrine and West African geography at Saint Michael's High School. That is when he got to know Sisters Joél Kolmer and Kathleen McGuire, as well as the other Adorers, who lived but a five-minute walk from his new home.

Tony fit nicely at the school. His seminary training served him well as he was called upon to counsel some of the children who had been traumatized by the war. "My being in Saint Michael's was providential," he said. He and the sisters "shared in the pains of our students, some of whom were badly wounded by the civil war."

And then, Operation Octopus began to rain death on their new home. Soon, Tony and his family were forced to flee. "I remember," he said, "that my mother, as old as she was, ran like an athlete," from the shelling. Only later did he learn that the sisters had not escaped the fighting. He was taking refuge at a friend's house in Paynesville when he heard the news of their deaths on the radio. He remembers the loss of the sisters as "a big blow." And while their deaths were painful, he says their presence until the very end "meant a lot" to the local people. In truth, he says, "The sisters should have fled" when they had the chance "but they remained." This last part is uttered almost reverentially. "They were part of the Catholic Church that never abandoned the poor," he said. The sisters were "like the legends of the Church of past centuries who laid down their lives. They believed that this life is important," he said, but they also believed "that there is a life after that is more important."

When the fighting eased up a bit, Tony Borwah went back to Saint Michael's School and took up Sister Joël's work. Once again, he began to counsel students through their grief —even as he wept along with them over their losses as well as his own.

Anthony Fallah Borwah went back to the seminary. He was ordained a Catholic priest in 1996. In 2011, he was ordained Bishop of Gbarnga. Bishop Borwah still remembers the kindness of the ASC sisters, who he says, "paid for the school fees of my nephew who is now one of the best medical doctors we have." Those who benefitted from the sisters' charity are many, he says, and they are now repaying this kindness through their own charitable works. "This is their legacy," said the bishop. "They will never be forgotten, especially by the people of Saint Anthony Parish and by the people of their schools. They are dead only physically, but their spirit is still around."

Today in Liberia there are a few reminders of the five murdered nuns. A white cross on Barnersville Road bearing the names of Sisters Barbara Muttra and Joël Kolmer, reads "In memory of the sisters killed here October, 1992." Another is placed at the former convent where Sisters Kathleen Mc-

Guire, Shirley Kolmer, and Agnes Mueller died three days later. There is a memorial library dedicated to Joël at Saint Teresa's School in Monrovia. The school in Gardnersville has been renamed for Shirley. Agnes is remembered in Gardnersville with the Sister Agnes Memorial Maternity Clinic and Barbara's name sits above the health center in Gardnersville run by the Catholic Archdiocese of Monrovia. Finally, a Catholic school in Cooper's Farm is named for Kathleen. In 2012, likenesses of the five were cast in metal along with a bust of a Liberian woman meant to represent all the innocents who also lost their lives in the war. The memorial is located at Holy Martyrs parish in Barnersville.

In 2008, former ASC missionaries Sisters Mary Evelyn Nagle and Raphael Ann Drone, along with Sister Elizabeth Kolmer, blood sister of Shirley and cousin of Joël, journeyed to Liberia for the first time since the slayings. (Raphael Ann would later return to Liberia in 2010. For two years she ministered in Bomi, helping the SMA fathers with the preparation and education of prayer leaders and catechists from the dozens of small parishes around the area. She returned again in 2014, this time to Gbarnga. However, her tenure was cut short due to the onset of the widespread Ebola crisis.)

The three ASC sisters were welcomed at the Presidential Mansion by Ellen Johnson Sirleaf. She presented them with a medal in honor of the humanitarian work performed by the martyrs in Liberia. The medal, the Grade of Grand Commander in the Order of the Star of Africa, is one of the "highest decorations that the government can bestow," said the then Monsignor Andrew Karnley in an email to Sister Raphael Ann Drone. Karnley, now the bishop of Cape Palmas, added, "it is an appropriate recognition of the work and sacrifice of the sisters by the government of Liberia."

And yet, I must ask: Is this enough? Wouldn't it be a more fitting memorial to the sisters to bring those who committed these crimes to justice? While that is not the focus of this book, the question must be asked. Though the sisters would never have demanded it for themselves, and their community and families seem to have made peace with the outcome over the years, there is still a grave injustice that has been done and gone unpunished. It is not just the five sisters but the quarter million Liberians too, whose lives were lost because those who could wreak havoc did wreak havoc. And now, many of the warlords and soldiers who were once the worst offenders profit from what they did; some even sit in their government's senate and hold state office.

Gerald Rose was the Deputy Chief of Mission at the U.S. Embassy in Liberia from 1991-93. He remembers the

ASCs from Friday night dinners the embassy held for the American expatriate community. Most Fridays, at least two or three of the sisters would show up for the conviviality and good food. At the peak of the dinners, 30 or 40 Americans attended, along with most of the embassy staff. Missionaries, business people, and once in a while even someone from the Firestone Plantation would be in attendance. "It was a way for us to interact with the expat community and see how things were going," he said.

It bothers Rose that no one in Liberia has been charged with the sisters' murders. Though the U.S. Federal Bureau of Investigation has considered the case, nothing has come of it. A 2014 *Front Line* and *ProPublica* story as well as a 2012 *Time* article have come to the same conclusion: initial delays in investigating the crimes and a lack of desire on the part of the current Liberian government to pursue the case mean that justice has been stymied. The *Time* article said, "Their deaths have gone unpunished, but not for lack of evidence. Investigators in Liberia and the U.S. identified some of the individuals they believed responsible, but for reasons both political and legal, it is unlikely that anyone will ever be brought to justice." (From "Why the Murder of Five American Nuns Will Go Unavenged.")

In the past, U.S. policy in Liberia complicated the situation, and even when the FBI came up with a credible suspect in the killings many years after the fact they were unable to proceed. Apparently, there was a statute of limitation of five years on prosecuting federal murder charges in Liberia at the time of the killings. The statute was lifted in 1994, but the situation remains murky. The FBI will not comment on the case and only say in a written statement: "The FBI always continues to diligently work and follow all investigative leads toward the service of justice." A 2014 request by *ProPublica* and *Frontline* for the release of case files on the murders was denied, apparently because some new leads were being pursued. It may be that a link is being explored between former Liberian Defense Minister under Taylor, Jucontee Thomas Woewiyu, and the nuns' killings. Woewiyu was arrested in 2014 for lying on his 2006 application for U.S. citizenship for failing to disclose his relationship to a violent political group in Liberia. He has been reportedly under house arrest in Pennsylvania. Another arrest made in Belgium in 2014 was that of Martina Johnson, a former commander of the rebel National Patriotic Front of Liberia (NPFL). She, too, has been implicated in the sisters' murders.

But in Liberia itself, there appears to be little stomach for pursuing those who did the most damage during the civil war, at least among those in government. Though the Truth and Reconciliation Commission submitted its final report to the Liberian Congress in 2009, little has been done to follow its recommendations. Parties identified in first-hand testimony of atrocities have gone unpunished. All sides in the civil war were guilty of gross human rights abuses. Perhaps that is one reason Liberia prefers not to address the issue of culpability and punishment.

Gerald Rose believes he knows at least one of the men responsible for the ASC murders: Christopher Vambo. He has been working since 1995 to have him extradited to the United States, where he could be tried for the murder of the three sisters killed at their convent. The responsible persons for the first two murders is less clear. Though he lays all of the killings at the door of Charles Taylor whose actions precipitated the slayings, Rose is not very hopeful of justice.

Bishop Borwah also longs for the day when the truth of the sisters' murders is fully known. "I want to get to the truth," he says. Were they targeted, he asks? If so, why? Was it to get even with a chief critic of Charles Taylor, Archbishop Michael Francis? And why, he wonders, has the United States government not pressured Liberia to do more? "I know you don't touch American citizens and go free," said the Bishop. He shakes his head sadly adding a single word, "Five!"

It is an indictment of the United States government that it was not vigilant early on; it took 10 years for the FBI to begin investigating, and now the Liberian government would rather look the other way than face the aftermath of the civil war. The truth is that war crimes were committed by the NPFL, the INPFL, MODEL, and a whole host of other rebel groups bearing incomprehensible acronyms. The Liberian army was guilty, too. With all of these guilty parties, who then is left to seek justice for the victims?

WAITING FOR SAINTHOOD

I find myself growing impatient with the machinations of the Catholic Church. Canonization, a promise dangled by its representatives in front of the families shortly after the sisters' deaths, has been working its way through the labyrinthine process for years after the initial petition was submitted shortly after their deaths by the now deceased Archbishop of Monrovia, Michael Francis. The road to sainthood is generally a three-step process in which a candidate is officially declared "Servant of God," "Blessed," and then "Saint." The last two steps are required to be accompanied by a miracle that can be directly attributed to the intervention of the Servant of God. But in the case of martyrdom the "miraculous" requirement, at least for beatification, is waived since martyrdom itself is considered a miracle of grace. In this case, a theological commission would establish the death of the Servant of God as true martyrdom, resulting in a Decree of Martyrdom by the Holy Father.

But here is where the waters get a little muddy. As I understand it, there are true martyrs of the Church, that is those who died because of their religious convictions, such as Saint Stephen, who was stoned to death in the first century. Then there are those who are deemed "martyrs of charity." They are men and women, who in spite of great personal jeopardy, chose to carry on in their ministry of service to their brothers and sisters. They are the ones who were actually living out their faith in the face of danger. In these instances, it was their actions, not their professed faith, that led to their deaths. Bishop Oscar Romero in El Salvador would be an example of this kind of martyrdom.

It is reported that the late Pope John Paul II did refer to the murdered Adorers as "martyrs of charity." However, that term is not an officially recognized category of canonization. In my opinion, this is a designation that does not fully acknowledge the sacrifice made by these five women for their faith. To me, it is a distinction without a difference, for without their faith none of these women would have been in Liberia in the first place, fulfilling the Scripture's directive to serve the lowliest among us.

For a moment let us consider the great courage it took Sister Kathleen McGuire to walk the 30 or so steps to the front gate on October 23, 1992. She saw the armed men on the other side of the fence waving their weapons. She heard their crazy rantings; the demands to unlock the gate. Yet she set one foot in front of the other surely at least suspecting that her death was imminent. Why would she obey? Perhaps she hoped her compliance would keep the young men from spraying the entire yard and everyone in it with automatic weapons fire. She must have been terrified. What reserve of bravery (and holiness) do you call forth in such a situation? And what of Abraham Nassar, the Lebanese man who dutifully accompanied her to the gate and earned a bullet that killed him for his effort? Little has been made of his sacrifice. He could have stayed back with his wife and been spared. What act of charitable humanity pushed him to accompany Kathleen on her final journey? Jesus told us: "There is no greater love than to lay down one's life for another."

Father Patrick Kelly, an SMA and former missionary, reflected on the sisters' martyrdom. "That's the deal," Father Patrick said to me rather matter-of-factly, "though it's nothing that you seek. The Lord I believe in promised us many blessings if we follow him, but he also promised we would be persecuted for his sake. It's a line we often skip over. I believe when the moment comes you are given great strength to accept: Alright Lord, I accept. But anybody who wants martyrdom is crazy."

The saints I grew up with, such as Maria Goretti, the 12-year-old who chose death over immodest behavior, and Francis of Assisi, a reformed twelfth-century playboy who turned his life around and received the marks of Christ (stigmata) as a reward for his devotion, are perhaps too remote for most of us today, though their lives make great stories for children. We need real saints, modern saints—people who fall down just like we do then somehow manage to summon the faith and strength to get up again and do battle with the forces of despair and hopelessness that would enslave us given the chance. We need saints we can put our arms around— real flesh-and-blood people whose stories will inspire us and remind us of what it is to be truly human in a broken world. We need saints who will show us that it is our very humanity that makes us holy.

In the end, the ASC sisters were not careless about their own safety; they just cared about it less than they cared about their duty, their dedication, and above all their love for their fellow human beings. Simple really; yet extremely profound. When the chips were down and the decision had to be made between "us" or "them," they chose them—the people they had come to Liberia to serve. Perhaps there was a niggling sense of fatalism at the back of some of their minds—they were in effect standing in the bow of a sinking ship of state—but they weren't just standing there wringing their hands, they were there trying to help others into the lifeboats. Today, we need saints we can embrace. I have found mine. Sisters Barbara Ann Muttra, Mary Joél Kolmer, Kathleen McGuire, Agnes Mueller, and Shirley Kolmer were women of stubborn grace, perfectly imperfect, and that is what makes them tangible for me. Whether they are ever officially recognized as saints by the Roman Catholic Church is a moot point.

To paraphrase Sister Shirley: We pray the Lord that we might always try to be *women and men* of the Lord; *women and men* who laugh and dance and sing.

It is enough.

ACKNOWLEDGMENTS

Foremost, thank you to the Adorers of the Blood of Christ, Ruma Province, who opened their hearts and shared their stories with me. Thank you especially to Sisters Elizabeth Kolmer and Mary Ann Mueller, who brought life to this project with their personal remembrances. Also, Sister Raphael Ann Drone for her humor and guidance and Sister Mary Alan Wurth for tirelessly answering questions and sharing the treasurers of the Ruma archives with me. I am especially grateful for the encouragement of Sister Marie Clare Boehmer, whose book *Echoes in Our Hearts* provided a roadmap when I was lost.

I owe a debt to the Mueller, Mudra, Kolmer, Weltig, and McGuire family members who entrusted cherished memories of their loved ones to my care, and to all who took the time to sit with me, either in person or by phone, to increase my understanding of Liberia, missionaries, women religious, and so much more.

Thank you to my family and friends who listened to my

numerous recitations as I was drawn more deeply into the lives of these remarkable women. Your comments and support were greatly appreciated.

When I was floundering early on, Robert McClory offered encouragement with a robust side dish of questions to guide me along. What would you think of the final project, I wonder, professor?

Sister Joyce Rupp, your voice rooted me on early in this project and then nudged me forward at the very end. My debt to you is immeasurable. And, Patricia Lynch, your beautiful design and layout made visible what had previously sat unseen in my mind's eye.

I am grateful to my publisher, Greg Pierce, who has championed this project and gotten it over the finish line.

And I am the most grateful for the fact that there are people in this world who can inspire us. When I needed them most, in my own life, they found me.

This book is a work of fact, not fiction. However, in a few instances I have taken the liberty of creating a dramatic scene and adapting some of the dialogue as told to me by those with direct knowledge of the events in order to bring to life the story being told. This book does not purport to be a history of the Liberian Civil War. It is meant to be a snapshot of particular people caught in a particular period of the war.

APPENDICES

COMMON ACRONYMS

ASC   Adorers of the Blood of Christ
           (a.k.a. Precious Blood Sisters)
AFL   Armed Forces of Liberia
ECOMOG   Ceasefire Monitoring Group for ECOWAS
ECOWAS   Economic Community of West African States
IGNU   Interim Government of National Unity
INPFL   Independent National Patriotic Front
           of Liberia
MODEL   Movement for Democracy in Liberia
MSF   Doctors Without Borders
NPFL   National Patriotic Front of Liberia
SMA   Society of African Missions
TRC   Truth and Reconciliation Commission
ULIMO   United Liberation Movement of Liberia
           for Democracy
WHO   World Health Organization

ADORERS OF THE BLOOD OF CHRIST
WHO SERVED IN LIBERIA

Province of Ruma

Sister Antionette Cusimano
Sister Raphael Ann Drone
Sister Martha Goeckner
Sister Rachel Lawler
Sister Julia Lengermann
Sister Kathleen McGuire
Sister Agnes Mueller
Sister Barbara Ann Muttra
Sister Mary Evelyn Nagle
Sister Mary Joél Kolmer
Sister Shirley Kolmer
Sister Alvina Schott
Sister Janet Smith
Sister Martha Wachtel
Sister Virginia Walsh
Sister Bonita Wittenbrink

Province of Schaan, Liechtenstein

Sister Zita Resch

PERSONAL INTERVIEWS

Leona Beckman
Sister M. Sponsa Beltran, OSF
Midge Biegler
Sister Marie Clare Boehmer, ASC
Bishop Anthony Fallah Borwah
Sister Barbara Brillant, FMM
Monsignor Robert Charlebois
Ramona Chebli-Virgil
Betty Cole
Sister Antoinette Cusimano, ASC
Father Brendan Darcy, SMA
Sister Alicia Drone, ASC
Sister Raphael Ann Drone, ASC
Father Joe Foley, SMA
Sister Barbara Jean Franklin, ASC
Sister Mildred Gross, ASC
Father Ted Hayden, SMA
Sister Cecelia Hellmann, ASC
Theresa Hicks
Sister Barbara Hudock, ASC
Sister Therese Anne Kiefer, ASC
Father Patrick Kelly, SMA
Sister Elizabeth Kolmer, ASC
Joe Kolmer
Sister Mary Rachel Lawler, ASC

Jim McHale (former SMA)
Chuck McGuire
Linda McGuire
Myrtle Merriman
Father Michael Moran, SMA
Jim Mudra
Joe Mudra
Bill Mueller
Sister Mary Ann Mueller, ASC
Sister Mary Evelyn Nagle, ASC
Sister Kate Reid, ASC
Eileen Rockensies
Gerald S. Rose
Sister Joyce Rupp, OSM
George Sabo
Beatrice Sawa
Father Gabriel Sawyer
Sister Kris Shrader, ASC
Ray Studer
Vic Weltig
Sister Mary Alan Wurth, ASC

WRITTEN SOURCES

Personal letters and papers
Sister Barbara Ann Muttra
Sister Shirley Kolmer
Sister Joél Kolmer
Sister Agnes Mueller
Sister Kathleen McGuire

ASC Convent Journals
Grand Cess, 1971-1990
Gardnersville, 1973-1990 and 1991-1992
Klay, 1983-1990

Reports
Chebli, Ramona. Eyewitness account of escape from Liberia in 1990.

O'Connell, Kay, SSND. The Northeastern Province of the School Sisters of Notre Dame 1970-1992. Evacuation of Liberia.

Catholic Relief Services. "CRS Continues Liberia Feeding Program on Two Fronts: Monrovia Situation Described as 'Horrendous' by UN." January 3, 1991.

Murphy, Sister Bridget. Report on Conditions in the Ganta Leprosy Center. February 28, 1991.

INS Resource Information Center. "Disintegration of the Liberian Nation Since the 1989 Civil War." November 1993.

U.S. Department of State. "Liberia Human Rights Practices, 1993." January 31, 1994.

Unite Steelworkers of America. "Preliminary Report: Bridgestone/Firestone's Role in the Liberian Civil War." September, 1996.

Reuters. "Liberia Troops Accused of Massacre in Church." *The New York Times*, July 31, 1990.

The Forum for the Establishment of a War Crimes Court in Liberia. "Liberia: Massacre, Summary Execution, and Other Gruesome Acts from 1990-2003." Re-published by Bernard Gbayee Goah President Operation We Care for Liberia. 2003.

Liberia: Freedom of Information Act Project Report. Prepared by Urban Morgan Institute for Human Rights University of Cincinnati College of Law. For Catholic Justice and Peace Commission and Robert F. Kennedy Center for Justice & Human Rights. 2010.

Testimony of Morris A. Padmore before the Truth and Reconciliation Commission of Liberia. January 2008.

James-Allen, Paul, Aaron Weah, Lizzie Goodfriend. "Beyond the Truth and Reconciliation Commission: Transitional Justice Options in Liberia." International Center for Transitional Justice, May 2010.

Books

Boehmer, Marie Clare, ASC. *Echoes in Our Hearts*. Adorers of the Blood of Christ, 1994 and 2012.

Members of the Province. *Congregation of Sisters Adorers of the Most Precious Blood*. Province of Ruma. The Mission Press, 1938.

Grady, Pauline, ASC. *Ruma: Home and Heritage, The Story of a Convent in Rural Southern Illinois 1876-1984*. Christian Board of Publication, 1984.

Pham, John-Peter. *Liberia: Portrait of a Failed State*. Reed Press, 2004.

Waugh, Colin M. *Charles Taylor and Liberia: Ambition and Atrocity in Africa's Lone Star State*. Zeb Books, Ltd. 2011.

Dries, Angelyn, OSF. *The Missionary Movement in American Catholic History*. Orbis Books, 1998.

Stur, Heather Marie. *Beyond Combat: Women and Gender in the Vietnam War Era*. Cambridge University Press, 2011.

Cabeen, Jerome, with Barbara Pawlikowski. *Memoirs of a Reluctant Servant: Two Years of Triumph and Sorrow in Liberia, Africa*. Trafford Publishing, 2011.

Sirleaf, Ellen Johnson. *This Child Will Be Great*. Harper-Collins Publishers, 2009.

Other Sources

Saigon-AP. "Doc Grandma Plots Return to Highlands." *Stars and Stripes.* Wednesday, May 3, 1972.

Kolmer, Shirley. "Out of Africa." *Ruma Bulletin,* vol. 39, no. 1, September 1, 1990.

Cooper, Helene. "Flight From Madness." *The Washington Post,* June 16, 1991.

McFadden, Robert D. "Five U.S. Nuns Are Shot to Death While Trapped by Liberian War." *The New York Times,* November 1, 1992.

Thompson, Cheryl. "Remains of Murdered Nuns to be Returned from Liberia." *Chicago Tribune,* December 23, 1992.

Berkeley, Bill. "Liberia." *The Atlantic,* December, 1992.

Press Release Ruma. "Reports Clarify Circumstances of Sisters Deaths." February 8, 1993.

Lamb, Betty, OP, and Ezekiel Pajibo. "Liberia, Land in Conflict." *Africa Faith and Justice Network,* February 1993.

Grimes, Charlotte. Special Report "Lives of Faith." *The St. Louis Post-Dispatch,* April 11, 1993.

Meyer, Richard E. "Seekers of Good Find Evil." *Los Angeles Times,* December 26, 1993

Meyer. "Days of Grace End in Terror." *Los Angeles Times,* December 27, 1993.

Dukule, Abdoulaye W. "Anniversary of Terror: October 12—Operation Octopus." *The Perspective,* October 12, 2001. http://www.theperspective.org/octopus.html.

Williams, Gabriel I.H. "Distortion the Liberian Reality: The Case of the Five Murdered American Nuns." *The Perspective*, November 20, 2002. http://www.theperspective. org/americannuns.html.

"Lutheran Church Massacre Victim: 'My Body Was Covered with Blood and Human Brain.'" Truth and Reconciliation Commission of Liberia. http://trcofliberia.org/press_release/129.

Jonny, Michael T. "Liberia: The Calamity of 'Operation Octopus' 20 Years After." *All Africa*, October 5, 2012. http//allafrica.com/stories201210151222.

Dwyer, Johnny. "Why the Murder of Five American Nuns Will Go Unavenged." *Time*. October 31, 2012. http:// world.time.com/2012/10/31/why-the-murder-of-five-american-nuns-will-go-unavenged/

Miller, T. Christian, and Jonathan Jones. "Firestone and the Warlord: The untold story of Firestone, Charles Taylor and the tragedy of Liberia." *ProPublica*. November 18, 2014. (a six part series)

Miller and Jones. "A Company That, Literally, Has Blood on Its Hands." *Pacific Standard*. March 19, 2015. https:// psmag.com/economics/a-company-that-literally-has-blood-on-its-hands.

Jones, Jonathan and T. Christian Miller. "Union Buried Evidence of Firestone Support of Warlord After Labor Deal." March 12, 2015. https//www.propublica.org/article/union-buried-evidence-of-firestone-support-of-warlord-after-labor-deal.

Miller. "Unsolved Killing of American Nuns in Liberia an Open Case Again." *ProPublica*. May 6, 2015. https//www. propublica.org/article/unsolved-killing-of-american-nuns-in-liberia-an-open-case-again.

"Waging War to Keep Peace. The ECOMOG Intervention and Human Rights." Human Rights Watch June 1993: Volume 5, Issue No. 6. https://www.hrw.org/reports/1993/liberia/#4

Charles Taylor. The Hague Justice Portal. http://www. haguejusticeportal.net/index.php?id=6414

"Easy Prey Child Soldiers in Liberia." Human Rights Watch. September 1, 1994. https://www.hrw.org/report/1994/09/01/easy-prey/child-soldiers-liberia

"How to Fight How to Kill Child Soldiers in Liberia." Human Rights Watch. February 2, 2004 https://www. hrw.org/report/2004/02/02/how-fight-how-kill/child-soldiers-liberia

Shaw, Russell. "Where Have All the Sisters Gone?" *Catholic Answers Magazine*, November 29, 2011. https//www. catholic.com magazine/print-edition/where-have-all-the-sisters-gone?

"ASCs Return to Liberia: A Time to Recollect and Reconnect." *New Vintage*. Fall 2008, volume 7, number 5.